THE SEEKER'S LESSONS

THE SEEKER'S LESSONS

A Memoir of Becoming Whole

WRITTEN AND LIVED BY
Rowena Sowders

QUIET CUP
PRESS

Copyright

For the girl who once felt lost, unseen, afraid, and unloved.
You were never truly any of those things.

You hadn't been given the kind of protection, the peace,
the quiet, or the love without fear that helps a person remember who she is.
You deserved more back then. You still do.
And through these words, you finally get to receive it.

This book is for you, the brave soul who made it through, who kept searching, who never
stopped listening for the echoes of her own voice.

And for every Seeker still out there, wandering through shadow and light…
This is for you, too.

May it remind you that lost was never the truth, you were already on your way home.

Contents

Before You Begin

A note on tarot, truth, and letting you in

There's something I haven't shared with most people in my life, not because I'm ashamed of it, but because it felt safer to keep it close. Tarot has been one of those things. Not for party tricks or predicting doom (though I've definitely pulled a few cards that made me mutter, *Oh, hell no.*), but as a way to reflect, ask better questions, and sit with what's real.

I know the word tarot makes some folks twitchy. Maybe you've been told it's evil. Dangerous. That it opens portals. It doesn't, unless we're talking emotional ones. And if that rattles you more than a noise in the dark when you *know* you're alone, well... that's between you and your therapist.

If you're already reaching for your judgment, hang on a minute. This isn't a conversion ritual. I'm not trying to sign you up for a coven or talk you into velvet robes (though no shade if that's your vibe). This book is about telling the truth. And for me, tarot has been one of the most honest mirrors I've ever held up to my life.

It helped me survive.
It helped me stay.
It helped me make sense of things I didn't even have words for.

Here's the thing: the cards aren't decoration in these pages; they're part of the way I lived, the way I listened, and the way I remember. If you want to walk this journey with me, I'd love for you to spend a little time with *My Interpretation of The Tarot*. It's the backbone of how I understand the cards, not as fortune-telling, but as story-telling. Without that lens, some of the threads in these chapters may feel thinner than they are.

And if tarot's not your thing? That's okay too. You don't have to believe in the cards to hear a story. But I'd be lying if I said the cards didn't help me tell it.

Author's Reflection

On Memory & What Remains

I've written mostly of storms. Not because the sun never showed up, but because my nervous system learned to track thunder. The body remembers what the mind can't always hold. Our brains, brilliant and protective, bury what overwhelms us. They blur what we're not ready to face; sometimes they even lock away the good, especially when it's wrapped too tightly around pain.

What I remember, and what I offer here, is shaped by survival, by trauma, and by healing. Some memories are fragmented; some moments are missing. That doesn't make them less real. These reflections, especially from my earliest years, aren't clean-cut recollections. They're soul impressions, shaped by body memory, family stories, reminiscing with old friends, emotional resonance, and the intuitive threads I've followed through meditation and reflection.

There are other stories too, nights and days that pressed themselves into me, yet refused to stay neatly marked in time. The edges blur. The details tangled.

What remains is the imprint: the bone-deep exhaustion, the demand to perform as if everything were fine, the silence I was expected to carry. Those memories are harder to hold, but they shaped me all the same.

They may not be snapshots, but they're still true in the ways that matter. Truth doesn't always come in sentences; sometimes it rises in sensation. This is why the writing in this book often takes a nontraditional, hybrid shape: not always paragraph after paragraph, but image by image, breath by breath. Line breaks became my way of breathing through memory, of offering space where words once failed. The rhythm of the page became the rhythm of my healing.

This isn't the whole story. But it's mine, the one my body kept; the one I'm finally ready to tell.

If you're holding your own gaps and silences as you read, know this: you are not broken. You're remembering, in your own time, your own way.

Prologue: The Seeker Awakens

"Your life is a deck of cards, shuffled by fate, dealt by time, and read by the soul."

This began as an experiment. A soul-mapping. A quiet remembering. One card for each month of my life, drawn from multiple decks - tarot, oracle, animal spirit, ancestral energy. From my first breath to age forty-seven, I laid it all on the table: one card, one layer, one truth at a time.

What started as curiosity became something else entirely, a conversation with the sacred within. A breadcrumb trail from my shadows to my strength.

But it didn't happen overnight.

I've been circling this work for decades. Writing in fragments. Whispering truths. Walking away when the weight felt like too much. Each attempt brought a trembling in my body: the shiver of fear, the sweat of memory, the sharp pangs of a nervous system still healing. I wasn't ready, not emotionally, not physically, not spiritually.

It took years of therapy. Of unlearning. Of re-parenting myself. It took education and experience, and the hard-earned skills I once thought I had gathered to survive. Only after that deep inner excavation, after I had truly come home to myself, could I return to these pages with clarity, compassion, and courage.

I didn't set out to write a book. But as patterns emerged, as voices grew louder, and as lessons repeated themselves in new disguises, I realized this wasn't just about me. This was about all of us, seekers, survivors, healers, mystics, and anyone trying to make sense of the invisible thread that winds through a life.

This is not a traditional memoir. It's not linear. It's not prescriptive. And it's not always easy.

What it is, is sacred.
What it offers is yours to receive.

Each section explores a recurring theme, rather than a specific year. While a single card was pulled for every month of my life, the cards featured in this book are a distillation of those yearly insights, a gathering of what rose to the surface. They weren't chosen at random. They revealed themselves through rhythm, memory, and meaning. This journey honors both what was drawn and what was deeply known.

Before we go any further, I want to share how this came to life, not in a flash of clarity, but through years of slow unfolding, card by card.

Though my path with tarot began long ago, I've always believed wisdom finds us when we're ready to receive it. As newer decks like *The Wild Unknown Animal Spirit* (2018), *Oracle of the 7 Energies* (2020), and *The Relative Tarot* (2021) entered my world, they offered fresh language for patterns I'd been carrying for years. They weren't part of my early practice, but when they arrived, they felt like long-lost companions. Their insights struck such a deep chord that I wove them retroactively into the story.

Through meditation, reflection, and intuitive dialogue, I revisited past chapters of my life with these newer energies in hand, not to rewrite what had already happened, but to illuminate it from angles I hadn't seen before. This book is both a record of the past and a testament to what continues to be revealed. Healing isn't static. Neither is insight. The cards, whether longtime guides or recent arrivals, spoke truths that had been waiting to be heard.

With every turn of the page, you'll step into a pocket of lived experience. You'll move through the energetic themes of the cards, my reflections, and most importantly, you'll be invited to pause, to journal, and to reflect.

Because this is your story, too.

Feel free to write all over these pages. This memoir was made to hold your story as much as mine. Use it as a working book. Journal in the white space, thread your own memories through the chapters, sketch a feeling, underline a sentence that hums, and let your truth mark the paper.

This book can hold it. I wrote to remember. You're invited to do the same.

And if you prefer to keep the pages clean (I understand, I'm a little particular about my books, too), keep a simple notebook nearby and let your story run there. What matters is that it finds its way out of your body and into the world.

Let this book be a mirror to reflect what's already within.
Let it be a map, not of where to go, but how to return.
Let it be a soft place to land.
A pause.
A breath.
A beginning.

You don't need to know tarot. You only need to know your truth.

And please, take your time. Move at your own pace. There's no finish line here, no hurry.
Just a space for what's sacred to rise in its own time.

Welcome, Seeker.

The Blueprint Beneath Me

"When the roots are deep, there is no reason to fear the wind."

The beginning of my story wasn't about being born; it was about everything that shaped me before I even had words. Family, culture, ancestry, even the quiet intention of my own soul. It was all there, forming a kind of blueprint. You can feel that kind of weight before you can explain it, like breath that never quite settles.

Those first years weren't only about where I came from. They were about the framework being built inside me, who I thought I had to be, long before I had a choice. It was a tug-of-war between the stability I longed for and the quiet strength already in me, waiting for me to notice. Beneath the noise of daily life, there was this steady hum, a vibration I didn't yet know how to name.

Movement came early, almost constant, like my body was already chasing truths my mind couldn't catch up to. I didn't know the word "resilience," but I recognized its rhythm: the clink of dishes in the sink, the hush of carpet under cautious steps, the way I studied my mother's moods like other kids might study the sky for signs of rain.

At the same time, I felt myself being pulled inward, toward stillness. Toward carrying more than a child should carry. Joy and responsibility showed up hand in hand, long before I could tell them apart. I braced. I built. I became reliable. Not because anyone asked me to, but because it felt necessary. By three years old, I was already the emotional maintenance crew. No salary. No training. Not even a juice box stipend.

Those years taught me effort. Endurance. Intuition. They showed me what it meant to survive, and hinted at what it might one day mean to truly live. Enduring felt noble. Safety felt rare. And claiming even the smallest bit of space for myself, that was rebellion, even if no one else noticed.

This part of my story isn't neat. It's tangled with inheritance, the truths passed down without words, the lessons stitched into my bloodline. These were the beams and scaffolding of my early identity; pieces I would later need to loosen and unlearn to find my way back to myself.

1977 – The First Breath

Cards That Held the Year.

- *Relative Tarot*
  Chariot (Karma) - I kept moving, even though I had no idea where I was headed. It wasn't vision that pushed me, just not wanting to stop.

- *Rider-Waite Tarot*
  9 of Swords - Some nights I couldn't sleep at all. My mind wouldn't settle, and the ache was there whether I understood it or not.

  4 of Pentacles - I clung to the little I had. It wasn't much, but it felt like the only thing I could count on.

  The Hermit - Being alone wasn't empty. I could still sense a faint light inside, even if I didn't know what it meant.

- *Oracle of the 7 Energies*
  Broken Open - Pain hit me in ways I didn't see coming. My heart didn't break clean; it bent and reshaped itself enough to keep going.

  The Power of Purpose - Even in those raw hours when I felt half-undone, there was still a pull toward something more.

  Into Me I See - Awareness didn't start with wisdom. It started with me finally daring to look at myself, even when I wasn't sure I wanted to

- *Animal Spirit*
  Whale - A weighty stillness, like standing at the edge of the ocean. So much depth underneath, and I felt it in my own chest.

∞ ∞

I didn't come into the world gently. From the start, there was this tension in the air, like the room itself was holding its breath. I couldn't name it then, of course, but I felt it. I was too new to understand any of it, yet it was as if my body had arrived already carrying memories my mind hadn't grown into. Somehow, I knew right away that safety wasn't something I could assume; it was something I'd have to create.

Even before I had words, I picked up on everything around me. The atmosphere, the mood, the way people carried themselves, I absorbed it all.

I didn't know what anxiety was, but my body sure did. I curled in, tense before I even knew what fear meant. My nervous system was already on high alert, noticing things no one else seemed to say out loud. I was born into a family that had survived so much. On the surface, things didn't always look chaotic, but underneath, it was there: the quiet tension, the silence, the watching, and the lack of softness where there should've been comfort.

So, my body responded by holding tight. Guarding. Scanning. Staying ready. But here's the thing, alongside that fear, something else lived in me too. A spark. A little voice that kept saying, *Go anyway*. Even when I was braced, I still moved forward. It's like momentum was stitched into me from the very beginning.

Now, looking back, I think my soul had weathered storms long before this life, and still chose to come here. I wasn't built for stillness; I was built for pausing, preparing, and then moving again. Even in the dark, something in me was already finding its way.

I wasn't born into ease. I was born into the leftovers of someone else's survival. But I was also born with purpose. With a story, I must've agreed to face head-on. Not because I wanted pain, but because I was ready to remember who I was underneath it.

There wasn't any clear guidance back then, no bright light leading me. But deep inside, something kept nudging me forward. I didn't know to call it sensitivity, but it lived in my body. I felt everything. I carried it quietly. And even in those first breaths, I wasn't empty. I came already full of memory, of direction, of a soul that didn't come here to shrink in fear, but to rise, again and again.

1979 – The Awakening of Voice

Cards That Held the Year

- *Relative Tarot*
  Hermit (Karma) – Solitude carried its own light. In the quiet, I began to hear a voice that was mine.

- *Rider-Waite Tarot*
  Wheel of Fortune – Cycles turned whether I wanted them to or not. Something larger than me was already in motion.

  Chariot – I started steering, even if the destination hadn't yet taken shape.

  High Priestess – A knowing that didn't need explanation. I couldn't name it, but I understood it.

- *Oracle of the 7 Energies*
  Beyond the Ordinary – A brief glimpse of who I was beneath the roles I'd been handed.

  Spirit of Gratitude – Quiet thanks for what was only beginning to take root.

- *Animal Spirit*
  Nightingale – A song rising from the shadows, fragile at first but brave enough to begin.

∞ ∞

I don't remember every detail of this year, but I remember how it felt, in sensations, in flashes, in emotional truths that come back like half-remembered songs. Something stirred in me then. It wasn't loud, not a sudden break, more like a shift. A whisper. The beginning of a voice I hadn't yet spoken, but was already starting to live.

I remember a train ride with my paternal grandparents. The hum of the wheels, the steady clatter beneath our feet, the wind rushing past the windows. It felt like music I couldn't hear clearly but somehow knew by heart. Ordinary on the outside, but to me, it was magic.

Their presence felt safe, their attention steady.

I was named after my grandmother, and even then, I understood that meant something. Her name wasn't just a sound; it was a thread. A link that carried weight and history. I could feel the strength of the women before me, women who had endured more than they ever said out loud. I felt those roots, even if I couldn't see where they began.

And then, everything shifted again: the day my baby sister was born. Her cry sounded like a squeaky hinge, and I was immediately convinced she needed me. I took the job seriously. Bodyguard, bedtime manager, spiritual advisor, all before I could even tie my own shoes. I remember holding her, how impossibly small she was, and feeling pride bloom in my chest so strong it surprised me. It wasn't just love; it was purpose.

That was when my voice began. Not in words, but in presence. In care. In instinct. I didn't speak it, I lived it. I didn't have answers, but I carried knowing, a deep certainty that what I felt was real. It didn't need volume to matter. It spoke through how I showed up.

My arms memorized her weight. My breath slowed to match hers. My body learned stillness so she could feel safe. Softness so she could rest. Strength so she could grow. That was the first time I belonged to someone. And after that, I kept belonging to my siblings who followed, to the family I tried to steady, to the roles I stepped into without hesitation: protector, soother, guardian. I never questioned it. I simply became it.

That quiet inheritance became my way of caring. It showed up in how I listened, how I paid attention, how I tried to carry what others couldn't put into words. Even my silence carried meaning. Looking back, I think there was something mystical about it, though I wouldn't have called it that then. A sense that I was being shaped by more than circumstance, that I was part of a story already unfolding.

Destiny wasn't a lightning strike. It was more like a quiet hand on my shoulder, turning me toward a path I was already walking. This was the year my voice awoke, not with sound, but with devotion. And my small body, soft and watchful, already seemed to know what it was here to do.

1980 – The Dance of Duality

Cards That Held the Year

- *Relative Tarot*
  Sun (Karma) – Light and shadow moved together, joy showing me not only what was healed, but also what still hurt.

- *Rider-Waite Tarot*
  Magician – I carried more power than I knew, though I hadn't yet learned where or how to direct it.

  6 of Wands – For once, I was seen. I didn't know what to do with that kind of recognition.

  7 of Pentacles – I waited for growth without realizing what I had planted in the first place.

- *Oracle of the 7 Energies*
  Quieting the Mind – Stillness felt foreign at first, but in it came a thread of clarity.

  Beyond the Ordinary – My truth was never going to be "normal," and neither was I.

- *Animal Spirit*
  Moth – Always drawn to the light, even when it singed. Restless with longing for something beyond what I had.

∞ ∞

Some years glow in memory. Others only flicker. For me, 1980 was both. It felt bright and full of motion, like something inside me had suddenly switched on, curious, confident, eager to be noticed. I wanted connection, attention, anything that shimmered with promise. What I really wanted, though I couldn't name it yet, was to be chosen.

And sometimes, I was. I have flashes of real joy from that year, laughter that came easy,

15

movement that felt free, applause I didn't have to earn but soaked up like sunshine anyway. There were moments when I sparkled, when I reached outward with pride, when I felt celebrated.

But even in those bright moments, something trembled underneath. I wanted the light, but I didn't quite trust it. Eyes watching me too closely made me shrink. Joy sometimes felt like a setup for disappointment. Applause rang too loud, like it carried a warning. The spotlight warmed me, but it also scared me; it felt like it could burn if I stayed in it too long.

That was the beginning of my lifelong dance with duality. I stretched toward the light and pulled back in the same breath. I learned how to adjust myself, shine enough to be seen, then dim just enough to feel safe. Laugh, but not too loud. Win, but don't take up too much space. My nervous system rehearsed disaster even in the middle of a celebration. Compliments came with a flinch. Achievements with a brace. I started to believe visibility was a double-edged sword: a place where you could feel powerful, but also far too exposed.

Still, under all that restlessness, something softer tugged at me. A sense that timing mattered, that not everything had to happen at once. A quiet voice inside kept saying: *Wait. You're still growing. Let it root.*

Around me, the air had begun to change. I didn't know the words yet, but I felt the weight of whispered arguments, the way tension clung to the walls. The ground didn't feel as steady anymore. People didn't feel steady. My body picked up what wasn't said and began to prepare.

So I chased warmth, but I winced when it got too close. I glowed, but I guarded. I reached out, then hesitated. Joy started to feel risky, as if light itself couldn't fully be trusted.

Still, I think a part of me knew I didn't have to force it. I could take my time. I didn't need to shine so brightly that it burned. I needed to keep growing, slow and quiet, until I was ready.

What the Body Carried, Even in Sleep

Before I had words, I had feelings I couldn't explain. A flutter in my chest when voices got sharp. A twist in my stomach when doors slammed. Cold hands when someone left too fast.

I didn't know the word "fear," but I knew when to freeze. When to shrink back. When to make myself small enough not to be noticed. My body learned the rules before I ever could: don't ask, don't speak, don't need too much.

I don't remember the dreams themselves, but I think my body did. It dreamed in silence, in tension, in instinct. Curling around danger that wasn't there. Flinching at sounds that never came. Bracing for storms no one talked about.

My nervous system knew the truth before I had language for it. The body holds the first stories. And those early stories taught me how to listen, not just with my ears, but with my skin, my breath, my stillness.

Even now, when nothing is wrong, I sometimes feel that same flutter, that same tightening, as if something invisible is still about to happen. The difference is: I'm not that child anymore. I can name the fear now. I can calm the flutter. I can remind my body, *We're safe*.

Long before I could speak a word of truth, my body was already living it. Quietly. Faithfully. Carrying it for me, even in sleep.

Letter to the Girl Who Remembered Without Words

Dear Little One,

When I think back on these earliest years, what stays with me isn't what happened, it's what my body held onto long before I had words for any of it.

I see you now, that small version of me, wide-eyed and soft-voiced, carrying more than anyone realized. You didn't ask for the role you stepped into, but you filled it with grace and grit. Even if the details faded, the weight stayed. I know that because I still feel it.

There's so much I wish I could tell you. Not to change what happened, but to honor what you carried.

You won't remember this time in pictures or clear stories, but your body will. It will remember in the way your shoulders tense when the room gets heavy, in the knot that forms in your stomach before storms, in the way your voice sometimes catches when you want to tell the truth. None of that was ever your fault. You were born into unfinished stories and unspoken grief, but you were never the chaos. You were the calm at its center. You were the pause in the storm that no one else noticed was sacred.

Even in your very first breath, there was something ancient in you. A kind of knowing that didn't match your size. A quiet strength that didn't need to shout to hold steady. A softness that listened when no one else did.

I wish you could have rested more. I wish the world had let you stay soft a little longer. But you, my fierce and tender girl, learned to build early. You built safety with your silence. Purpose with your protection. Identity through your care for others.

You became the quiet center of every storm, hoping that if you were good enough, helpful enough, quiet enough, maybe things wouldn't fall apart. But, Little One, you were never meant to hold it all together. That was never your job.

Still, I marvel at you. I see you clutching your baby sister, your very first sacred bond. You didn't understand the weight of that responsibility. You felt it in your bones and knew the importance. That urge to nurture, to soothe, to protect, it wasn't placed on you. It was simply you.

Yes, the role grew heavy. But it also became your gift. You became the one who listened, who steadied, who understood without explanation. You began singing before you could speak. Your soul whispered in dreams and symbols; in longings you didn't yet know how to name.

Those dreams, strange, haunting, sacred, were never random. They were maps. You weren't lost. You were remembering.

I wish I could wrap you in the warmth you didn't even know you needed. Hold you until the world quieted. Tell you that stillness isn't failure. Softness isn't weakness. And you don't have to prove your worth by wearing yourself out.

You are not the walls you built to hold things together. You are the light that stayed when everything cracked. You're not broken. You're becoming.

One day, you'll return to these roots, not to fear them, but to honor them. You'll dig into what was buried, not to carry it again, but to finally set it down. And when you do, something will click into place.

You'll know you were never meant to be the fireproof wall. You were always the spark.

With tenderness and pride,
Me

The Seeker's Lesson

We start learning before we even know we're learning. Before we're fully conscious, we've already absorbed whether the world feels safe or not. We learn when to speak, when to stay quiet, when to reach out, and when to pull back. None of it feels like a choice at the time, but it becomes part of us.

We adapt. We bend ourselves to fit whatever atmosphere we're dropped into. And yet, even then, there's always a part of us that remembers, a truer self, an ancient knowing, a seed planted before anyone told us who we were supposed to be.

That part never disappears. It waits. It tucks itself deep down, growing quietly in ways we can't always see, until one day we notice ourselves leaning toward the light.

For me, that's what this reflection is about, the early pieces of me that were forming long before I knew what they were becoming. My foundations weren't soft or easy, but they were fertile. The soil was made of both shadow and love, and from it, I rose.

Rooted. Wounded. Resilient. And always reaching.

Reflective Journaling Prompt

Before we even knew who we were becoming, we were already absorbing things, stories, expectations, and survival strategies all dressed up as personality. Those early imprints shaped us quietly, often without our permission. They taught us who we needed to be to belong. To be safe. To feel loved.

Now, we get the chance to go back to them. Not to blame, but to understand. To gently look at the roots of our becoming and ask: *Does this still serve me? Did it ever?*

This is the work of reclaiming, sorting through what was passed down, and this time deciding for ourselves what to keep and what to let go.

Reflect on these questions as a starting point:

- What stories did you inherit from childhood that you now see were only half-true, or maybe not true at all?
- What roles did you slip into without realizing, just to keep the peace, earn love, or stay invisible?
- How do those early "roots" still show up in your choices, your relationships, or how you see yourself today?
- What are you ready to rewrite?

Take your time with this. Answer honestly. There's no right way to do it; this isn't about performance. It's about remembering.

Let this be gentle.
You're not digging for blame; you're simply getting curious about what lies underneath. There's wisdom in the soil of your beginning, even in the messy roots, especially in the ones you were told to hide.

Some truths may be soft.
Some may sting.
Some may surprise you with their silence.

But whatever you uncover, it will be yours to claim. And reclamation is power. Not because it rewrites the past, but because it reshapes your relationship to it.

You are allowed to know.
You are allowed to question.
You are allowed to become.

Author's Note

I've given you this page as a place to begin: to jot, sketch, list, or map whatever rises as you reflect. But don't feel limited by these margins. Your thoughts deserve more space.

Keep a larger journal nearby. It doesn't have to be fancy. A composition notebook, a few loose pages, even the back of an envelope or napkin will do. And if words don't feel right, choose another medium, paint it, sketch it, sing it, or stitch it into something with your hands. What matters is that what lives inside you makes its way into some form outside of yourself. That way, you don't have to carry it all alone.

Your Turn to Speak
Say it your way: words, sketches, fragments, arrows, messy lists. Let it out of your body and onto paper.

Child of the Storm: Through the Shadow Years

"Sometimes, the darkness is not a place to escape, but the womb of your becoming."

The storms in my life didn't start with thunder. They showed up smaller. A chill across my skin before the clouds even rolled in. That metallic taste in the air that says rain is close. I felt it before I could name it.

The shadows stretched long over my childhood before I even had words for loss or fracture. I grew up learning how to walk through that terrain, lightning flashing in the distance, a door slamming so loud it echoed longer than the silence after, a family cracking under pressure we couldn't hold.

Those years tested me in ways I couldn't understand at the time. It felt like collapse, but sometimes it felt like clearing too. I survived both. The storms pushed me to let go of what no longer fit, even when it was all I'd ever known. They asked me to keep moving through fog without answers, to live with endings I didn't choose, to face truths I wasn't ready to see.

Patterns repeated themselves, wearing new faces. The same lessons circling back, asking: Can you see it now? Are you ready this time? Sometimes I caught the warning. Most times, I didn't. Danger flashed. Sometimes it whispered. And I ignored both more often than I should have. Looking back, what stayed with me most was this: silence can bruise just as much as the truth. It's a different kind of sting, but the ache is the same.

And yet, there were softer moments, too. Small invitations that said, *It's okay to break here. It's okay to set this down. You don't have to carry everything to matter.* I began to learn that sometimes things have to crack before something real can rise.

That's the strange gift of it. Even as life came apart, I was uncovering parts of myself I thought were gone. Not after the storm, but right there in the middle of it. My grit. My fire. My voice. They weren't lost; they'd only been buried. And finally, there was room for them to breathe again.

This is the story of those storms. Not what they tore down, but what they made possible.

1981 – The Shattering Foundation

Cards That Held the Year

- *Relative Tarot*
  Judgment (Karma) – A reckoning I had felt building for years. Out of the wreckage, my soul began to rise.

- *Rider-Waite Tarot*
  Tower – Nothing felt steady. What fell apart wasn't only walls or structure, it was trust itself.

  5 of Pentacles – Even when people were around, I still felt cut off. It was a kind of loss I didn't have language for back then.

  The Lovers (reversed) – What should have been love often came with distance. The choices I made weren't out of freedom, but out of fear of being left.

- *Oracle of the 7 Energies*
  Broken Open – Grief tore me apart in ways I hadn't imagined. And yet, through those cracks, something unexpected slipped in and reminded me I was still alive.

  Smoke & Mirrors – The stories I told myself blurred what was real. They dulled the pain, but they also kept me from seeing the truth clearly.

  Exposed & Revealed – The truth didn't wait until I was ready. It landed hard, and I had no choice but to face it.

- *Animal Spirit*
  Scorpion – I struck out quickly when I felt cornered. It was my way of protecting myself long before I understood what actual safety meant.

∞ ∞

This was the year everything broke. Not the house, not the family, but something inside me too. My sense of safety, my trust, my idea of love, all of it started to fall.

In May, my mother left my father. By December, she had married someone new. A man who would never really choose my sister and me. He could be verbally cruel, but we felt the deeper wound in what he never said. It was the kind of chill you get when you're tolerated, not wanted. I couldn't have explained it then, but my body knew. The quilt of warmth that had once held us together was gone. What replaced it was tight, conditional, unfamiliar.

That's when I learned something I wish I hadn't: love doesn't always protect. Sometimes it vanishes. Sometimes it wounds. I began watching everything more closely, reading between words, scanning rooms the way some kids scan for permission. The house looked the same, but nothing inside it felt steady. The ground had shifted, and nobody said a word.

So, I adapted. I made myself small. I held my breath without even realizing. I learned to walk softer, to talk less, to fold myself down to fit whatever version of "okay" the room demanded. Maybe if I stayed quiet, helpful, invisible, things would hold together. Maybe then I'd be safe.

But it didn't work. Silence never made me seen. Good behavior never made me chosen. What hurt wasn't the divorce. It was the erasure of softness, the loss of clarity, the sudden absence of any assurance that I mattered. The house hadn't just cracked, it had been stripped bare, and we were expected to move through it like nothing had changed.

I remember how sharp the air felt, how love turned into a room I couldn't step into. I was inside the house, but outside the warmth. And even at four years old, I understood what it meant to be left out of love's circle.

That year rewired me. It taught me that love could be dangerous, that trust had to be earned, that safety was never guaranteed. After that, joy always carried a flinch. Gratitude and fear lived in the same breath.

I don't remember the dreams I had that year. But I remember the way I woke: sheets twisted, jaw clenched, heart pounding. Not from monsters, but from absence. From knowing something had left and wasn't coming back. Even in sleep, I braced. My body carried the grief I couldn't name.

I didn't understand the wound, but I lived inside it. This was the year I learned that the people you love most can walk away, replace you, pretend not to see you. This was the year I started to disappear in plain sight.

1983 – The Breaking Point

Cards That Held the Year

- *Relative Tarot*
  Emperor (Karma) – Order pressed down on me, more imposed than chosen. It looked like protection on the outside, but it felt like control underneath.

- *Rider-Waite Tarot*
  4 of Swords – Stillness wasn't a choice; it was forced. I paused because I was depleted, not because I was at peace.

  Tower – Once again the collapse came, tearing apart what I thought was solid. The truth had a way of rearranging everything.

  Emperor – The father archetype, fractured in front of me, mirrored back in ways I both embodied and resisted.

- *Oracle of the 7 Energies*
  Healing the Heart – The wound rose to the surface. It didn't want pity; it wanted me to finally look at it and name it.

  A Tall Tale – I told myself stories just to get through. Sometimes I even half-believed them, even when I knew they bent the truth.

  Smoke & Mirrors – What was real slipped in and out of focus. I held onto the distortions because they felt safer than what lay underneath.

- *Animal Spirit*
  Rabbit - My body stayed on high alert, always bracing. Fear lived in me so long it felt stitched into my skin.

This was the year I started to understand things no one would say out loud. By six, I had already learned to translate tension, not the obvious kind, with raised voices or slammed doors, but the quieter kind. The kind that makes you tiptoe because the air feels sharp.

28

That makes you second-guess your laughter. That teaches you not to be too much of anything.

That was also the year my mother was pregnant again, and my stepfather's resentment became harder to ignore. We weren't a family; we were pieces that didn't fit. My sister and I weren't chosen. We were tolerated. Extras in a story he hadn't asked for. Even at six, I knew what that meant. Children always do.

My parents weren't just fighting; they were waging a war. Not only with each other, but over us. No explanations, no clarity. A shifting landscape of moods and rules, where love showed up disguised as control and tenderness had no place. Authority ruled the house, but it wasn't protective. It was rigid. Cold. Impersonal.

Home became a place where I tried to stay invisible. I wasn't afraid of monsters. I was afraid of being noticed at the wrong time. So, I got good at reading the room, hearing anger in a footstep, sensing accusation in silence, decoding affection for what it really was: performance. I kept my head down. I became the model child. The helper. The peacemaker. Not because I thought it would make me safe, but because it seemed like the only way to keep the peace.

I carried blame I didn't understand. Absorbed emotions that weren't mine. My body never stopped buzzing. My breath stayed shallow. My stomach knotted more often than not. By then, hypervigilance had become my baseline. I knew how to flinch without sound, how to freeze without notice, how to smile like nothing was wrong while everything burned under the surface.

I missed my dad in a way no one let me say. He was on the outside, looking in. I was stuck in the middle, loyal to everyone, understood by no one. They used me as a bridge, an emotional courier, passing messages in tone, silence, and sideways glances. I wasn't a child. I was part of the strategy.

At night, the tension followed me into dreams. I wandered houses with too many rooms, some locked, some endless. I searched for someone who had already left. I followed invisible rules. I tried to find the door out of a place that looked like home but never felt safe. Even asleep, I couldn't rest.

That year didn't shatter me, but it taught me how to live in pieces. How to split truth from expression. How to tuck the tender parts of myself behind a polite smile. How to carry the weight of a lie so well that even I almost believed it.

And that's when I began to realize: sometimes the story you're told to believe isn't the same one your body already knows is true.

1984 – The Unseen Shift

Cards That Held the Year

- *Relative Tarot*
  Hierophant (Karma) – Lessons arrived in silence; in rules I never agreed to but had to follow. Authority loomed larger than safety, and my truth curled inward, sacred but unseen.

- *Rider-Waite Tarot*
  5 of Cups – I grieved what was never spoken and mourned what never fully became.

  2 of Pentacles – I kept balancing without realizing how much I was already carrying.

  8 of Cups – I turned away, not because I wanted to reject, but because I had to.

- *Oracle of the 7 Energies*
  A Deep Breath – A pause that felt borrowed from somewhere softer, a rare moment of stillness.

  The Land Between – I wasn't here, and I wasn't there. I lived in the uncertain space of becoming.

- *Animal Spirit*
  Black Egg – The truth was still curled inside, a voice waiting to form, present even before I could speak it.

∞ ∞

My youngest sister was born that year. A new life, a fresh start, that's what it was supposed to be. But I didn't feel joy. I felt myself getting smaller. Not out of jealousy, but out of gravity. As if love had limits, and her arrival meant there wasn't enough left for me.

Around that same time, something else happened. Something I can't forget, because my body won't let me. A trusted caregiver crossed a line. I told my mother. I remember that clearly, I said the words. And then came silence. A silence louder than anything I'd spoken.

It wasn't empty silence. It was uncomfortable. Dismissive. A silence that said what I'd shared was inconvenient. The person who hurt me was tied to my stepfather, and that connection seemed to matter more than my safety.

There was a big tree in our front yard. I used to climb it, not for fun, but for refuge. I've never liked heights, still don't. My body would shake on the way up, but once I reached the branches, I felt steadier than I ever did on the ground. Safer than in rooms where I wasn't believed. Safer than with adults who turned away.

Up in the leaves, I didn't have to explain myself. I didn't have to smile or soften. I could disappear. The fear of falling was real, but it was nothing compared to the ache of being unseen.

No one ever brought it up again. But I did, in my own way. I folded my hands in my lap. Softened my voice. Read the room for signals instead of warmth. I made myself small, agreeable, easy. Not because I wanted to, but because I was learning the rules of survival.

That year, something sacred was crossed. And no one came for me. So, I went for myself. I stopped expecting to be held. Stopped assuming someone would step in. By then, I knew they wouldn't.

Care stopped being something I received. It became something I gave to my siblings, to strangers, to anyone but me. I wasn't retreating for space. I was retreating because being visible had become too dangerous.

My grief didn't scream. It lived in my stomach, tightened my shoulders, fluttered in my chest whenever footsteps came too fast.

Even my dreams shifted. They grew quiet or buried themselves deep. When they surfaced, they were strange. Sometimes I stood in a room and faded away, trying to speak but having no voice. Other times, I floated in still water, silent, waiting for someone to notice I was gone. No one ever did. I'd wake with that emptiness pressed against my chest.

I wasn't afraid of monsters. I was afraid of being forgotten. Of being erased while still in plain sight. That was the year I learned to live in the in-between, between being and not being, between knowing and pretending not to know.

My voice didn't vanish. It curled inward, sacred and waiting. Holding the truth like a seed. That year didn't silence me. It taught me to whisper. And the whisper carried everything no one else wanted to hear.

1985 – Learning to See

Cards That Held the Year

- *Relative Tarot*
  Lovers (Karma) – Clarity arrived in an instant, turning blur into detail, confusion into choice. I began to see differently, the world, myself, and the possibilities waiting once vision opened.

- *Rider-Waite Tarot*
  The Moon - Shadows whispered louder than truth. I could only see what I was ready to face.

  10 of Cups - The dream of family, whole, bright, unbroken, flickered for a moment and then faded.

  Strength - A gentle kind of power, one that looked like softness from the outside but was anything but.

- *Oracle of the 7 Energies*
  Endless Possibilities – Small glimpses of something larger than the life in front of me.

  Beyond the Ordinary – A quiet sense that I didn't fully belong, and maybe that misfit was the gift.

- *Animal Spirit*
  Moth – I was drawn toward what glowed, hungry for light, learning too that not all of it was safe.

∞ ∞

I didn't know I was blind (not technically blind, severely near-sighted, with really bad dyslexia) until the day I saw leaves. Not green blobs, but actual leaves, with sharp edges, flickering light, a thousand tiny shapes moving in the wind. It was the spring of second grade, and I had recently gotten glasses. I looked up at a tree outside my school, and the world shifted. Everything suddenly had detail.

34

Texture. Clarity. Until then, I thought everyone saw life like I did: blurry, colors bleeding together.

School had already been a battle; letters moved, numbers slid, nothing stayed put, no matter how hard I tried to focus. Add in a lazy left eye and a patch over one lens, and I looked like a tiny, bookish pirate. *Arrr, matey!* Who needs vision to read?

It wasn't traumatic, just tiring. School was already hard, and now it came with blurry frustration and endless eye appointments. But I'll never forget that tree. That was my first moment of real vision, emotional as much as physical. What used to be a shapeless canopy became a thousand tiny miracles I hadn't even known were missing.

Reading was still frustrating. Learning felt like quicksand. But I didn't complain. I figured I wasn't trying hard enough. That tree changed something in me, though. The world hadn't transformed; I had. That clarity, that sudden awareness of what had always been there but hidden, wasn't about eyesight. It was the beginning of a deeper truth I couldn't name yet: there's more than you can see. And once you see it, you can't go back.

I repeated second grade that year. At first, it felt like failure, but eventually it became a gift. That extra time gave me space to breathe, to catch up, to rebuild what I hadn't realized was crumbling. It wasn't only my grades that improved. It was my sense of self. For the first time, I felt capable. Maybe I wasn't broken. Maybe I was wired differently.

Once I could see, my world opened twice: the physical one, and the imaginary one. Books became my lifeline. I couldn't get enough. Science fiction, fantasy, anything that let me step into another life. I lived in other galaxies, walked through portals, befriended dragons, fought battles that weren't mine. Every page was an escape hatch. Every story was a survival tool. And that saving grace carried me through more times than I can count.

School got better after that. I learned tricks to keep the words from sliding, little workarounds no one else saw. I started bringing home straight As. For once, I felt like I belonged there. Home was still chaos, unpredictable and sharp, but school had rules, structure, recognition. It was the one place I felt steady.

I worked harder than anyone realized. Not just in academics, but emotionally. I memorized moods, patterns, faces. Even when I couldn't read the board, I could read the room. That year, my strength took on a new shape. It wasn't endurance anymore. It was a strategy. Adaptation. Quiet resilience built through effort.

The challenges didn't vanish. Words still danced. Math is still tangled. But I had tools now, and a little more breath in my lungs. That was the year I picked up the reins. Clumsy, shaky, but determined.

School became the one place where I felt seen. Capable. Strong. And for a child who lived between two worlds, one blurry, one sharp, that clarity meant everything.

1987 – The Fire Beneath the Surface

Cards That Held the Year

- *Relative Tarot*
  Strength (Karma) – I held steady when it would've been easier to break. Courage burned quietly beneath the surface, mostly unseen.

- *Rider-Waite Tarot*
  The Moon – The truth was there, but it slipped under the surface. I kept reaching for it and coming up with shadows.

  The Lovers – My heart stood at a split in the road. The choices I made about love in those days shaped what I thought love was supposed to be.

  Queen of Swords – Clarity didn't come free. Boundaries stopped being optional; they became the only way I could survive.

- *Oracle of the 7 Energies*
  Ears Wide Open – I learned to listen differently, past the noise, catching the things no one said out loud.

  Spirit of Gratitude – Gratitude wasn't pretty; it was what I used to hang on when everything else was unraveling.

- *Animal Spirit*
  Wolf – I guarded others as much as I guarded myself. Loyal and protective, but it left me standing apart.

∞ ∞

By 1987, I had already started to mother myself. Not because I wanted to, but because I had to. My body knew it before my mind did. My shoulders squared. My spine stiffened. My heart grew guarded without anyone telling it to.

I lived in contradiction: strong and scared at the same time, wise beyond my years yet still aching to be held. There were moments I wanted to collapse into someone's arms, but I already knew there was no one to catch me. So, I held the line. I carried the weight. I stayed composed.

Strength didn't feel like power. It felt like armor. Something I strapped on every morning to make it through the day. Inside, I felt like fire and steel, burning quietly, never allowed to spark out loud.

There was no room for breaking. Nobody around me had the bandwidth to notice, and I didn't feel like I had the luxury to fall apart. The air in our house was thick with things unsaid. Silence that pretended to be peace but hummed with secrets. I picked up on what I couldn't explain, reading the glances, the tones, the doors that shut too hard.

I didn't know the full story, but my body did. I was always listening, not just to people, but to energy, to something bigger. Even while I shrank under the weight of my reality, another part of me kept reaching for a future I couldn't name yet, but still believed in.

Gratitude became survival. Not the loud, shiny kind, but something quiet and practiced. I counted what I could: a moment of quiet, a teacher's smile, a walk outside that didn't end in punishment. Not because things were okay, but because I needed something to hold onto so I wouldn't unravel.

That year, my body never fully relaxed. My muscles stayed tight, even in rest. My lungs never filled all the way. Even asleep, I stayed on alert.

My dreams came in symbols. Sometimes I ran through forests, fast and silent, like something wild. Sometimes wolves followed me, not chasing, watching, waiting to see if I'd lead or flee. Sometimes I did both.

Other nights, I saw fire, not destructive, distant. A bonfire glowing beyond reach. Warm. Familiar. Untouchable. Maybe that was my truth. My rage. My instinct. The parts of me I'd buried, burning quietly in the background.

And sometimes, I carried my siblings through dreamscapes, dark hallways, winding rivers, mountains I didn't know how to climb but did anyway. Even in sleep, I was never off duty.

That's what no one saw: the labor beneath the stillness. The fire beneath the composure. The strength that didn't roar but endured. I held space for others long before I knew how to hold it for myself. Nobody taught me. I just knew.

The truth is, I wasn't weak. I was tired. I was scared. I cried in secret and smiled in public. I kept my needs quiet because I didn't think they mattered. But I endured. I carried more than I should have, and I still rose.

That year taught me how to lead quietly. How to survive without recognition. How to stand firm when softness felt impossible.

1988 – The Role of Protector

- *Relative Tarot*
  Hermit (Karma) – Silence became my teacher. I carried grief no one named and made space for others while tucking away my own questions in the quiet. I began to guide myself, holding hope like a hidden lantern no one else could see.

- *Rider-Waite Tarot*
  10 of Wands – I ended up carrying things that didn't belong to me. Responsibility pressed down on my shoulders before I was ready for it.

  Page of Pentacles – I didn't have much to work with, but I tried anyway. Every small step taught me something new.

  The Star – Hope showed up quietly, almost shy. I felt it at the edges of my life, though I barely trusted it enough to name it.

- *Oracle of the 7 Energies*
  Roots of Abundance – Stability grew slowly, hidden underground, before I ever saw it on the surface.

  The Uncharted Sea – My emotions had no edges that year. It felt like being dropped into water with no map, just learning to move with it.

- *Animal Spirit*
  Hyena – Humor was the mask I wore. Laughter kept the tears at bay. A shield I leaned on more than I let anyone know.

∞ ∞

My brother was born in February. I loved him instantly, fiercely, instinctively, completely. It wasn't something I had to think about. It was primal, like a soul-bond that didn't ask questions.

But that love carried weight. Not because of him, but because of the role I stepped into without hesitation. Protector. Soother. Keeper of calm. I wasn't just a sister. I was a second mother. Not because anyone told me to, but because my body already knew how to carry what others couldn't. I quieted his cries, anticipated his needs, and made myself the buffer between him and the chaos. I was ten and a half.

That fall, my uncle died. I still remember how the house went quiet. Not peaceful, still. Grief slid in like fog, low and heavy, settling over everything without a word.

I had questions. I always had questions. But no one answered. They said I was too young to understand. The truth is, I did understand. I learned to pretend I didn't. It was safer. If I didn't ask, I couldn't upset anyone. If I didn't speak, I couldn't make anyone angry. So, I stayed silent. Again.

His death cracked more than my heart. It cracked the atmosphere of the whole family. No one talked about it. No one offered comfort. Grief sat there, thick and unspoken. That year, I learned silence can be as heavy as sadness, and I carried both.

There was no one to hold space for my confusion, so I made space for everyone else's. I became the capable one, the good girl, the steady presence. My back curved, my shoulders drew in, and my voice softened into something background, steady, and soothing, yet forgettable.

Sometimes I dreamed of laughing and no one noticing. Of smiling while something inside me split apart. I carried too much, emotionally, physically, energetically. My dreams told the story: boxes I couldn't lift, children in my arms while I searched for a place to rest. Always moving. Always responsible. Never still.

Even asleep, I was on duty. Grief followed me into those dreams, formless but constant. Sometimes I woke with tears on my cheeks; I didn't remember crying. Sometimes I stood at the edge of a funeral with no casket, holding silence like a secret. I think my soul was mourning something I hadn't been told I was allowed to grieve: the death of my childhood.

And yet, hope never disappeared. It went quiet. It lived in the breath between breakdowns, in the way I still looked up at the night sky, searching for light.

Once, in a dream, I saw a star. Far away. Unreachable. But I reached for it anyway.

That's the kind of girl I was. Carrying too much, but still believing there had to be more. I didn't stop hoping. I learned to wish quietly.

There was something deeper in me then, stronger than exhaustion, older than fear. A kind of sacred persistence. A strength not born of glory, but of necessity. A resilience not for show, but for survival.

The lessons came early. You don't fall apart when people are counting on you. You don't cry if no one will wipe your tears. You don't rest when there's still something left to carry. So, I carried it. Without complaint. Without applause.

I became the girl who made space. Who absorbed sorrow like air. Who stayed soft only in the smallest, most private corners, because that was the only place softness felt safe.

And still, even then, I dreamed of being loved without condition. Of being seen not for what I could do, but for who I was underneath it all.

That year, I learned what it meant to carry more than my share. And I learned how to do it without breaking. Which is its own kind of miracle. And also, a wound.

1992 – Fracture and Resignation

Cards That Held the Year

- *Relative Tarot*
  Emperor (Karma) – Power and order shaped my world, even as it cracked beneath me. I built small structures inside chaos. I adapted quietly within authority. And I learned to hold my ground in spaces that weren't built for me.

- *Rider-Waite Tarot*
  3 of Swords – The break cut deeper than just my heart. Pain came without explanation and left me reeling.

  7 of Cups – Options blurred together, and most of them weren't real. I kept reaching anyway, not even sure what I was reaching for.

  10 of Swords – The ending came hard, even though I saw it coming. It was a defeat that didn't shout; it settled in quietly

- *Oracle of the 7 Energies*
  Time Machine – The past kept showing up dressed in new clothes. Different on the surface, but underneath it was the same old hurt.

  Smoke & Mirrors – leaned on confusion to protect myself. Even the so-called kindnesses, the lies told out of love, left me in the dark.

- *Animal Spirit*
  Frog – I craved a clean slate. Part of me wanted to peel off everything I'd absorbed, like it had seeped too far into my skin.

∞ ∞

My youngest brother was born this year. My mother wanted that baby with everything in her, her last chance, her hope, her redemption. But my stepfather had never wanted children. Not really. And with each new life in our house, he pulled back further. Colder. More bitter.

The fracture in our family didn't explode; it widened. Slowly. Quietly. Like a seam coming undone, thread by thread. Nobody said it out loud, but we all felt it, the stretch, the silence, the sense that something essential had unraveled, and no one knew how to stitch it back together.

This year broke me in a different way. Not with dramatic heartbreak. Not with sudden loss. But with resignation. I stopped expecting to be loved. I started hoping not to be hurt. Warmth felt too much to ask for, so I settled for neutrality. And I accepted it even when I didn't get that.

Stillness became my shield. Not the calm kind, the bracing kind. The kind that comes from holding your breath too long. From making yourself invisible because being unseen felt safer than being seen and misunderstood.

I floated through life that year. Smiling when I had to. Staying out of the way. Doing the work. Avoiding conflict. Not quite here, but not gone either. Untouchable, not out of strength, but out of numbness. Not because I didn't feel, but because I felt too much and couldn't risk letting it show.

I didn't collapse; I folded. Quietly. Efficiently. A kind of spiritual origami: smaller, smaller, still smaller. It wasn't an accident. It was survival.

I built entire worlds inside my mind. Not daydreams, exits. Doorways into softer lives. Landscapes where tenderness wasn't a prize you had to earn, but something freely given.

At night, my dreams turned strange. Deserts, cracked and dry, where I searched for someone I never found. Staircases that led nowhere. Doors opening to empty rooms. Phones that wouldn't dial out. Every dream whispering: *you are reaching for something that will not answer.*

Other nights, the dreams were sharper. Office buildings. Conference rooms. Cubicles under fluorescent lights. I didn't understand them then; I was still a teenager. But years later, walking into those exact spaces, I felt it, that eerie jolt of recognition: *I've been here before.* What I thought were dreams had been glimpses. The future, circling back.

It was disorienting. How do you explain knowing something that hasn't happened yet? Even the dreams that made no sense were trying to show me something. They weren't escapes; they were blueprints. A place to prepare. A soft echo that whispered: *You're not crazy. You're awake in a world that wants to stay asleep.*

During the day, I barely spoke. At night, my dreams wouldn't shut up. They poured into me, symbols, feelings, truths I couldn't yet translate. Even my silence was trying to say something.

That year, I stopped believing anyone was coming to fix it. The break had already happened. We just weren't naming it. So, I adapted. I learned how to stay while vanishing. How to feel everything and show nothing.

That wasn't giving up. It was strategy.

And beneath all the stillness, a truth kept pulsing. Faint, but stubborn. *One day, this won't be all there is.*

1993 – The Truth Comes Forward

Cards That Held the Year

- *Relative Tarot*
  Hierophant (Karma) – The systems I had trusted started to show their cracks. Through them, truth began to rise, slipping out from behind old teachings.

- *Rider-Waite Tarot*
  10 of Swords – The ending came quietly. It wasn't only pain; there was also the strange release that followed.

  Judgment – A call to rise from the wreckage. It wasn't brand new, but this time I was awake enough to hear it.

  The High Priestess – A knowing sat beneath the silence. I couldn't ignore it anymore, no matter how hard I tried.

- *Oracle of the 7 Energies*
  The Oracle's Gift – Insight that didn't come from logic. A deeper sight began to unfold in me.

  Close Encounters – Intimacy came closer, both with myself and with others, raw, disarming, and real.

  Broken Open – The breaking hurt, but the crack became the opening. What shattered also started to teach me.

- *Animal Spirit*
  Dolphin – Healing didn't come heavy. It slipped in through laughter, through play, through lightness that let me breathe again.

∞ ∞

That summer, I was sent to New Jersey to attend prom with my mother's best friend's son. It was supposed to be special, a gesture of trust, tradition, connection. On the surface, it looked like a celebration. Underneath, I was trying to get through it.

Her friend was kind. I stayed close to her whenever I could, because near her I felt safe. But her son? The moment I met him, my body lit up with alarm. My breath went tight. My chest felt shallow. My pulse raced, and I couldn't calm it. I didn't know how to explain that kind of knowing, so I didn't. I counted the days until I could go home.

I smiled. I played along. I monitored every interaction like a guard on duty, back straight, eyes scanning, heart pounding. That summer, my body spoke louder than my voice. I didn't yet know how to listen to it out loud. Anxiety lived in my breath. My posture was polite but braced. My jaw ached from holding it all in. And still, I stayed silent.

Nothing happened. And yet, everything did. Because I knew. Fear doesn't need proof to be real. Sometimes it's a hum in your chest that won't shut off. That summer, I learned that instinct itself is evidence, even when no one else can see it.

At night, my dreams picked up where my body left off. I wandered through unfamiliar houses, called out to voices I couldn't reach, searched for exits that disappeared when I got close. In those dreams, I was always the only one who noticed the danger, and no one ever believed me.

I woke with fists curled, jaw clenched, like I'd been arguing with silence all night. Not nightmares with monsters. Warnings dressed as symbols. My spirit was showing me what I wasn't allowed to say out loud.

And there was something else in those dreams, too, a presence. Silent. Strong. Watching. It reminded me: *what you know is real, even if no one else understands it.*

I was the seer no one wanted to believe. But I still listened. Not with words, but with knowing. Even my silence had sight.

That summer didn't just unsettle me. It woke me up. I wasn't rescued. I was revealed. Tradition told me to stay quiet. My spirit told me to trust what I felt. And I chose the latter, not with noise, but with clarity.

That year, I learned survival sometimes means sticking close to the safest person in the room and praying they don't leave. I learned joy can't always be reached when you're busy watching your back in a dress.

And most of all, I stopped doubting my gut. I started trusting what I knew. And I've never let that go.

1995 – The End of Innocence

Cards That Held the Year

- *Relative Tarot*
  Chariot (Karma) – I was pushed forward by force more than choice. The movement came hard, without mercy.

- *Rider-Waite Tarot*
  Tower – Everything collapsed at once, the illusions, the hope, the sense of safety I thought I had.

  7 of Wands – I found myself defending ground I never would have chosen, but there I was, holding it anyway.

  The Fool – I stepped into the unknown, not out of joy but because there was no other way forward.

- *Oracle of the 7 Energies*
  Great and Full – A fullness that came for a moment and slipped away just as fast.

  Willing Release – I learned to let go of things that were never really mine to hold.

  Waking the Lion – A roar I didn't expect rose through my chest, stronger than I thought I had in me

- *Animal Spirit*
  Camel – I endured in barren places, carrying reserves no one else could see.

This was the year everything broke, for the second time. The illusions. The hope. The little bit of safety I thought I had.

That summer, I left home with nothing but a garbage bag of clothes and a spirit barely stitched together. I ended up in Texas, terrified and free at the same time. I enrolled in my senior year of high school. Got a job. Took my first shaky steps toward independence.

And then I went back.

Not because I'd failed, but because I still loved the people I'd left behind. Even then, I could hold two truths at once: I needed space, and I needed connection. I was afraid, and I was brave. Lost and found. Running, yet returning.

That year, I heard myself say: *You can do hard things.*

And one of the hardest? Testifying against my mother.

In that courtroom, I spoke words I never wanted to speak. Not to punish her, but to protect myself. To protect my siblings. To say the truth out loud in a place that had long demanded silence.

My voice shook, but I spoke anyway.

I'll never forget her eyes. That glare, sharp as a blade, cold as judgment. Like I had betrayed her simply by surviving. My stomach still knots remembering it. My skin crawls thinking about how her stare sliced through me as I finally told the truth of what was happening in our home.

I cried on the stand. I tried not to break. Not because I wasn't breaking, but because my sister was there too. She testified, and I saw it, the same glare, the same daggers in our mother's eyes, this time aimed at her.

We were teenagers. Doing the unthinkable because no one else would. Trying to protect our three younger siblings. Trying to stop the cycle.

That day was the hardest thing either of us had ever done. No one acknowledged our strength. No one said, *I'm proud of you.*

But we did it anyway.

I wasn't just carrying my story that day. I was carrying hers. Theirs. And the heavy truth that no one was coming to save us.

With every sentence, a piece of my childhood cracked. What I had clung to, what I had tried to protect, shattered. The illusion of safety fell away, hard and public.

And in that wreckage, I stood. Shaking, but upright.

My body bore witness. My stomach twisted. My legs locked. My throat burned. My breath came fast and shallow. And still, I spoke. Not because I wasn't afraid, but because I was.

Truth cost me something sacred. And I paid it.

That year, I learned freedom doesn't always bring peace. Sometimes it brings terror. I was always scanning for stability, even when I was the one building it from scratch. Resilience became something I rationed, a hidden reserve I drew on quietly. Not in grand gestures, but in steady survival.

I didn't feel strong. I felt hollow. But I kept moving.

Even my dreams split in two: the ones before I testified, and the ones after.

Before, I ran. Not away, but toward something. Fields. Highways. Empty houses where I could breathe. They whispered: *freedom is real, even if you haven't touched it yet.*

After, I fell. Off cliffs. Out of windows. Through collapsing floors. Always waking before I hit the ground, lungs frozen, heart pounding. Those dreams weren't subtle. They told me what I couldn't yet say: telling the truth had shattered something inside me.

But not all my dreams were about falling. Some nights I stood barefoot in the dirt, planting something I didn't recognize. Roots pressed into the earth beneath me. A future I hadn't imagined yet, already asking to grow.

I didn't lose my innocence that year. I gave it up, piece by piece, in exchange for something fiercer: clarity. Self-trust. The first taste of sovereignty.

1996 – The Year Everything and Nothing Was Left

Cards That Held the Year

- *Relative Tarot*
  Strength (Karma) – Survival looked quiet from the outside, but it carried its own weight. This was endurance without applause, courage forged in silence, and a power born of staying when leaving would have been easier.

- *Rider-Waite Tarot*
  9 of Swords – Nights without rest, caught in the kind of pain that loops when no one else can hear it.

  The Empress – Creation still lived in me, even without having been mothered. I found ways to nourish where I hadn't been fed..

  Strength – Survival looked quiet from the outside, but it carried its own weight. Endurance without fanfare.

  2 of Pentacles – I juggled more than I could hold, keeping the motion going even when it felt like chaos.

  Death – What ended gave no instructions. Only space, only silence

- *Oracle of the 7 Energies*
  Smoke & Mirrors – Survival blurred the truth. I saw only what I was able to handle at the time.

  Broken Open – The breaking split me wide, but through it, something sacred pushed its way through.

  Waking the Lion – Fierceness didn't arrive early, but it showed up when I needed it most.

- *Animal Spirit*
  Sea Serpent – Healing curled inward first, like a spiral. Sometimes beginnings are tucked inside endings, in ways we can't yet see, much less make sense of.

∞ ∞

January: My stepfather divorced my mother.
May: My mother went to prison.
Two weeks later: I graduated from high school.

Those are the facts. Clean. Chronological. But the truth was never that tidy.

I didn't step into adulthood like my classmates, full of plans and possibilities. I stepped into survival. And survival didn't stop at my front door. It followed me onto highways, into classrooms, into places that were supposed to help but didn't.

After graduation, I took a road trip to Iowa with a friend to visit my sister for her own graduation. Somewhere under a stormy sky, a tire blew. No cell phones. No towns nearby. Two teenage girls in the rain, stranded. When a Sheriff pulled up, I thought maybe, just maybe, someone would help. Instead, he circled us, his questions cutting sharper than the wind. "What are you doing out here? Is it just you two? Where are you going? Why are you alone? You know it's going to storm? What's taking so long?" Then he went back to his cruiser, unwrapping food while the rain came down harder. He aimed his spotlight on me like a warning, a test, while I wrestled with the jack and the rusted lug nuts, my hands slipping, clothes soaked through. His voice came again, "Hurry up." He never lifted a hand. Safety had pulled up beside us, and still, I was on my own.

That night, I understood again what life had been teaching me all along: the people meant to protect you often don't. No rescue. No safety net. Just me, a rusted jack, and the kind of grit you don't choose, but inherit. I fixed that tire myself. And I learned: when the road gets rough, you fix what you can, and you move. Even when no one helps. Especially then.

When I came back from Iowa, everything around me looked the same, but inside I'd cracked open. I had smiled through the ceremony, clapped, hugged, and posed for pictures. But afterward, I felt hollow. The celebration noise had faded, and all I could hear was the echo of what I'd lost and what I never had.

I was still reeling from my mother's sentencing. Still waking in cold sweats, wondering if I had done the right thing. Still haunted by the faces of my little siblings, twelve, eight, and three, not understanding why they couldn't see their mother. They didn't understand fully, but they knew she was gone. And in my bones, I felt like I had pulled the trigger.

The town made sure I didn't forget where I came from. "That's her daughter," they whispered. Not Rowena. Not a girl fighting to survive. Just her daughter. Like a curse sewn into my name.

One day in the grocery store, I snapped. I marched up to two men, fire in my throat: "I have a name! I am not her. I am my own damn person." They stammered apologies, but the damage had already worked its way into my skin.

I wanted so badly to be seen for who I was, not where I came from. To be loved. Accepted. Chosen.

For a while, I thought maybe I had that. A boyfriend who stayed through the chaos, who didn't flinch at my story. We even started imagining a future. But when I got pregnant, despite precautions, his answer wasn't "We'll figure this out." It was, "If you keep it, I'm gone." I couldn't lose one more person. So, I said yes to something I didn't want. Because I wasn't ready to say goodbye to him.

That same friend who went with me to my sister's graduation went with me again, this time to another state, to hold my hand. She was the only one who knew, and she carried the silence with me for years. I told no one else. I carried it like a secret stitched into my ribs. The grief didn't arrive right away. It came later, like an aftershock, silent, devastating. And the cruelest part? He left anyway. Two months later. For someone else.

At nineteen, I was exhausted. Raising kids who weren't mine. Working multiple jobs to fill the hours while they were in school or asleep. Stillness felt dangerous. Silence, unbearable. I grieved a child I'd never meet, a choice I hadn't wanted to make, and a boy who was never planning to stay.

Some days, I could barely breathe. Some nights I didn't think I'd survive. But something small and stubborn inside me kept whispering: *You can do this. You have to do this.* So, I did.

Later, someone gave it a name: childhood PTSD. Back then, I didn't know the words. I just knew I was living in fragments. My body always braced. My mind always scanning.

Sleep was never rest. It was vigilance with my eyes closed. I startled at sounds other people ignored. I read rooms the way other kids read comic books, always looking for danger.

Memories came jagged, out of order, sometimes not at all. But the feelings stayed: the knots in my stomach, the racing pulse, the deep belief that safety was temporary, always about to be taken away.

I learned to leave my body long before I understood dissociation. To float above. To disappear inward. To survive by becoming unreachable.

And beneath it all, shame I couldn't name. Shame for not being able to live lightly. Shame for carrying storms even when the sky was clear.

That's what PTSD looked like in a child. Not war stories or explosions. Flinches at slammed doors. Silences too sharp. A body carrying truths no one wanted spoken.

And still, under all that weight, something shifted. Not peace, not yet. But surrender. The kind that isn't giving up, but letting go. Letting go of rescue. Of return. Of the hope that someone else might swoop in and make it all okay.

That year, I didn't rebuild. I endured. I survived in the quietest, fiercest way possible: by staying. By breathing. By not giving up on a life that hadn't yet made room for me.

Even my dreams carried it. Roads that never ended. Storms I drove into with white knuckles. The message was never subtle: *you are on your own. Keep going anyway.*

Other nights, I tried to speak, and no sound came out. I walked through houses underwater, arms full, trying to save what mattered most. Always the only one who noticed we were sinking.

But sometimes, in fragile nights, I dreamed of fields under stars. No demands. No noise. Just stillness. Just breathe. Just me.

The dreams weren't escapes. They were reflections. They told me the truth gently but without apology: *You are not crazy. You are awake in a world that keeps trying to sleep through your story.*

And the whisper that rose with them was the same one that had carried me all along: *don't stop now.*

What the Body Carries

They say the body keeps the score. Mine wrote it in tension, in silence, in the stillness I didn't choose but learned to survive by. Before I could form memory, I had already formed armor.

Silence lived in the clench of my jaw. My stomach twisted with shame. My shoulders carried responsibilities too heavy for a child. I didn't know these weren't mine to hold. I only knew that being small, quiet, and useful kept me safe. Even now, when I speak my truth, my throat tightens. When I rest, something inside whispers, *Shouldn't you be doing more?*

Because once, I believed that stillness would undo me. So, I worked. I overworked. I filled every hour I could to keep from feeling what might rise in the silence. That wasn't laziness I feared, it was the collapse I was trying to outrun. Even learning was survival. I trained my brain to navigate a world that didn't bend for kids like me.

The letters moved. The numbers slid. My left eye lagged behind the right, covered with a patch that made me look like a tiny pirate. I found workarounds anyway. What my eyes couldn't track, I compensated for in determination. Even now, decades later, that eye still twitches when I'm stressed, tense, or bone-tired. And let's be honest: as a middle-aged woman, when am I *not* tired?

I pause more now. I listen. I thank my body, not for surviving, but for staying with me when I didn't yet know how to stay with myself.

Some of the ways I protected myself still live in me. Not because I'm broken, but because they worked. I still cry in the shower, the safest place to fall apart, where no one can walk in, where the sound of sobbing is drowned by water, where grief can flow without explanation. Even now, when the world gets heavy, I find my release behind a locked door, under running water, where my pain doesn't echo.

And when the world feels sharp, I still disappear into my mind. I create entire internal worlds, not for fantasy but for refuge. Places where I don't have to earn tenderness. Where protection is assumed. Where I get to be soft, whole, unobserved.

Now, as a middle-aged woman, I return to those imagined spaces not to escape life but to remember I can still choose safety when it's missing from the outside world. This isn't regression. Even safety has a memory, and mine lives in my skin.

I am a grown woman with a voice and a life I've built with intention. But the girl in me still needs her places, her exits, her soft landings. That's not weakness. That's wisdom. That's memory. That's survival turned sacred.

Dreams That Told the Truth

Long before I had words, I had dreams. I ran barefoot through dark woods, always searching, always unseen. Water rose too fast. Stairwells crumbled as I climbed. Doors jammed shut. Voices stayed out of reach. And then, sometimes, there was a hand, a voice, a light just beyond the tree line.

As a child, I thought dreams were scraps, random pieces of a tired brain. Now I see them for what they were: messages, warnings, promises, letters I couldn't send. My soul was mapping exits when none were visible. Even asleep, I was problem-solving. My dreams weren't passive; they adapted, shaping survival strategies with whatever symbols they could find.

The dreams didn't rescue me, but they didn't lie either. They carried truths I couldn't say out loud, grief I had no space to release. They whispered: *You're not weak. You're wounded. And still walking.* They didn't just mirror fear, they honored it.

I dreamed of drowning, lungs filling not just with water but with everything I couldn't say. Of mirrors that refused to reflect me. Bridges that fell apart halfway across. Endless hallways where the doors disappeared. Sometimes I screamed into voids where no sound came out. Sometimes I carried people I loved through storms that swallowed us whole. Other nights, I tried to save what dissolved in my hands while houses sank around me.

But not every dream was terror. Some were visitations. Ancestors waiting quietly at the edges. Symbols surfaced, too, animals, stars, paths I wouldn't understand until much later. Even then, my spirit was practicing hope. Remembering who I was. Rehearsing wholeness. Whispering of a peace I hadn't touched yet, but still believed in.

Dreams weren't just stories. They were survival. Soul-maps sketched in metaphor and moonlight. When life caged my body, my spirit found another language. And even when I wasn't ready to listen, my dreams told the truth anyway.

Letter to the Girl Who Carried More Than Her Share

Dear Me, in the years of storms,

You should never have had to learn those lessons so early. But you did, and you learned them well. You learned that love could vanish without warning. That family could fracture in a single sentence. That silence could be a weapon, and truth a risk. You learned to hold secrets in your bones and smile in rooms where everything hurt. None of that was your fault. Not the chaos. Not the abandonment. Not the things they asked you to carry, or the ones you picked up on your own. You were just a child.

And still, you mothered. You protected. You endured. I see you standing small but steady, watching more than anyone realized. Feeling everything. Trying to make sense of a world that offered no sense, only stories you were told to believe. I see the girl who went quiet after her voice was dismissed. The one who whispered warnings through migraines and asthma. Who flinched at footsteps and found safety in order. Who built control in closets because the rest of the world spun too fast.

I see the girl who couldn't read the words as they were written, so she invented her own ways to make them make sense. Who couldn't see the board but learned to listen harder. Who passed the test with the odds stacked against her, not because someone made room for her, but because she carved space for herself. You weren't just surviving. You were solving. And that, too, was sacred.

I ache for her. But I also admire her. Because despite everything, she never gave up. While others dismissed her quiet, she paid attention. She followed her intuition. She named what no one else dared to name. And even in the thick of it, she hoped, not because it made sense, but because something in her refused to stop believing. She held her siblings close, not because anyone told her to, but because love lived loud in her, even when it wasn't returned.

She made choices no one should have to make alone, believing love meant sacrifice. And when it all fell apart, she blamed herself, quietly and completely. But still, she kept going. And when the world broke open, she found her way through the cracks.

I know you thought it was just survival. But it wasn't. It was becoming. Every time you endured without explanation. Every time you held your own hand when no one else would. Every time you whispered, *keep going* through clenched teeth, you weren't breaking. You were forging something sacred.

There will come a time when your body no longer flinches at softness. When your voice rises without apology. When love finds you, and you don't have to earn it through pain. Until then, keep dreaming. Keep trusting that your knowing is enough. That your worth was never tied to their choices. That the girl who watched the sky split open at age four was already a phoenix, she just hadn't stretched her wings yet.

With fierce love and unshakable awe,
Me

The Seeker's Lesson

We often imagine survival as fire, loud, fierce, defiant. But sometimes survival is quieter. Sometimes it's simply the choice to keep breathing when the weight of the world dares you to stop.

Child of the Storm: Through the Shadow Years wasn't only about chaos or collapse. It was also about what grew in the aftermath. It wasn't the story of me fighting my way through. It was the story of enduring when there was no fight left. Of carrying what no one saw. Of becoming, even when I thought there was nothing left to build from.

This season didn't arrive with one big collapse. It came in pieces, a slow string of surrenders. I gave in to truths I didn't want but couldn't keep pretending away. I stepped into roles I never asked for. I held grief in silence because I didn't know how to speak it yet, or if I was even allowed to.

That's when I learned: sometimes no one comes to save you. And that's when you discover you can save yourself.

Somewhere in that darkness, I started to see differently. Not with my eyes, but with something deeper. Even in confusion, I could sense where to step. I built tools. Strategies. Quiet systems of survival, in school, in life. Learning became a lifeline, not because it was easy, but because it was mine.

This wasn't the season where I found my light. It was the season where I learned to see in the dark.

I didn't come out of the shadow years untouched. I came out aware. Aware of my strength. Aware of my limits. Aware of that sacred, stubborn will to keep going when everything else says stop.

Aware, too, of the love I gave without return.
The choices I made alone.
The ones I still grieve.

If the first section was about roots, this one was about fire and ash. About learning that survival isn't weakness, it's alchemy. And that sometimes, endurance itself is the bravest kind of becoming.

Reflective Journaling Prompt

Some moments split us wide open. Sometimes it happens in a flash; other times it sneaks up on us so slowly we barely notice until the crack is there. Storms come in both kinds, sudden and sharp, or quiet and grinding. And when they pass, yes, they leave pain, but they also pull back the layers on things we didn't know were there: resilience, truth, identity, the sound of our own voice.

The fiercest storms don't only uproot. They reveal.

Take a moment to reflect:

- What storms have shaped you, not just in what they destroyed, but in what they uncovered?
- What did you learn to carry that was never really yours?
- Which survival roles became your armor, caretaker, peacekeeper, overachiever, invisible one, and which pieces are you finally ready to set down?
- How does your body still carry the language of those storms? And how might you begin translating that into healing?

Remember: survival was never your whole story.

So, ask yourself:
What sacred truths rose from what you outlived?

This isn't about reliving the hurt. It's about noticing who you became inside it. There's a certain strength in looking back and realizing, *I actually made it through that.* It's in moments like that that we begin to take back what the storm tried to strip away. Not just peace, but identity. Not just healing, but truth.

You were never only the one who endured. You were also the one who transformed.

I carried the storm in my body long after the sky cleared. Maybe you did too. But somewhere in that rubble, there is always a whisper waiting to be heard: *What now?*

That whisper can become a voice. And that voice, once buried, is ready to speak.

Your Turn to Speak

Say it your way: words, sketches, fragments, arrows, messy lists. Let it out of your body and onto paper.

What the Silence Held

"Your voice is the echo of everything you've survived and everything you still believe is possible."

Silence is never really empty. It hums in the ribs like bees caught in glass. It thickens the air of a room until even breathing feels like trespassing.

As a child, I learned to fold myself into that silence. To press my back against the wall and pretend it kept me safe. But silence is both a shield and a prison, and I carried its weight until my own voice finally cracked the glass.

It wasn't about safety anymore. This was the season of speaking, softly at first, then with more fire. The season of whispering truths I had buried for years.

I didn't roar right away. My voice began small. A lullaby. A soft request. A note scribbled in the margins of a textbook, ink smudging my fingertips. A fragile truth hummed under my breath when no one was listening.

That was the beginning of taking my voice back, little by little. I spoke even when the rule was to stay quiet. And in time, I realized something I hadn't known before: words can cut, yes, but they can also help heal. Even the quietest truths carried power.

I didn't stand on mountaintops declaring my story. I dreamed it out loud, piece by piece. I wrote it in notebooks. I whispered it in classrooms, chalk dust in the air. I breathed it into therapy rooms and late-night journal pages. Slowly, I began to believe what I was saying.

This was the turning point. Silence loosened its grip. Words became more than survival; they became spells. Speaking wasn't just about sound. It was about selfhood.

At first, I spoke for my son, because love made bravery non-negotiable. And then, little by little, I spoke for me.

These years taught me that truth doesn't always arrive as a roar. Sometimes it waits under layers of fear until you're ready to claim it. I began moving through the world with curiosity, with quiet knowing, with a rekindled fire. With softness and strength braided together.

I learned that healing isn't linear. That wisdom often whispers. That survival sometimes means burning the rulebook you were handed. Here is where I began to believe in my own story, and in the power of sharing it.

I stopped waiting for an invitation to speak. I realized: I *am* the conversation. I *am* the story worth telling. My voice was never gone. It was waiting for me to remember it had always been mine.

1998 – The Year I Remembered My Own Voice

Cards That Held the Year

- *Relative Tarot*
  Wheel of Fortune (Karma) – A turning point came, the cycle shifting. This time I chose not to spin with it.

- *Rider-Waite Tarot*
  The Magician – I started reclaiming my tools. The power was shaky, but it was real.

  The Devil – I saw the chains, and I saw that they weren't locked.

  10 of Swords – The betrayal landed hard. But with it came a sharp kind of clarity.

- *Oracle of the 7 Energies*
  Exposed & Revealed – There was nowhere left to hide. Truth showed itself, stripped bare.

  Wish Upon a Star – Hope bloomed quietly, like a secret I hardly trusted.

  Healing the Heart – Healing had started, though it wasn't easy and it didn't move in straight lines.

- *Animal Spirit*
  Panther – Fierce clearing energy. It burned down what I could no longer carry forward.

∞ ∞

There comes a point where survival isn't enough. Where the quiet voice you've buried for everyone else's comfort starts rising whether you're ready or not.

1998 was that point.

I loved my siblings fiercely, but I was disappearing inside a life that asked me to be everything for everyone, except myself. That year, I didn't run away, but I did step away. I moved into an apartment down the street. Close enough to still be their safe place, but far enough to begin remembering I was a person outside the caretaker role.

Even that small distance stretched wide with guilt. I wanted space and I wanted connection. I needed both. And I was learning to let that be true.

At first, my body moved on autopilot. I worked, paid bills, cleaned the kitchen, and kept everything running. The rhythm was familiar, steady, reliable. My spine carried the posture of responsibility; my jaw held the tension of constant readiness. My nervous system didn't understand rest; it only understood vigilance.

But underneath the routine, something stirred. Something wilder. Something alive. A flicker of creation. A whisper that maybe I could build something just for me. It wasn't loud or dramatic, but it was persistent. I felt it in my fingertips, in the way I started writing again, imagining again. Daring, even if only in small ways.

And then, just as I stretched toward that light, I got tangled in a relationship that mirrored everything I thought I'd escaped. It wasn't obvious at first. But piece by piece, the control crept in. Criticism. Manipulation dressed up as care. My body recognized it before I did. My shoulders rounded. My breath shortened. My voice dimmed. I flinched at tones that felt too sharp. Dissociated through conversations. My body remembered.

That year, something cracked in me. Not because of the relationship itself, but because I finally lost the illusion that I could survive it unchanged. I wanted to leave. Desperately. I felt it in my bones; in the way I went still whenever he walked into the room. I knew this wasn't love. It was survival dressed in patterns I already knew too well.

Then I found out I was pregnant. And suddenly leaving didn't just feel hard, it felt impossible. I was twenty-one, exhausted, tethered to a life I knew was hurting me. And now there was a baby, a heartbeat I would protect with everything I had. So, I stayed. Not because I didn't know better, but because I couldn't see another way.

The heartbreak wasn't about the relationship ending. It didn't end. The grief was in realizing that hope had. I stopped waiting for him to change. I started grieving the part of me that believed love could fix what was already broken. My body carried that truth the way it carried the child, silently, heavily, and with a strength no one else could see.

The pain wasn't one moment. It was a long ache, like a breath that never reached the bottom of my lungs. And still, I endured. But I also shifted. I didn't collapse. I stood. Trembling, but upright. That was the real turning point.

For the first time, I was learning to walk without certainty, only commitment. I didn't have a map. I only knew I couldn't stay where I was. I let the sun touch my skin again and didn't flinch. I laughed louder. I said *no* more often. Sometimes that "no" was met with arguments, glares, fists, holes in walls and doors, but I still said it. Not as frequently as I should have, but I said it.

And the dreams came back, sharper than before. Not just stories, maps. I dreamed of homes I couldn't enter, doors locking behind me, keys I couldn't find. I stood outside houses I once called home, knocking, watching life unfold inside without me. I woke with that ache pressed against my ribs.

But there were other dreams, too. Dreams where light spilled from my palms. Where journals filled themselves with my handwriting. Where doors swung open the moment I dared to speak. Sometimes, shadows showed up, familiar faces cloaked in dread. I'd wake breathless, heart pounding, like I'd just outrun something that had lived inside me too long.

Even those dreams carried truth: *You are still repeating old patterns. You still think pain is the price of love.* Even in sleep, I was waking up.

By the end of the year, I stood at a crossroads. One hand holding the weight of everything I'd survived, the other reaching toward something I couldn't yet name. I didn't have a map. I didn't need one. I had a voice. And for the first time, I was learning to use it, not just in defense of others, but as a declaration of myself.

I stopped waiting for permission. I lit a candle in the dark and whispered, *This way. I'm going this way.*

1999 – Becoming a Mother

Cards That Held the Year

- *Relative Tarot*
  Justice (Karma) – A reckoning I hadn't expected, life balancing itself in the form of love and new responsibility.

- *Rider-Waite Tarot*
  The Empress – Creation in its rawest sense, both physical and spiritual.

  Page of Cups – Innocence showed up again, this time reflected back through my child's eyes.

  King of Cups – Emotional steadiness didn't come easy, but it rose in me during the storm. It was a deeper kind of strength than I'd known before.

- *Oracle of the 7 Energies*
  Great Big Love – Love rewrote me from the inside out, changing everything I thought I knew.

  Roots of Abundance – What held me up came from devotion. It wasn't flashy, just a steady ground beginning to take shape under my feet.

- *Animal Spirit*
  Butterfly – The change didn't come with noise or force. It was gentle, almost fragile, and through that tenderness I realized I was becoming someone new.

∞ ∞

Becoming a mother cracked my heart wide open. It changed what love meant, not something to chase anymore, but something to live inside. But before the tenderness came chaos. Not metaphorically. Not memory. Actual chaos.

It started with back pain. Sharp. Consuming. I figured it was just another long shift, another ache I could muscle through. I cried at my desk. I told my boss I needed to see a doctor. "I think I've got a bad UTI." I was twenty-one, pregnant, still believing I could push through discomfort the way I always had.

At the clinic, my midwife looked worried. She sent me for labs and told me to rest. But as I walked out, something gripped me from the inside. Not just pain, knowing. A voice rose in me, urgent and quiet at once: *Go back*. So, I did.

Another doctor examined me, paused, and looked up slowly. "You're in labor." Ten weeks and ten days too soon.

They admitted me on the spot. IVs, medication to stop the contractions. Then my lungs gave out. I remember the panic, the rush of voices, my body refusing to cooperate. They resuscitated me. Brought me back, not just for me, but for him.

After that, I stayed. First in labor and delivery for a week, then in a recovery ward meant for the elderly, where antiseptic and grief seemed to seep from the walls. Strict bed rest. A month of it. Every breath became a plea: *Stay in. Stay safe. Stay with me*.

One night, across the hall, an elderly woman screamed, "NO! STOP! GET OFF ME!" I hit the call button. Nothing. I wasn't supposed to leave bed, but I couldn't lie there listening. I stood, weak, IV pole in one hand, the wall in the other, everything spinning from low blood pressure. I screamed as I slid down the wall until the staff finally came running. At first, they yelled at me, "You are not supposed to be out of bed!" I responded in kind, through gritted teeth, "I know. That lady across the hall has been screaming that someone is hurting her. She needs help, and no one has been responding to the call button." It turned out to be a nightmare, not an attack. Relief washed over me. I had no regret about almost passing out in the hallway. Survival had taught me this: when others freeze, I move. Even when it costs me.

Eventually, they sent me home on strict bed rest. I lasted three weeks before I was back in the hospital. My little boy still came early, three weeks ahead of schedule. But he was healthy. Whole. Alive. That was everything.

Outside the hospital walls, life was chaos, bills piling, accounts drained, his choices unraveling everything in their path. But inside, all that mattered was keeping my son safe. I refused to let the storm eclipse the quiet truth I was building.

I gave birth without the woman who gave birth to me. My mother wasn't there. Her absence echoed louder than I expected. Grief hummed beneath the joy of my son's first cry. But even in that ache, I showed up. I mothered him the way I had always needed to be mothered: fiercely, gently, consistently.

Pregnancy rewrote how I lived in my body. For the first time, I wasn't at war with it. I was in awe of it. Every flutter, every ache, every shift felt sacred. And still, grief lingered. Her absence wasn't just emotional; it was physical. I felt it in the hollow beside me, in the silence where guidance should have been.

When my son was born, something opened in me. My chest expanded, not just with breath, but with spirit. I didn't just feel love; I became it. The kind that protects without question. The kind that nurtures without permission. My hands, once sharpened by survival, softened again. My breath deepened. My presence steadied.

I wasn't just showing up for him. I was showing him what safety looked like.

This wasn't only tenderness. It was strength braided into softness. I became the anchor I never had. Leadership didn't come with titles or authority; it came with choosing, over and over, to soothe instead of control. To guide with compassion instead of fear.

I had spoken for years, for my siblings, for survival. But no one had really listened. In 1999, everything shifted. I stopped hoping to be heard. I started expecting it.

I would not let my son endure what I had. I became his safe space. And in doing so, I finally became my own. It didn't feel like flight, not yet. But I could sense the wings forming. My body, once a vault for fear, became a sanctuary for him, and for me. It carried love the way it once carried danger. And with each breath, I taught myself: healing isn't always loud. Sometimes it's a lullaby. Sometimes it's a quiet promise, *You are safe here.*

My dreams softened that year. The sharp edges didn't disappear, but they blurred. The darkness didn't vanish, but it no longer threatened to swallow me. I dreamed of water, not drowning, but floating, holding something close to my chest, keeping it safe. I dreamed of walking barefoot through a forest, lantern in hand, shadows behind me, quiet ahead. The message was simple: *Keep going. You're not alone now.*

My mother appeared in some dreams, not as herself but as absence, a hollow shape at the edge of the dreamscape. She never helped, never harmed, just wasn't there. That silence said everything.

I dreamed of singing lullabies to a child I hadn't met but already loved. Of animals gathered close as I gave birth. Of stars aligning above me. Of doors opening as I held someone's hand. I didn't understand them all, but I woke with the same knowing: *This matters*.

Those dreams weren't escape. They were preparation. They didn't teach me how to mother. They reminded me I already knew.

2000 – Claiming the Path

Cards That Held the Year

- *Relative Tarot*
  Empress (Karma) – I began reclaiming my power to create, not only life, but a sense of direction for myself.

- *Rider-Waite Tarot*
  Ace of Pentacles – A beginning rooted in something real, like planting in soil I trusted to hold me.

  Page of Swords – Curiosity turned into my compass. I stumbled, but I was learning how to ask the right questions.

  The High Priestess – Intuition had been there all along. That year, I finally started listening.

- *Oracle of the 7 Energies*
  Call of the Muse – Creativity stirred again, not randomly this time, but with a sense of purpose.

  Spirit of Gratitude – Gratitude became a practice, a way of grounding myself and marking the way forward.

- *Animal Spirit*
  Shark – My instincts sharpened. I moved with more precision and stopped pretending I was shallow when I knew I wasn't.

∞ ∞

I didn't just leave a marriage that year. I walked away from a lie. Not one big betrayal, but a slow erosion of self. The belief that I was too much, too loud, too ambitious. The lie that I couldn't raise a child, finish school, or build a life without leaning on someone else. The expectation that love should hurt and that stability meant silence.

I walked out with my son on my hip and a trembling kind of clarity in my chest. It wasn't rage that fueled me, but something quieter, a knowing. I couldn't keep shrinking inside a life that made me disappear. My father's presence gave me the anchor I needed, the out my husband could never control. Without my father, I don't know if my son and I would have made it.

There were no grand declarations, no dramatic exits. Just steady steps: signing forms, finding childcare, going back to school. At night, I opened books while my son slept in the next room. At first, I chose practicality. I enrolled in business classes. But the material fell flat, like chewing cardboard. When I switched to criminal justice, something in me ignited. Every lecture, every case study, every theory, I absorbed it like oxygen. It wasn't just education. It was reclamation.

My voice shifted that year. Not louder, but sharper. More deliberate. I started asking the questions I used to swallow. I began connecting dots I had once been told not to see. I wasn't just learning, I was remembering. I was remembering and acknowledging the girl who asked why. The young woman who knew how to lead. The truth-teller who had always sensed what was broken in the systems around her. I finally had the language to name it.

My body moved differently, too. My hands carried groceries and textbooks. My legs walked me into classrooms and across courtroom thresholds. My back, already trained to hold weight, now carried the pressure of rebuilding. Of showing up. Of saying yes to a new life. I still flinched sometimes. Still braced at unexpected noises. I still held my breath in moments of rest. Trauma doesn't vanish with a degree. But something shifted. I began to walk straighter. To speak without apology. To feel my spine hold not just history, but pride.

Sleep came in pieces, but my dreams spoke in a new voice. I dreamed of staircases, long and spiraling, climbing ever upward. I never reached the top, but I wasn't afraid of the climb. I dreamed of ancient women at chalkboards, pointing to equations I didn't understand but felt were mine to solve. I dreamed of my son, older, watching me from a distance, not needing me to save him, just witnessing me become.

Other dreams were stranger. Keys hidden in books. Whispers in mirrors. Torches pressed into my hands. I didn't always know what they meant, but I woke with a steady pulse behind my ribs. A quiet *yes*.

One night, I fell asleep at my desk, face pressed into a textbook, and dreamed I was in a courtroom. Not as the accused. Not as the witness. As someone who knew the rules, who could name the harm, dissect it, and offer justice. It didn't feel like fantasy. It felt like a premonition.

That year, I was bone-deep tired. But it wasn't the exhaustion of despair. It was the weariness of effort, of moving toward something better. Underneath it all, I carried a sense of purpose I hadn't felt since childhood. I wasn't just surviving anymore. I was building. Brick by brick. Class by class. Breath by breath.

There were plenty of doubts, bills stacked too high, nights when my son wouldn't sleep, papers still waiting to be written. I questioned everything: my worth, my sanity, my right to want more. But then I'd remember her, the girl who survived the silence, the woman who walked away from the lie. And I'd keep going.

Because I had already lost everything that wasn't real. What remained was mine. Because I had already died the deaths required to live more fully. Because I had already learned I wasn't too much. I was finally just enough.

And this time, I wasn't asking for space. I was taking it. Making it sacred. Making it mine.

2001 – Liberation

- *Relative Tarot*
  Emperor (Karma) – I began reclaiming sovereignty. Authority wasn't something to fear anymore; it was something I could stand in myself.

- *Rider-Waite Tarot*
  Chariot – I moved with direction this time. Determination took the place of drifting.

  Death – Something old finally let go of me. I didn't just keep breathing, I changed.

  Queen of Wands – I stepped into my own fire, bold enough to carry heat without apology.

- *Oracle of the 7 Energies*
  Wish Upon a Star – I gave myself permission to want again. Hope itself became a sacred act.

  A Merry Motive – I started choosing joy, not as a mask but as a way to lead with light.

- *Animal Spirit*
  Unicorn – The magic hadn't left; it was only hidden. My truth came back through wonder.

∞ ∞

My divorce was finalized in May, but the leaving happened long before the paperwork. Separation doesn't begin with a signature. It begins in the body, in the breath that catches one too many times, in the moment your voice dies mid-sentence, in the quiet knowing that the only way to survive is to walk away.

But this time, I wasn't just walking away. I was walking toward myself.

It wasn't graceful. It wasn't clean. It was wild, raw, burning. A rebirth that came not with celebration but with reckoning. Something inside me snapped, not in surrender, but in clarity. The life I had been living could no longer contain who I was becoming. So, I burned it down. It wasn't rage. It was instinct. Not violence, but liberation. The kind that rises when you finally say: *No more.*

I stopped whispering my boundaries and began speaking them. My hands trembled, but my spine held steady. I had molded myself to fit someone else's shape for so long that I'd forgotten I had a shape of my own. That year, I began reclaiming it.

Freedom didn't feel soft at first. It felt sharp. Like noise and silence colliding. Like shaking while still choosing to move forward. As if I were standing in front of the wreckage of everything I once clung to and saying, *I choose me.*

Every step I took away from that old life was its own declaration: I will not disappear for anyone again. I carved a new structure from scratch, not out of rigidity, but resolve. I gave myself permission to rest. To rise. To rebuild. Not from ashes; there was nothing left to burn. But from bone. From will. From knowing.

I didn't wait for a map. I didn't need one. I had my own hands, my own voice, my own direction. For the first time in years, I became my own compass.

My body remembered its own force that year, not as something to fear, but as something to trust. I moved with purpose, not apology. My spine stayed steady even when my heart shook. I walked into rooms without shrinking. I stopped curling my shoulders to take up less space. I could sit in a restaurant alone and breathe freely. If people noticed, that was their problem, not mine. I didn't need their validation. I needed air. And I gave it to myself.

The fire inside me didn't rage. It focused. It sharpened into purpose. Into truth waiting too long to be spoken. I let myself speak rather than hide. Not all at once, but in steady sentences. In decisions that prioritized peace. In mornings where I no longer questioned my worth. My breath deepened. My muscles loosened, then firmed again, not braced in fear, but ready in strength. My body had carried fear for so long that it didn't recognize freedom at first. But it learned. And once it did, it didn't forget.

That summer, my dreams shifted. They weren't about escape anymore. They were about arrival. I walked barefoot through burning landscapes and didn't flinch. I stood on cliffs and didn't fall. I saw my reflection crack open and didn't shatter. I drove through winding roads in the dark, headlights cutting through shadow, unsure of the destination, but certain of the direction.

I dreamed of mirrors falling away, revealing something older, wilder, more whole beneath. I dreamed of wings I hadn't realized were mine. These weren't fantasies. They were knowings. Ancient. Wordless. Mine.

My dreams no longer begged for rescue. They whispered reminders: *You are not lost. You are choosing.* I dreamed of packing bags and not looking back. Of standing in a crowded room and knowing I didn't need anyone's approval to belong.

That year, I didn't just break free from a marriage. I broke free from every lie I had ever believed about who I was allowed to be.

I didn't rise quietly. I didn't glide toward peace. I ran, barefoot and bold, toward a life I wasn't sure I was allowed to want. And then I claimed it anyway.

Because 2001 wasn't just the year I survived the end.
It was the year I embodied the beginning.

What the Body Carries

There's a reason truth burns on its way out. For years, I swallowed silence like medicine, bitter, numbing, and most often, necessary. I wore obedience like a second skin, mistaking stillness for safety. My voice wasn't gone. It was caged inside a body that had learned to flinch before it ever learned to speak.

This body carried every silence I swallowed. The remembering lived in each held breath, in my posture, in every pause, in every stifled scream, in every *I'm fine* that was anything but. It remembers survival not as a single moment, but as a posture. As tension. As teeth clenched so tightly, the jaw forgot how to release.

And it remembers the first time I told the truth. Not in a courtroom. Not in a classroom. But alone, whispering words into the dark that I had never dared to say out loud. My hands shook. My spine trembled. But I didn't take it back.

That was the shift.

At first, my body responded the only way it knew how: fear, trembling, bracing, flinching. But then something else came. Not ease, not yet. But a softening. A little more air. A space inside me I hadn't known existed.

Each season brought new language, but the pattern stayed the same: speak, shake, soften, repeat.

There were years my body carried guilt like gravity, holding paradoxes I couldn't name. Years it became a sanctuary, cradling both life and grief at once. Years it moved with the determination of a woman rebuilding her world from bone and breath. And finally, years where it stopped apologizing altogether, becoming not just shelter, but a compass. A home.

This body, my body, has carried so much. Not only pain, but possibility. Every truth I dared to whisper. Every dream I refused to bury. Every time I said *no more* and meant it.

This body, tired, tender, resilient, carries a voice that was never lost, only waiting.

And now, it doesn't whisper. It echoes.

Dreams That Told the Truth

There were nights when my dreams spoke the words I couldn't. They didn't come as stories. They came wrapped in symbols, strange places, strange images, but always heavy with meaning. I couldn't ignore them.

At first, they felt like warnings. Rooms pulsing with silence. Endless hallways where sound disappeared. I knocked on doors that never opened. I ran through forests thick with fog, my voice caught before it reached the trees. I'd wake breathless, heart racing, certain I'd been shown something, even if I couldn't name it yet.

But slowly, the tone changed. I stopped waking with clenched fists. The dreams didn't chase me anymore. They began to guide me instead. They weren't only about fear. They were about becoming.

One night, I dreamed I was running barefoot, the earth cool and alive beneath me. Back then, I told myself it was just an escape, the freedom of moving fast without carrying weight. Now I see it differently. My body wasn't only restless. It was reaching for what it needed most: roots under me, ground steady enough to hold me. Even in sleep, I was searching for solid earth.

Later, I dreamed of staircases, spiraling upward. Of lanterns I carried without trembling. Of my own voice rising, steady and certain. I dreamed of singing lullabies to a child I hadn't met but already loved. Of being seen, and not apologizing for it.

These weren't escapes. They were rehearsals. Each night, I trusted just a little more. The visions edged closer. Not fantasy, but memory. I dreamed of floating instead of drowning. Of mirrors reflecting me clearly. Of women older than time pressing keys into my hands and calling me by name.

In the stillness after waking, I heard it: *Keep going. You're not imagining this. You're remembering.*

Those dreams saw the rooms I would one day walk into. They carried the truths I would one day speak. They reminded me of the self I was always becoming. I held onto them, not because I always believed, but because they believed in me.

And I know now: the wildest dreams aren't fantasies. They're futures, finding their way back home.

Letter to the One Who Chose Truth

Dear Me, no apology necessary,

You were afraid. Terrified, even. And still, you spoke. Your voice didn't roar, it trembled, it cracked, it whispered truths into rooms that weren't ready to hear them.

But you spoke anyway.

I want to honor you for that, because I know the cost. The way your body shook with every word. The way your eyes searched the room after each sentence, bracing for silence, for rejection. The way love and loyalty kept trying to drown out your clarity.

You didn't take the easy path. You took the honest one. And that choice, shaky, costly, brave, was the beginning of everything.

You left what was familiar but suffocating. You dared to believe in something better. You whispered, *I want more*, before you even knew how to reach for it. That's the bravest kind of becoming.

I see you on that small apartment floor, trying to rebuild something no one ever modeled for you. I see you holding your son, vowing quietly, *It stops here*. I see you balancing college supplies with sippy cups, writing papers with one arm while cradling a future in the other.

You weren't ready. How could you be? But you didn't wait. You carved a path in the dark, your toddler's food on your shirt, fire in your belly, hope tucked into your pocket like a promise no one else could see.

And yes, there were stumbles. People who mirrored the past. Choices born from wounds instead of wisdom. But none of that defined you. Because every time you were knocked down, your voice came back stronger. Louder. Steadier. More your own.

You never spoke to wound. You spoke to heal. First, for your son. Then, for yourself. Then, for all the parts of you that had never been invited to speak before.

You enrolled in classes that lit your mind back up. The same questions that once got you in trouble became the very ones that carried you forward. And this time, no one stopped you.

You remembered how to wonder. To dream. To choose. You began to become the woman you always needed.

And you did it in the dark, in courtrooms and classrooms, in therapy rooms and journal margins. You turned pain into purpose, one word, one breath, one choice at a time.

Let me tell you this, from where you're headed: that voice you found? It doesn't fade. It gets stronger. Clearer. Wiser. You will speak in rooms that once would have terrified you. You will write stories that make others feel less alone. You will become the safe space you never had.

And one day, you'll look back, not just with pride, but with awe. Because you didn't simply *find* your voice. You remembered it was yours all along. And no one can take it from you again.

With deep love and lifelong gratitude,
Me

The Seeker's Lesson

There is a kind of reckoning in reclaiming the voice you were told to silence. The one buried under obligation, fear, and the weight of keeping other people comfortable. The voice that bent itself into survival until, one day, it whispered through clenched teeth: *Not anymore.*

My voice wasn't born here. It was remembered. Each word I spoke, each line I wrote, each thought I dared to let surface was an act of reclamation. Not just of sound, but of self. This wasn't about convincing others to hear me. It was about hearing myself, fully, fiercely, without flinching. About naming truths I had once been punished for seeing. About stepping out of survival and into embodiment.

I learned that voice isn't volume. It's presence. It's claiming space in rooms that once asked you to shrink. It's being able to say, *This happened,* and standing steady in the silence that follows.

I found mine in fragments. In the tiny apartment I moved into, just a block away, trying to keep my siblings close while finally beginning to choose myself. In the relationships that mirrored my past until I could finally name the pattern and say, *Enough.* In the courtroom, in the classroom, in the hush beside my son's crib, whispering promises I wasn't sure I knew how to keep.

I didn't roar. I built. Word by word. Class by class. Choice by trembling choice. Somewhere between heartbreak and homework, between dreams of being silenced and visions of speaking truth, my voice sharpened. Not into a weapon, into a compass.

I stopped speaking to please. I started speaking to live. To protect. To name. To become. Motherhood didn't mute me; it clarified me. Leaving didn't break me; it set me free. Education didn't distract me; it reminded me that I had always been the one asking questions.

The more I trusted my words, the more I saw the truth: my voice had never really left. It had been waiting, for safety, for sovereignty, for me. Because voice isn't just what comes out of our mouths. It's the knowing we refuse to abandon, the truths carried in our bodies, our breath, our very bloodlines.

And once that voice rises, there is no going back. Not to silence. Not to shrinking. Not to stories that demand our disappearance.

This season didn't just return my voice. It gave me vision. A life where I belong to myself. A life where my words aren't a liability, they're a legacy.

Reflective Journaling Prompt

After a while, silence feels like a bigger burden than the truth itself. When the words you buried start to stir, not to wound, but to free. Speaking doesn't have to be loud. Sometimes it's just a trembling whisper that says, *This matters*. Sometimes it's a quiet vow to stop shrinking in the presence of your own knowing.

This isn't about shouting. It's about returning to your voice. To your story. To the truth that's been waiting to rise.

- What truth have you carried in silence that now asks to be spoken aloud?
- What stories were you handed that no longer fit the life you're building?
- What part of you is no longer willing to whisper?
- Where have you mistaken silence for safety?
- If your voice could speak without fear of consequences, what would it say first?

Let this page be a permission slip, not because you need one, but because sometimes we forget we're allowed to begin. There is no perfect moment to use your voice. There is only the quiet pull that says: *Now*.

Readiness isn't about applause. It isn't about agreement. It's about honesty.

Your voice has waited patiently. It has endured silence. It softened when it needed to keep you safe. And now, it is ready to rise. Not to persuade. Not to defend. But simply to exist, whole, steady, and your own.

Speak, not because the world is ready. Speak because *you* are.

And remember: finding your voice is only the beginning. Once you speak, the deeper question often follows: *What is my voice truly longing for?*

For me, it wasn't attention. It was sanctuary. The space to face the ache I had carried all along. The chance to choose love that didn't demand I disappear in order to be safe.

Your Turn to Speak

Say it your way: words, sketches, fragments, arrows, messy lists. Let it out of your body and onto paper.

What the Ache Was Always Saying

"To love after loss, to hope after heartbreak, that is the bravest kind of magic."

Love, in all its forms, has always been both a longing and a lesson. This isn't a fairytale; it's a reckoning. It reaches into something deeper, the longing to be protected, the ache for mothering, the hope of being chosen not for what I could offer, but for who I was, without effort, without audition.

I didn't yet know I was searching for safe love, the kind I had never really known. Love that doesn't ask you to earn your place. Love that stays when it's inconvenient. Love that softens the edges instead of sharpening them. From the grief of my mother's absence to the terror of protecting my son from inherited pain, those years became a masterclass in boundaries, in resilience, in redefining what love means.

Not romance, sanctuary.
Not attention, devotion.
Not fireworks, a hearth.

The ache lived in my body before I could ever put words to it. It sat heavy in my shoulders, wound tight as breath. It hummed in my jaw when I clenched too long, curled in my stomach when hunger wasn't about food. The ache was its own language. A throb, a pulse, a warning. Every year it seemed to ask the same thing: *Will you listen this time?* And most years, my answer came too late.

And then, like light breaking through a long storm, I met my husband. He didn't arrive as a savior. He arrived as a witness. A steady presence who didn't flinch at my story or my son. For the first time, love felt like ease, like exhaling after years of holding my breath. He didn't save me; he made space for me to save myself. To unfold. To be seen. He didn't see my son as baggage. He saw him as sacred. A bond. A beginning.

Together we built something both fragile and luminous. Not perfect, but ours. Not in spite of what had fractured, but because of it. This is for the nights I held love with trembling hands and chose to keep holding it anyway, knowing it might cost me, knowing it might split me. Even when it meant breaking cycles. Even when it meant breaking open. Maybe that was always the point.

2002 – Fierce Protection

Cards That Held the Year

- *Relative Tarot*
  Hierophant (Karma) – I began building structure out of what I'd learned the hard way. New traditions grew from old scars and hard-won wisdom.

- *Rider-Waite Tarot*
  Queen of Swords – I was clear-eyed and sharp when I needed to be, but there was compassion in it too. The boundary I drew turned out to be a blessing.

  9 of Wands – I was worn down but not finished. What I defended came from love, not just survival.

  Strength – Power showed up in restraint. I protected fiercely, but I didn't need to roar to do it.

- *Oracle of the 7 Energies*
  Tender Embrace – Softness returned slowly. I felt it in the safety of being held, something my body hadn't trusted for a long time.

  The Uncharted Sea – My emotions ran deep that year. I stepped into them anyway, moving through places I didn't fully understand.

- *Animal Spirit*
  Bat – The dark didn't give me much to see, so I felt my way through instead. I listened to the small cues in my body, following them one step at a time. My instincts weren't perfect, but they carried me, and somehow that was enough.

∞ ∞

This was the year I became a warrior. Not the kind who shouts or swings in daylight, but the kind who sharpens in silence. The kind who protects not with panic, but with presence.

After my son came home from time away, I was giving him a bath. He was splashing, telling me about his summer in his little three-year-old voice, when I noticed a mark on his back, a burn, edged with a bruise.

I asked what happened. He answered the way only a small child can, with simple words that landed like thunder: someone who was supposed to protect him had hurt him.

I wanted to shatter right there. But I didn't. I kept my face calm, my voice steady. I finished the bath. I tucked him into bed. And then I picked up the phone and made the call that changed everything.

I said there would be no more visits. When threats came: court, custody, intimidation, I met them head-on. *Bring it on. I'll see you in court.* I knew he wouldn't press it any further. He never did.

What followed wasn't silence, but it was different. Harassing calls, petty antics, yes. But fear? That was gone. My intuition had carried me through, and it worked. I saw him clearly then, shaped by violence he had never unlearned. But the cycle stopped with me.

When I learned my son had been hurt, not in the ways I had been, but struck by someone meant to protect him, the world didn't collapse. It reassembled. The floor didn't fall away; my body rooted itself deeper. I didn't scream. I moved. I didn't tremble. I focused.

Something ancient rose in me that day. Not rage, not chaos, but precision. My spine straightened. My jaw set. My breath slowed. This wasn't fear. This was ignition. A vow: *Not again. Not ever.*

And vows require action.

I changed phone numbers. I packed boxes. I studied locks. I didn't ask for advice. I acted. My voice turned to steel, not in volume, but in structure. Short sentences. Final ones. I didn't soothe. I didn't explain. I enforced.

The mother I became that year wasn't born from tradition. She was forged from trauma, turned into intention.

Even in sleep, my body carried the knowing. My dreams screamed when my waking voice could not. I ran through endless halls, heard his voice but couldn't reach him, saw his room wrapped in thorns. I woke soaked in sweat, heart pounding. The message was clear: *He is not safe. You cannot stay silent.*

But not all dreams were warnings. Some were visions. I stood between him and the dark, not with fear, but with fire. I glowed. I held ground. I became immovable. Those dreams didn't soothe me. They prepared me.

The tension I once mistook for collapse became readiness. The bracing wasn't fear. It was foundation.

My body stopped being a place of hiding and became a place of knowing. And that knowing said: *This ends with me. Not just the harm, but the silence. Not just the pain, but the pretending.*

So, I moved us. Not to erase the past, but to rewrite it. To live the truth I had longed for: *You are safe now.*

Because I will never again be the girl who didn't know she could fight. I was exhausted, yes. But unbreakable. Afraid, yes. But unwavering. I wasn't just surviving. I was protecting with intention. And that intention became identity.

That year didn't make me hard. It made me clear.

I wasn't just guarding my son. I was guarding every version of myself who had ever wondered if someone would show up.

And I showed up.

2003 – A Light in a Dark Room

Cards That Held the Year

- *Relative Tarot*
  Lovers (Karma) – I began choosing myself. Love became both a mirror and a doorway, showing me where I stood and where I could go.

- *Rider-Waite Tarot*
  Judgment – A call echoed in me, and something inside rose to meet it.

  4 of Swords – In the quiet, I noticed my body starting to mend. Rest didn't feel natural at first, but it began working on me anyway.

  The Empress – I kept nurturing others, but slowly, I began learning how to offer some of that care back to myself.

  8 of Swords – The cage was inside me. I started testing the lock, unsure if it would give way.

- *Oracle of the 7 Energies*
  Smoke & Mirrors – So much of it was confusing. I couldn't always tell what was real, though sometimes the truth showed itself for a moment.

  Willing Release – Letting go hurt every time. I kept trying anyway, though part of me still held on tight.

  Healing the Heart – Healing came unevenly. Some days the ache let up, other days it came back just as sharp.

- *Animal Spirit*
  Shark – Its presence carried weight without needing to announce itself. I kept circling my own expression, knowing there was more power in me than I was showing.

∞ ∞

On July 23, 2003, I walked into a doctor's office thinking I had a UTI. I walked out pregnant.

After so many miscarriages, that word felt like a miracle, small, sudden, sacred. A whisper of *yes* after years of silence. That day I floated, light-headed and light-hearted. Not because I was naïve, but because I was hopeful. For a moment, I let myself believe joy might stay.

That night, everything changed.

The pain came sharp, fast, unmistakably wrong. Not the dull cramp of uncertainty, but the lightning-strike rupture that takes your breath away. At the ER, they told me what I already felt: ectopic pregnancy. Internal bleeding. A loss already happening. The rupture had been bleeding inside me for days. Time was now of the essence. Twelve hours after hope bloomed in my chest, devastation hollowed it out.

What broke me wasn't only the pain or the cruelty of timing. It was what could have happened. I might have died. My son, only four, might have been left behind. Left vulnerable. Left unprotected. Even as doctors worked, my mind spun in terrifying circles, picturing the unthinkable. The fear carved itself into me deeper than the wound in my abdomen. It lived in my breath, my bloodstream, the tremor that stayed long after the monitors went quiet.

I lay in the hospital bed, hand resting on the hollow of my belly, trying not to sob too hard because I needed my body to heal. I needed to survive. But grief doesn't stay neat. It seeps into muscle, into bone. My chest clenched every time I pictured my son alone, every time I imagined him handed to someone who once hurt us. The wound was physical, but it carried echoes far older than that night.

And then came the dream.

Not a dream, exactly. A visitation.

A room bathed in golden light. A rocking chair. A newborn in my arms, wrapped in pink. My son standing beside me, beaming. And then a voice, not mine, not imagined, but clear, certain: *"It's alright, Mom. My name is Peni. I wasn't meant to be more than what I was. I will always be with you. You will know when I am near."*

I woke with peace in my chest. Not numbness. Not denial. Peace. I hadn't just lost something. I had been visited by someone. My daughter. A soul never meant to stay, but never truly meant to leave.

Since then, she has returned. Sometimes as a toddler. Sometimes grown. Always her. Always arriving when I needed her most.

And in waking life, she leaves traces. Pennies. On pillows. In shoes. On the floors of rooms I hadn't stepped into for days. Especially when my son was far away, serving in the Army, beyond my reach, that's when they came most often. Small copper notes from the other side.

Peni. The one who named herself.

I stopped trying to explain it. Truth doesn't always make sense. Sometimes it just feels like love.

The healing didn't come from the hospital, or even from time, though both mattered. The real healing came from that room in the dream. From the light. From the permission to grieve someone I never held, and the mercy to recognize she was still with me.

I still carried the scar of survival. But it wasn't only a wound anymore. It became a thread, stitching grief and tenderness together in the same breath. My body remembered almost dying. But it also remembered choosing to stay.

That dream didn't just change my nights. It changed my days.

It taught me that presence doesn't require permanence. That motherhood isn't limited by breath or heartbeat. That some souls arrive only to remind us love doesn't need time to be real.

Peni became the light in a room I thought would remain dark forever.

The Seeker's Lesson: Peni's Light

There are losses so profound they split time in two. Days that begin with joy and end in silence. But even in silence, we are not alone.

On the day I came close to death, something sacred was born. This wasn't just a miscarriage. It was a threshold. A soul brushed mine, named herself, and left peace behind.

From that moment on, I saw differently. I listened differently. I mothered differently. Because not everything that ends is gone. And not everything unseen is absent.

Some love lives in light.
Some in pennies.
Some in dreams.
And some in the choice to stay.

2005 – A Love That Felt Like Home

Cards That Held the Year

- *Relative Tarot*
  Strength (Karma) – My vulnerability was finally met with warmth. Love didn't need pretense; it felt steady and real.

- *Rider-Waite Tarot*
  2 of Cups – It felt like recognition at the soul level, love offered in equal measure.

  6 of Swords – I made a quiet crossing into something safer, leaving old waters behind me.

  Page of Cups – The beginning felt tender, almost fragile. My heart agreed before I could find the words.

- *Oracle of the 7 Energies*
  Great Big Love – The love that came felt wide and familiar, like it had been circling close for a long time. It found me once I finally stood still.

  The Rose's Kiss – Intimacy showed up in small things, a glance, a hand brushing mine, the quiet moments between words. That kind of softness stayed with me.

- *Animal Spirit*
  Bat – I was finally crawling out of the old emotional caves I'd lived in. The past didn't fall away all at once, but I was breathing new air.

∞ ∞

When my now-husband came into my life, I didn't recognize what he was offering at first. Safe love doesn't show up with fanfare or a warning label. It arrives quietly, steady hands, patient eyes that don't flinch when you forget how to trust.

I waited for the turn. For the shift. For the punishment, I had learned always followed closeness. In my past, love was conditional. It came tangled in tension, followed by silence, blame, or need.

So, when he stayed calm, present, and kind, I braced. When he listened without trying to fix, I tensed. When he didn't disappear, I panicked. Ease made me suspicious. Kindness set off alarms. Consistency felt like the prelude to abandonment.

But this was different. There was no storm hiding behind his stillness. No cost attached to his affection. He didn't ask me to shrink or twist. He simply stayed. Walked beside me. Met me as I was.

At first, my body refused to believe it. My shoulders wouldn't drop. My breath stayed shallow. I scanned for danger. But slowly, like ice softening in spring, something in me began to melt. My jaw loosened. My laughter sounded lighter. I stopped bracing for impact every time he reached for my hand.

Love started to feel less like a test and more like a place to rest. Not a leap, but a steady crossing. A series of small choices: to believe in calm, to move away from harm, to let ease become familiar.

Something tender stirred inside me, something I thought had gone quiet forever, that childlike part of me that still believed in good things, that still hoped even after everything I'd endured. A fragile ember, but glowing all the same.

He didn't ask me to collapse into him. He invited me to stand beside him. Not as someone to rescue, but as someone to walk with. If I needed him, he showed up. Always. At the end of every day, no matter what else had happened, we returned to each other. Sometimes it was on the sofa, watching TV. Sometimes at the kitchen table, talking until the words slowed into silence. Even now, when work takes him far away, we still end our days together, a call, a text, a ritual of return.

At night, my dreams shifted. Not because the fear was gone, but because something gentler had arrived to hold it. I dreamed of still water, of rooms without corners, of hands that held but never claimed. I dreamed of walking next to someone in silence, not chased, not rushed, just walking. And the absence of fear felt like a revelation.

It was as if my soul had started practicing a kind of peace I had never lived but always longed for. A love that didn't demand. A presence that didn't shift. A home I didn't have to build alone. Sometimes I woke with tears, not from panic but from relief. My body didn't fully trust it yet, but it was listening. It was learning.

I didn't leap into the light. I emerged from the dark, blinking, unsteady, but whole. This was new. And terrifying. And exactly what I'd been waiting for.

He never asked me to earn his love. He offered it freely, quietly, again and again. And I began to believe: love can be soft. Safety can stay. Peace doesn't need permission.

That year, I didn't just fall in love. I began to *understand* it, not as fantasy, but as practice. The sacred, imperfect act of showing up. Of staying.

2006 – The Sacred Yes

Cards That Held the Year

- *Relative Tarot*
  Hermit (Karma) – It was a year of inner confirmation. My soul said yes long before my voice managed to catch up.

- *Rider-Waite Tarot*
  The Lovers – For the first time, my heart, my mind, and my spirit weren't at odds. Choosing felt steady, like something I could finally trust.

  2 of Cups - Love didn't tower over me or leave me chasing it. It met me eye to eye, in a way that felt steady and human.

  10 of Cups – Joy surprised me in small places, meals, conversations, and laughter I hadn't expected. It wasn't something waiting at the end; it was already here.

- *Oracle of the 7 Energies*
  A Higher View – I began to see things differently, like pulling back far enough to catch the bigger shape of my life.

  Willing Release – Letting go of fear didn't happen all at once. Each time I loosened it, a little more room opened for love.

- *Animal Spirit*
  Scorpion – My intensity was close to the surface. I protected fiercely, but I was trying to learn how to carry that fire without always burning.

∞ ∞

That year, we left everything behind. Packed up our lives in boxes, carried our hope right alongside them, and headed to the Southeast. We got married. We began again.

My son gained a father. I gained a partner, a co-creator in life. Not someone who tried to complete me, but someone who walked beside me, steady and present.

I'd never known love like this. Not quiet love. Not lasting love. Not the kind that grows roots without demanding blood in return. Part of me kept waiting for it to break, for the shadow to fall, for the old patterns to show up. But they didn't.

Instead of chaos, I found peace. Instead of testing, I found tenderness. Instead of proving, I simply belonged.

When we stood in that little rustic venue, the county commissioner cracking jokes, our "yes" wasn't just paperwork or romance. It was something deeper, a recalibration of the soul. A full-body knowing: love doesn't have to hurt to be real.

For so long, I had equated commitment with control. With losing myself. With silencing my needs to keep the peace. But this was different. This was presence without pressure. Intimacy without invasion. A shared future that didn't come from fantasy but from trust.

Still, I carried my past with me. Not to sabotage it, but to see the difference. My body didn't know how to rest right away. It approached this love like a traveler in a new country, curious, cautious, hopeful. Every gesture felt foreign. Every day was both a relief and a risk. Could I really be all of me here, and still be loved?

It took time, but slowly, my breath deepened. My shoulders lowered. The tension I thought was permanent started to ease. I watched my son take to him, not as if meeting someone new, but as if recognizing someone he'd always known. They built trust at their own pace, and I stood back, quietly amazed, watching us shift into something stable. Something sacred.

In our new home, I caught myself humming for no reason. Laughing from my gut. Letting my voice rise without apology. I didn't just say yes that year. I lived it.

Even my dreams shifted. They stopped testing me with mazes and escape routes. I dreamed of open doorways, sunlight falling across new floors, warm and inviting. I wasn't running anymore. I wasn't hiding. I was arriving.

In one dream, we stood together in a field, no guests, no ceremony, just us, exchanging something older than vows. In another, my son ran ahead on a beach, laughing, not checking if we were following, trusting we were. My mother appeared once, not angry, not ashamed, just watching. I woke with sadness, but not pain. More like recognition: some things can't be repaired, only witnessed.

Those dreams weren't fantasies. They were practice. My spirit rehearsing how to live inside something that didn't demand suffering as proof. Slowly, practice turned into reality.

That year, I began to unlearn the flinch. To release the belief that love had to be loud or painful or earned. I began to trust that love could be ordinary and sacred at the same time.

Not everything healed at once, but something essential shifted. I stopped waiting for apologies that would never come. I stopped needing proof that I was lovable. I stopped gripping so tightly to grief that had already done its teaching.

Because now, I wasn't just loved. I was held by a man, by a family, by a life I had helped create. My yes wasn't spoken once. It was in the way I exhaled. In the way I stayed. In the way I began to believe that love, real love, doesn't demand your abandonment. It invites your return.

2007 – I'll Show You

Cards That Held the Year

- *Relative Tarot*
  Wheel of Fortune (Karma) – Life shifted, not softly but with force. The turn came with teeth.

- *Rider-Waite Tarot*
  6 of Swords – I moved toward something freer, even though leaving cost me.

  The World – I closed a chapter with conviction. It was the end of who I wasn't.

  7 of Wands – I stood my ground, fighting for my right to change the story.

- *Oracle of the 7 Energies*
  The Land Between – I wasn't where I had been, and I wasn't yet where I was going. Still, I kept moving.

  Awakening Genius – My voice came back with an edge, sharp, certain, and mine.

- *Animal Spirit*
  Bear – Strength rose slowly, like waking from a long hibernation. My will was reemerging, steady and alive.

∞ ∞

I thought law enforcement was where I belonged. My degree was finished. My résumé was stacked with grit, experience, and intention. I walked into the sheriff's department with a folder in my hand and purpose in my chest.

And then I heard the sentence that would change everything:
"We've met our quota of women. But there's a secretary position if you want it."

For a second, I froze. My fists curled tight. My jaw locked. My breath caught mid-chest. I didn't cry. I didn't beg. I didn't even argue. I stood there, feeling the heat rise in my body, a burn I knew too well, the sting of being dismissed, underestimated, pushed aside.

102

I left that building with one clear thought: *Oh, hell no.*

I hadn't survived this much to sit behind a desk and type someone else's reports. I hadn't carried all that fire to take notes while the boys' club carried on. If this was the door, then fine. I'd stop knocking. I'd build my own.

So, I pivoted. I applied to graduate school for mental health counseling. Not because it was easy, not because it was convenient, but because it was mine.

The rejection still hurt, of course. But not in the way it used to. This wasn't shame. This wasn't collapse. This was ignition. A spark that said: stop auditioning for belonging. Stop waiting for permission. Choose yourself.

The whispers came, the doubts, the questions. *You're not qualified. You don't belong there. Who do you think you are?* Some came from the outside. Others whispered inside my own head. But I didn't argue. I didn't defend. I just kept moving. One application. One choice. One breath at a time.

There's a kind of defiance that isn't about shouting. It's steadier than that. Built from muscle memory, from every slammed door you've ever walked past. That year, I walked differently. Chin up, spine straight, not out of arrogance, but out of refusal. Refusal to keep making myself smaller just because someone else was afraid of my strength.

I wasn't rising out of flight; I was rising out of sleep. Something ancient stirred, aching, ready. My body remembered the sting of dismissal before my mind could even process the words. My spine straightened on instinct. My breath deepened. My feet turned toward something better.

I couldn't name the destination yet, but I knew the direction: I wasn't going to stay where I wasn't seen.

Even my dreams began to shift. They weren't about hiding anymore. They were about power. I dreamed of staircases, spiraling upward, me climbing two steps at a time, breathless but unstoppable. I dreamed of podiums where I spoke without notes, words flowing steadily, the whole room listening. I dreamed of fire, not destruction, but intention. Flames that lit torches, marking trails for whoever came next.

And sometimes the dreams were quieter, but just as sure. I saw blueprints unrolling across tables. Keys pressed into my palm. Doors opening into wide, bright spaces. They weren't fantasies. They were instructions. Proof that I already carried what I needed.

This wasn't the year I gave up on law enforcement. This was the year I redefined justice. Not as a badge or a title, but as a way of living fully, fiercely, without apology.

That year, I stopped waiting to be chosen. I stopped knocking on doors that were never meant to open. And I started building my own.

2008 – Between Worlds

Cards That Held the Year

- *Relative Tarot*
  Justice (Karma) – The balance between control and surrender revealed itself in motion. I learned that fairness isn't safety, and protection isn't perfection, only presence, steady and true, when life demands reckoning.

- *Rider-Waite Tarot*
  Five of Pentacles – Body and security were shaken. I looked for the door in the dark and found it by feel.

  Queen of Swords – Clean edges, clear speech. I named what was true and let the rest fall away.

  Three of Wands – Not a parade, but momentum. Small signs on the horizon, arrival, beginning.

- *Oracle of the 7 Energies*
  The Land Between – One foot in what was, one in what would be. I learned to breathe in the in-between.

  It Is What It Is – Acceptance without resistance. The moment met as it stands, unbent, unargued, simply true.

- *Animal Spirit*
  Black Egg – The truth in my throat. Fewer words, deeper ones. I spoke from the place that cannot lie.

∞ ∞

We had just moved into a new house when the accident happened. Barely a week and a half in, boxes still half unpacked, routines not yet settled. I left for work that morning, watching my son wait for his school bus at the end of the neighborhood. He knew his phone number. He knew his address. I had drilled it into him, wanting him safe, prepared, and grounded in the world. What I hadn't counted on was that safety isn't always something you can rehearse.

He told me later that he'd heard an engine, thought it was his bus, it was a garbage truck, and panicked at the thought of being late. My son has always loved school; maybe it's from growing up with me in college most of his childhood. I could be wrong; it happens. So, he started walking to the next stop. When he described it afterward, his voice was calm, precise, almost matter-of-fact. *"I waited for the stoplight to change,"* he said. *"I waited for the green man to say it was my turn to cross the street. That MAN did not pay attention to the rules!"* Imagine wide eyes, shaking head, and wild arm gestures as the story is being told. He was furious. (I can laugh at the image now, but I absorbed every word back then with a heavy heart).

That MAN was from the neighborhood. His windows were fogged with dew, his phone in his hand, all of it keeping him from seeing the boy who was doing everything right. And just like that, my son was on the pavement.

As I pulled into the parking garage, a strange number kept lighting up my phone. When I finally parked and answered, a woman's voice came through, a stranger who had witnessed the accident. She told me she was with my son, keeping him still. *"He keeps trying to get up,"* she said, *"but I told him to stay down."* He was insistent on making it to the bus on time. Inside, I was unraveling, terrified, furious at the universe for requiring me to be in this moment, yet grateful to this woman for staying by his side.

I was already at the children's hospital. I worked there, just in a different building. I reached the emergency department before the ambulance. The staff looked at me, puzzled, unsure why I was standing there, waiting for a child they hadn't even admitted yet. I explained the situation, showed my credentials, and they immediately shifted from confusion to action, guiding me to the chairs outside the trauma bay already assigned to him.

When my son finally arrived, he was calm. Almost irritated, as if the whole thing were an inconvenience that might make him late for school. His tibia and fibula had pushed through skin, a compound fracture that made my stomach lurch and my knees weaken. But he stayed steady. When he asked the nurse if they would need to remove his leg, he didn't cry. He just wanted to know the truth, to prepare me for the worst.

He was a month shy of nine, and already carrying himself with a composure that shamed the chaos around him. The police officer who accompanied him chuckled when he told us, "He rattled off his phone number and address like a pro, but when I asked for his zip code, he said, 'How am I supposed to know that? We've only lived here a week.'" Even in crisis, his clarity showed.

But the healing wasn't only physical. Months in a cast passed slowly, but it was the car rides afterward that left their mark.

He didn't trust the road anymore. Didn't trust drivers. He would crawl to the floorboard in the backseat, hiding, shaking, convinced that any moment another car might veer off course. Watching him fold into himself that way broke something in me. I wanted to fight every reckless driver on the road. I wanted to shield him from engines, from wheels, from every unpredictable thing I could not control.

Not long after, I switched from days to nights in the same children's emergency department, the one where I'd waited for him. I wanted to be home with him during the day so my husband could be there at night. It was the only way I knew to keep our world steady while his body, and our hearts, learned how to heal.

That was the year I learned the hardest truth: you can't bubble-wrap the world. You can teach the phone number. You can steady your voice. You can wear yourself out with hope. And still, life comes roaring with engines you can't hear in time.

What I could do was meet his fear with presence. Sit in the driver's seat, calm and steady, while he hid on the floorboard. Wait until he slowly, carefully, climbed back into the seat. Tell him, again and again, "You're safe. I've got you. The roads are unpredictable, but I am not."

It wasn't clean. It wasn't quick. But little by little, he trusted again. He sat up. He buckled in. He let the world move around him without hiding from it.

And me? I stopped pretending I could protect him from everything. I started learning that sometimes love isn't in the shield, it's in the steady hand, the unwavering presence, the voice that says, even in the wreckage: We're still here.

My dreams carried the same unease that rode with us in the car. In one, I pressed the brake but the pedal sank to the floor, useless, while the road curved faster than I could follow. Another night, I dreamed of standing in the middle of an intersection, arms outstretched, trying to stop traffic with my body alone. I woke with my heart racing as if I'd already been struck.

Only later did I understand: these weren't warnings of what might happen. They were mirrors of what already had. They showed me the limits of my control, the futility of trying to bubble-wrap a world that was always in motion.

And here's the part that still makes me smile: the boy who once hid on the floorboard now loves cars. After the Army, he became a mechanic. He rides a motorcycle. He's the most responsible driver I know. What once terrified him became the very thing he claimed as his own.

2009 – The Body Breaks the Silence

Cards That Held the Year

- *Relative Tarot*
  Hanged One (Karma) – In the stillness, I saw what all that rushing had blurred. When I let go, the angle shifted. What I'd called loss began to feel like balance, and surrender took on the weight of peace.

- *Rider-Waite Tarot*
  10 of Wands – I carried too much, weight that should have been shared. The load bent me low before I even realized it.

  Queen of Cups – My feelings ran deep. I didn't always speak them, but they were there, steady and strong beneath the surface.

  The Star – After everything cracked, a faint light appeared. Healing came in whispers, not declarations.

- *Oracle of the 7 Energies*
  Broken Open – My body split before my heart could. The breaking made space for breath again.

  Sacred Reverence – I started treating my body differently, honoring pain as a kind of message I needed to hear.

- *Animal Spirit*
  Bear – Recovery moved slowly. Strength returned one heartbeat at a time.

∞ ∞

By the time 2009 arrived, my body was done pretending. I had carried trauma in every form: emotional, physical, mental, spiritual, and generational. Though I thought I'd learned to outpace it, my body had other plans. The pain wasn't sudden. It had always been there, layered and silenced. But that year it sharpened. It spoke.

I had a partial hysterectomy. A decision made with both clarity and sorrow. It was survival and surrender at the same time. On the surface, it was a medical procedure, but for me it was a reckoning. My body was saying out loud what my mouth had been too stubborn to admit: *I can't hold this anymore.*

I didn't just grieve the surgery. I grieved the illusions tied to it, the idea that I could carry everything forever, that I could outrun what had already shaped me, that endurance was the only measure of strength. For years, my body had been a container of pain, of legacy, of responsibility. Now it wanted to be something else. Tended. Rested. Heard.

And strangely, in that unraveling, something aligned. I began to notice how the pieces of my life were not random, but connected. The rejection in 2007, the slammed door that burned, had pushed me into graduate school. And now, my degree wasn't just coursework; it was a lifeline. Each class mirrored my own life with uncanny precision: grief counseling while I was walking through my own losses, geriatric studies while my grandfather's dementia deepened. Over and over, life and learning folded into each other like coordinates on a map.

I realized then that this wasn't a coincidence; I'd never believed in it. This was guidance. Every closed door had been steering me here, not where I thought I should go, but where I was meant to go.

I walked through that year exhausted, scarred, but reverent. Healing didn't arrive with clarity or celebration. It came in collapse, in stitches and scar tissue, in long silences. It came in listening.

At night, my dreams wept for me. Asleep, the dam broke; awake, I held it together. I sobbed in ways I couldn't during the day. I dreamed of slipping beneath water, my ribs sore but my body held, weightless in a way I hadn't felt in years. Of pulling thorns from my skin, no blood, only release. Of houses cracked wide open, ribs splitting to reveal secret gardens inside. Of women I didn't know, gathered in a circle, wrapping me in fabric and light. They didn't speak. They didn't need to. Comfort was simply given.

These dreams weren't nightmares. They weren't warnings. They were truths. Sacred truths. My soul wasn't running anymore; it was grieving.

And grief, I learned, isn't the end. It's the thaw. It's the way reverence creeps back in, not only for what was lost, but for what was survived. For the body that carried it all without breaking, until finally, blessedly, it asked to be heard.

That year broke me open, not as punishment but as passage. I stopped pushing. I started listening. And in that listening, I found something small but steady, a flicker, a whisper, a reminder: *You are not done yet.*

2010 – Crowned by the Climb, Carved by the Flame

Cards That Held the Year

- *Relative Tarot*
  Emperor (Karma) – I began claiming structure for myself, stepping into leadership that had been shaped by fire.

- *Rider-Waite Tarot*
  Queen of Swords – Pain had sharpened me. Clarity turned into both shield and compass.

  4 of Swords – Rest wasn't optional anymore. Healing became something I had to take seriously.

  Strength – Power showed up in presence, not force. Discipline looked like grace I had to practice daily.

  4 of Wands – A moment of celebration came, brief, but I let myself have it.

- *Oracle of the 7 Energies*
  Healing the Heart – Healing didn't come all at once. Some days I felt pieces of myself returning, other days it was harder to believe it at all.

  A Grand Symphony – I began to notice that what I said mattered. My voice wasn't alone; it was part of something bigger moving around me.

- *Animal Spirit*
  Cobra – The energy of transformation coiled inside me. I was rising into something older, wiser, and more precise.

That year felt like a marathon I hadn't trained for. I started my counseling internship in January, graduated in October, and finally walked across the stage in December with my Master's degree in Mental Health Counseling. On the outside, it looked neat: a straight line of progress, tassel swinging, degree in hand. But the truth? It was anything but smooth.

I was interning, mothering, and studying all at once, every role overlapping, none of them optional. My body was already carrying years of trauma, and then the old pain came back with a vengeance. The endometriosis I thought I had escaped after the partial hysterectomy returned sharper than ever, pain climbing my spine, curling around my ribs, demanding attention I didn't have time to give it.

In August, right in the middle of my internship, I had a full hysterectomy. I was thirty-three, lying in a hospital bed, body stitched and scarred, trying to heal while still showing up for clients. Pausing wasn't an option (and really, when had it ever been?). Bills still needed paying. My son still needed me. My internship hours weren't going to complete themselves. So, I did what I'd always done: pushed through. I sat in sessions with a heating pad tucked under my desk, smiled while my insides screamed, and reminded other people to breathe while forgetting to take my own full breaths.

I need to backtrack for a moment. When it came time to apply for internships, I cast my net wide, twenty applications sent out, twenty hopeful tries. Only one came back. The Sheriff's Office. A different county, a different set of doors, but still. The irony wasn't lost on me. Life has a dark sense of humor sometimes. Years earlier, I'd been told by another Sheriff that they had already "met their quota of women," as if justice could be tallied that way. And yet here I was, accepted, welcomed into the very system that once shut me out.

At first, it felt strange, almost cruel, like a cosmic joke. But as the months unfolded, I began to see it differently. This was placement with purpose. I wasn't meant to police, I was meant to heal. And the healing began right there, in the most unexpected of places.

I didn't feel fearless, far from it. But I stood steady anyway. And in that steadiness, something shifted. Every session was more than a job. It was a reckoning. It was healing I didn't know I needed.

As if the universe wanted to drive the point home, while I was holding that ground in the Sheriff's Office, my classes were unfolding with almost eerie precision. Grief counseling, while I was grieving the losses etched into my body. Geriatric studies while my grandfather's dementia worsened. Trauma courses while my own trauma roared to the surface. It wasn't coincidence; it was alignment. As if the universe was saying: *Pay attention. This isn't just coursework. This is your life's curriculum.*

By the end of the year, I realized my degree wasn't only about work. It was about reclamation. It was proof to myself that I could carve out something different, that I wasn't only what had been done to me, that my mind could expand even while my body was begging for rest.

Sleep was fractured, but my dreams kept pace with the transformation.

I dreamed of fire, not the chaotic kind, but ritual flames lining long roads, as though I was marking a path for someone else to follow. I dreamed of pain winding up my spine like vines, curling tight, loosening, curling again, teaching me that transformation doesn't arrive all at once, it coils and uncoils until you learn to live differently.

Some nights I dreamed of strangers handing me keys hidden in books or torches pressed into my palms, like reminders: *You're equipped. Keep going.*

And then came the dream that told the truth the loudest. I dreamed of handing my degree to someone who touched my chest and said, "Now heal this." That dream landed heavier than any lecture. It reminded me that education was never the finish line. Healing was.

By December, when I crossed the stage, my smile was real, but it wasn't the whole story. Beneath it lived scar tissue, sleepless nights, whispered promises to myself that I wouldn't quit even when quitting would have been easier. The degree didn't erase the ache. It honored it.

When I looked out into the crowd that December, it wasn't just my degree I saw, it was my son's face, watching me, proof that everything I carried had led us here.

2010 wasn't just the year I earned a degree. It was the year I stopped measuring strength by how much I could carry and started learning that sometimes the bravest thing you can do is set something down.

2011 – The Yarn That Saved Me

Cards That Held the Year

- *Relative Tarot*
  Hierophant (Karma) – I learned through experience. Wisdom wasn't given to me; I had to live it first. The lessons that year weren't taught in books, but in life itself.

- *Rider-Waite Tarot*
  Tower – Another break came, but this time it showed a doorway instead of just wreckage.

  Strength – I didn't roar; I stitched. Power took a quieter form in my hands.

  6 of Pentacles – Giving and receiving finally balanced out. Healing became something shared, not carried alone.

- *Oracle of the 7 Energies*
  A Beautiful Uncaging – The rules that bound me began to fall away, and the real started to push through.

  Call of the Muse – At first, creativity kept me alive. Later, it began to bring me joy.

  Spirit of Gratitude – Gratitude met me in the smallest places, in each stitch, in the breath I let out, in the softness I could finally hold.

- *Animal Spirit*
  Gazelle – I stayed alert, still sensitive, but at last I felt safe enough to stop running.

∞ ∞

That year, I thought I was having a heart attack. My chest clamped down, my breath went shallow, and the room tilted. I ended up in the emergency room, wired to machines, waiting to hear if my body was about to betray me for good.

The doctor came in, calm, almost casual: "It's not your heart. Just a panic attack." Just. As if terror is less real when no one else can see it.

But I knew better. My body wasn't lying. It was sounding an alarm. And honestly? I already knew what it was about.

My first boss at the Sheriff's Office. A woman who smiled while she cut me down. Micromanagement dressed up as mentorship. Gaslighting disguised as guidance. Punishment disguised as professionalism. I'd survived abuse before, but this was the first time I'd seen it institutionalized. Normalized. With a paycheck attached.

At first, I just watched. I saw how she treated my co-workers, sharp words and calculated cruelty delivered with a smile. I remember thinking, *What have I gotten myself into?* And then it turned on me. I told myself I had the fortitude to deal with it; after all, I'd already survived my mother. But I was wrong. This wasn't resilience training. This was erosion.

The doctor looked at me and said, "Whatever you're doing to deal with stress, it's not working." And he was right. I was journaling. Meditating. Reading all the self-help books. But none of it unclenched the fist in my chest.

One night, I researched ways to destress and then typed three words into my computer's search engine: *how to knit*.

I felt ridiculous, desperate even. But when I picked up the yarn, something shifted. The rhythm steadied me. The drag of the thread slowed my pulse. Loop by loop, my breath deepened. Knitting wasn't a hobby. It was a lifeline.

And because nothing that saves me ever stays just mine, I carried it into the jail.

The room was gray, fluorescent, and sterile, but once we gathered in that circle, it changed. Women shuffled in hesitantly at first, some skeptical, some curious. I set out bags of donated yarn, odds and ends, colors mismatched but vibrant against the dull concrete walls. The air smelled faintly of disinfectant, but the scrape of chairs and the soft rustle of yarn bags shifted the atmosphere.

Hands, many of them scarred, tattooed, trembling, picked up looms and yarn. Some fumbled, frustrated, muttering that they "weren't crafty." Others found a rhythm almost instantly. The sound was soft but steady: yarn sliding, wooden hooks scraping, laughter spilling out when someone dropped a stitch and had to unravel.

It wasn't just about making hats or scarves. It was about what happened in between the stitches. Conversation slipped in sideways, casual at first. A comment about a child at home. A sigh about court dates. And then, without fanfare, the harder truths: the abuse, the addiction, the grief. Trauma unraveled the way the yarn did, one loop at a time.

Sometimes I teared up. Sometimes I wanted to scream. But mostly, I listened. We all did. The yarn gave us something to hold, something to do with our hands while our hearts cracked open.

What we made wasn't just fabric. It was softness in a place that had none. Everything we made was donated to shelters for women fleeing violence, sending comfort outward, a stitch of solidarity from one survivor to another.

I watched their faces change. Shoulders dropped. Breath slowed. A stillness came over the room that had nothing to do with silence and everything to do with presence. For an hour each week, the jail wasn't just confinement. It was communion.

Even my own body began to unclench. Not all at once, but slowly. My panic didn't vanish; it transformed. Instead of caging me, it became the doorway back to myself.

At night, my dreams shifted too. I dreamed of glowing threads weaving through my hands. Of women passing scarves and stories to each other in silence, all of us knowing exactly what was being said without a word. I dreamed of my chest splitting open, not from pain this time, but release. Smoke rising. Breath returning.

Looking back, I know the panic attack wasn't failure. It was a reckoning. My body saying, *No more pretending.* And the yarn? It didn't just give me something to do with my hands. It gave me rhythm. It gave me breath. It gave me grace.

That year, I didn't just learn to knit. I learned to let softness save me. And maybe for the first time in my life, I started believing that survival didn't have to be sharp. Sometimes, it could be gentle.

2012 – Living the Love I Longed For

Cards That Held the Year

- *Relative Tarot*
  Lovers (Karma) – This time love was chosen. It felt like a sacred yes, like finally coming home.

- *Rider-Waite Tarot*
  The Star – Hope didn't stay in my imagination anymore. Healing started to live in my body.

  Queen of Pentacles – I gave care freely, and for once I could receive it without fear.

  Temperance – Balance didn't happen by chance. I learned to practice it, one intention at a time.

- *Oracle of the 7 Energies*
  The Oracle's Gift – Intuition kept showing up, steady and clear. It gave me small glimpses of what was ahead.

  Beautiful Uncaging – My heart opened wider than it ever had. I wasn't hiding anymore.

- *Animal Spirit*
  Firefly – The joy didn't last long, but it was bright while it was there. Those quick flashes reminded me what light felt like.

∞ ∞

By this year, the ache that once haunted my chest had softened. The longing that used to burn had turned into something steadier, quieter, woven through with gratitude. Not the kind you perform. The kind you live. Breath by breath. Gesture by gesture.

I wasn't chasing love anymore. I was nurturing it. Giving it. Becoming it. There was no single, cinematic moment of realization. Just the slow unfolding of presence, mine, and his. Love wasn't a finish line anymore. It was the ground beneath my feet.

I began to understand that peace isn't passive. It doesn't magically arrive once everything calms down. Peace is what you choose, again and again, when the noise quiets and you decide to stay soft.

This love didn't ask me to sacrifice myself. It asked me to bring my whole self forward. I didn't feel like I had to twist or disappear to be chosen. Instead, I found myself loved exactly as I was, fully, freely, without audition.

I didn't just love my husband. I loved the version of myself who could finally stay in the moment. The one who reached out without flinching. Who asked for what she needed and didn't apologize for it.

My body knew before my mind did. I woke in the mornings and realized my jaw wasn't clenched. I reached for him without bracing for withdrawal. I moved through my days not waiting for the other shoe to drop, but grateful that, for once, there was no shoe. No drop. Just steady ground.

Evenings felt different, too. Folding laundry while he joked across the room. Stirring a pot on the stove with my son telling me about school. Simple moments, but they landed differently. I wasn't tensing for interruption or punishment. I was here, really here, living inside the softness I'd always thought was out of reach.

My nervous system, once trained to expect rupture, began to learn rhythm. Safe rhythm. The kind that hums like background music instead of alarms. That year, my body stopped preparing for loss and started making room for love. Not a love that demanded proof, but a love that mirrored truth.

I no longer had to carve myself into pieces to belong. I brought all of myself to the table, and there was room for it. My hips carried stillness. My breath held grace. My spine straightened, not in defense, but in dignity. I wasn't proving anything. I wasn't chasing anything. I was home.

And at night, my dreams reflected that arrival. I dreamed of open fields and easy mornings. Of holding a warm cup in both hands. Of laughter that didn't carry tension. Folding clothes, planting seeds, holding a child's hand, and each act felt sacred.

No villains. No storms. No locked doors. Just unshaken breath. Belonging.

Sometimes my younger self appeared, standing at the edges of the dream. She didn't look scared anymore. She looked amazed, like she was whispering: *So, this is what it feels like.*

And once, under a wide tree, I dreamed of resting in sunlight with someone beside me. This time, I didn't flinch. I didn't tense. I didn't explain. I just let myself be held.

Those dreams didn't rescue me. They mirrored me. Whole. Soft. Still here.

Maybe most truthfully: finally, home. Finally arrived. Finally at rest.

What the Body Carries

My body knew long before I did. It clenched. It braced. It whispered through shallow breath and restless sleep. It held the story I hadn't yet learned to tell. Years of survival lived in my shoulders, hypervigilance in my spine, grief in my jaw. And still, I kept moving.

Even in moments when I tried to steady someone else, my body carried the tremor. At the hospital after the accident, I felt my chest tighten, my knees threaten to give, even as I kept my voice calm for my son. His body, a month shy of nine, carried its own strange wisdom. A broken leg, bones jutting through skin, and still he held himself with a composure that steadied me. He asked clear questions, sought the truth, and sat inside his pain without flinching. While my body shook, his stayed still, as if he understood instinctively that panic would not help.

But healing is not just bone and scar tissue. In the months that followed, his body carried fear differently. Car rides became battlefields. He folded himself into the floorboard, small, hidden, bracing for the next crash. His muscles remembered what his mind could not yet reason away: danger might come again at any moment. Watching him taught me what the body holds and how long it takes for that grip to loosen.

Healing didn't arrive as ease, not at first. It came with trembling. With rupture. With softness that felt like risk. But as safety grew, my body began to loosen. Where there was once flinch, there was pause. Where there was once armor, there was breath.

I noticed it in small, ordinary moments. Waking up and realizing my jaw wasn't locked. Feeling my shoulders drop without forcing them. Letting a breath reach all the way down to my belly. Even something as simple as my husband's hand in mine no longer made my pulse race with suspicion. It just felt warm. Steady. Safe.

And then there was knitting. Loop by loop, I could feel my heart rate slow, and my breath deepen. My hands moved in rhythm while my body remembered how to rest. The yarn wasn't just fiber; it was a tether. Each stitch reminded me I could create calm, that I could make beauty in real time, that peace wasn't only something I had to long for, it was something I could hold.

My body didn't forget. His didn't either. But slowly, both of ours stopped reliving. He sat up in the backseat again, trusting the road. I let my shoulders fall, trusting the moment. The ache became a memory, not a warning.

This body, mine, had carried it all: the silence, the fight, the fire. And now, it carried something else, knowing. Knowing when to rest. When to release. When to trust the hands that held me. When to stop gripping peace like it might vanish.

Healing didn't erase the past. It taught us how to live with it without becoming it. Memory still lives in the muscle. But so does the letting go. And mine? Mine has finally learned how to stay.

Dreams That Told the Truth

Back then, when I was still learning all the ways love could hurt, my dreams started showing me something else; something softer.

I dreamed of quiet rooms, curtains stirring in a slow breeze, sunlight spilling across wooden floors. I dreamed of hands, warm, steady, open, meeting mine without demand, without condition. In those nights, I wasn't chosen for what I could give or how well I performed. I was simply… chosen.

Sometimes it felt like being wrapped in a blanket after years of cold, the kind of warmth that doesn't scorch but settles, lingering like afternoon sun on skin. In those dreams, I wasn't managed or measured. I was met.

And sometimes, the dreams stretched further. I dreamed of steadiness when waking life cracked wide open. Of being held when I couldn't hold everything together. I dreamed of safety, not the kind you rehearse with phone numbers and addresses, but the kind that meets you where the world breaks and still whispers: you're not alone.

In waking life, everything felt like performance, sharp edges, constant vigilance. But when I slept, something shifted. Tenderness wasn't another test to pass; it was a resting place. Safety not as an illusion of control, but as presence. A way of being where I could set the weight down.

The dreams whispered what I couldn't yet believe: that longing wasn't weakness, it was direction. That love didn't have to crash in with thunder. It could arrive like a hush, a whisper, a steady hand that stayed.

And when that love finally did show up in my life, I didn't doubt it. I had already felt it in my bones. Already practiced the exhale in its arms.

My spirit had been rehearsing for years before my body knew it was possible. These weren't just dreams. They were memory. A reminder of the life I was always meant to recognize. A love I brushed against behind closed eyes long before I could name it out loud.

Letter to the One Who Believed in Softness After Survival

Dear Me, in the years you dared to believe love could be safe,

I know how long you waited for this. Not just for love, but for rest. For a touch that didn't leave bruises, seen or unseen. For a voice that didn't rise when it didn't get its way. For a place where you could finally set your armor down and not be punished for being soft.

You never asked to be rescued. But you did hope, quietly, achingly, that someone might see you. And then, he did. Not with grand gestures. Not with promises too big to keep. But with presence. With steadiness. With a look that said, *You don't have to flinch anymore.*

At first, you didn't trust it. How could you? You tried to outrun it, tested it, waited for the blow that never came. But he waited too, not for you to be perfect, but for you to believe you didn't have to be.

You were a fiercely protective single mother, and later, a wife. Not because you needed completing, but because you finally felt safe enough to choose it. You built a life from scratch, one word, one stitch, one sacred yes at a time. And you did it all while still healing.

I want you to know how proud I am of the way you protected your son. How you gave him what you rarely had. How you turned pain into a pattern for peace. You changed your name, your address, your story. Because your love for him was louder than your fear.

And even when the world tried to shrink you again, when it said, *We've met our quota of women*, you didn't disappear. You evolved. You built a new path. And when that path buckled under the weight of stress, when your body said, *no more*, you finally listened.

You picked up yarn like it was a lifeline, because it was. You healed in loops and rows, in yarn spun like breath between trembling fingers. The needles clicked like a second heartbeat. Softness gathered in your lap. Order formed where chaos used to live. And then, because that's who you are, you shared it with women the world had forgotten. With hands that also knew pain. Together, you created warmth from what once broke you.

I see the way your body carried the ache of longing, the scars of sacrifice, the echoes of all the times love had meant pain. And I see how slowly, almost imperceptibly, your shoulders began to soften. Your jaw unclenched. Your breath deepened. Because you were learning: this love is real. This peace is yours. And you don't have to earn it by enduring.

You were never too much. Never not enough. Never foolish for dreaming of softness, of safety, of sanctuary. That longing wasn't weakness. It was prophecy. It was the map to everything you were becoming.

You stopped waiting to be chosen. And in doing so, you became the one you were waiting for.

And even on the day you almost died, you were not abandoned. You didn't just lose something. You met someone. A soul who would never walk beside you, but would never leave you either. You weren't weak because you wept. You weren't broken because you dreamed. You were witnessing the sacred in the unbearable. You stayed. And she did too.

With a full and reverent heart,
Me

The Seeker's Lesson

Love, in all its forms, has been both my deepest ache and my greatest teacher. It was never simple. Never easy. It didn't come to rescue me. It came to wake me up.

There was the hunger for the mother I longed for. The fire to protect my son from the pain I once endured. The longing to be seen, not for what I could carry or perform, but for the whole of who I was. For years, I thought love meant sacrifice, that to be worthy, I had to disappear. But real love doesn't ask you to vanish. It asks you to return. It says: *Come home to yourself first.*

These years became a radical reclamation. I said no to systems that tried to shut me out. I said yes to a man who saw my son not as baggage, but as a bond. I earned a degree not to prove my worth, but to rewrite the story I'd been told I had to live. My voice grew sharper, softer, stronger. Longing changed shape over time. It stopped pointing to what I lacked and began pointing to what was already mine to claim. And love kept reminding me: safety was never in control, but in being steady when life shook. Safety was never guaranteed, not by vigilance, not by silent bargains. What I could offer was presence: a steady hand, a calm voice, the truth that even when the world broke open, he was not alone.

Strength wasn't in pushing through or in pretending I could carry it all. Strength lived in the pause, in listening inward, in trusting that presence mattered more than control. My body knew this long before I did. It clenched. It braced. It whispered the lesson I had resisted: love does not erase fear, but it gives us the courage to stay.

My body was never the enemy. It was always the map. And once I stopped trying to silence it, it led me home. Home to the truth I had overlooked: that love can be soft, steady, healing. That longing was never weakness. It was direction. The soul's compass pointing me back to what I was always worthy of. Love that is not conditional or punishing, but whole, steady, and mine.

Reflective Journaling Prompt

Love, especially after hurt, can feel strange in the body. We carry memories of when it wasn't safe, when it left without warning, when it required us to disappear to preserve it. But beneath those memories, there's another layer of knowing, an ancient map your body still holds of what safe love could feel like, if you let yourself imagine it.

This isn't only about longing. It's about giving yourself permission to redefine, to reimagine, to receive.

Ask yourself:

- What has your body been trying to tell you, through pain, fatigue, tension, or silence?
- What part of you is still waiting to be noticed, named, or nurtured?
- When you picture love that feels safe, what comes up? Is there one small step you could take toward it?
- When love feels unfamiliar but safe, how does your body respond? What sensations, images, or memories surface?
- What does choosing yourself look like in the smallest, most ordinary moment of your day?

This is where the ache gets a voice.

You're not asking for too much. You're asking for what has always been yours. Maybe this is the moment when longing stops being an ache and starts becoming direction. Maybe this is the moment it roots itself quietly, like a seed, not in striving, but in softness. In the quiet, in the sacred ordinary.

Let this be the moment you stop waiting to be chosen and begin choosing yourself. Let this be the reminder:

You were never too much.
You were always the way back.

When I began choosing myself, everything shifted. I realized love isn't earned by holding on longer than you should. With every soft no and every sacred yes, I found a rhythm I hadn't known before. Not romance. Reclamation. That's where power started for me, not in shouting, but in knowing.

Your Turn to Speak

Say it your way: words, sketches, fragments, arrows, messy lists. Let it out of your body and onto paper.

The Space I Stopped Shrinking In

"I stopped asking permission to take up space. And started building something new from the fire they tried to put out."

There came a moment when I stopped waiting for an invitation. I stopped apologizing for my presence and began building something sacred from the silence they once used against me. I discovered power wasn't always a roar; sometimes it was the steady pressure of my feet planted firm on the ground. Sometimes it was the way my spine refused to bend, the way my chest widened with breath I hadn't let myself take in years.

This part of my journey wasn't about dominance or performance. It was about sovereignty, choosing myself again and again in the smallest, most ordinary moments. Standing in a doorway and not moving aside. Holding eye contact without softening my truth. Letting my voice fill the room without first shrinking it down for someone else's comfort. Soft edges, sharp truth, steady ground beneath me.

After years of surviving storms and learning how to speak at all, I became something new: not the victim, not the bystander, but the architect of my own life. The firekeeper, the builder of a hearth no one else could extinguish. Boundaries became bricks. Boldness became mortar. Every "no" laid another stone. Every "yes" lit another flame.

It wasn't always easy. Some truths cost me company. Some days, being visible felt less like freedom and more like standing under a spotlight I didn't ask for. My knees shook, but I stayed anyway. What I came to understand was clear: real power isn't about controlling anyone else. It's about refusing to disappear. It's about choosing to stay visible in your own way, even when fading feels easier, because that's what you were always taught to do.

In this season, clarity came bright, unafraid. Creativity ran wild, unfiltered. The glow I carried then didn't just fall into my lap; I had worked for it. It came slowly; in the way I trusted myself a little more each day. I began to picture possibilities I once thought were out of reach, like a bird testing its wings after too long in a cage. Every choice I once doubted started to feel different, less like a risk and more like a step toward who I was already becoming.

It became a balancing act: holding structure where I needed it, but also letting myself want things and enjoy them without apology. I learned to stand tall and soften on my own terms. To hold space for others, and finally, finally, hold it for myself. My chest expanded. My shoulders held. And this time, I did not shrink back.

2014 – The Collapse

Cards That Held the Year

- *Relative Tarot*
  Strength (Karma) – My resilience was tested again. Survival didn't look the same this time; it bent me in ways I hadn't known before.

- *Rider-Waite Tarot*
  Tower – The break came hard, not gentle. But in its wreckage, things became clearer.

  10 of Wands – I burned out under the weight. Carrying too much for too long left its mark.

  4 of Swords – Rest wasn't a choice anymore. My body shut me down until I finally listened.

- *Oracle of the 7 Energies*
  The Uncharted Sea – My emotions pulled me into unfamiliar places. Half the time I felt lost, just trying to stay afloat.

  A Tall Tale – The stories I used to tell myself couldn't hold up anymore. When they fell apart, what was left wasn't easy, but at least it was honest.

- *Animal Spirit*
  Lion – During the collapse, I held onto whatever dignity I could. My strength didn't look fierce, it was mostly staying steady when I wanted to break.

∞ ∞

I was in the middle of a workday when it hit. At first, I brushed it off as a stomachache, something water and an hour of quiet would fix. A coworker drove me home. I told her I'd be fine, that I just needed to lie down. Pain was familiar; I'd worked through grief, surgeries, and heartbreak. What was one more wave?

I lasted thirty minutes. By the time I called my husband, I couldn't stand. Folded in on myself, I felt the pain sharpen into something undeniable. He rushed home, his face pale, eyes wide, and literally carried me into the ER. I was still in uniform, having collapsed in bed when I got home, still clinging to composure, but my body had stopped performing hours before.

The fluorescent lights hit me as the sliding doors opened, sharp and sterile, humming like static. I didn't make it through the waiting room. My body folded into the chair, uniform wrinkled, hair damp with sweat. The receptionist's fingernails clicked against the intake keyboard, my husband's hand never leaving mine, his worry etched deeper with every minute.

When they finally got me into a room, the questions came rapid-fire. Where does it hurt? How long has it been? I answered the only way I could: "Just make it stop." They gave me Tylenol and sent me for labs, suspicion written on their faces. I could feel it; they thought I was drug-seeking. When the bloodwork came back, proving something real was wrong, I spoke up. I told them I understood their hesitation, but this wasn't that. This was different. This was serious. Something inside me had broken open, and I wasn't asking for a fix; I was asking for help.

The diagnosis: appendicitis. Sudden. Painful. Unplanned. An emergency appendectomy.

When they wheeled me down the corridor, I caught sight of myself reflected in the dark glass of a window. Pale. Disheveled. Tethered to IV lines. Later, after surgery, I recall shuffling to the bathroom in oversized hospital socks, which were sticky-bottomed with the sides sliding against the tile. That sound stayed with me more than the surgery itself, the soft slap-slap of being alive. In the mirror, I smirked at my reflection. Not joy. Not pride. Relief. I was too tired to pretend. Too worn out to perform. Just breathing and standing was enough.

Looking back, I realize my body had been whispering warnings for years: exhaustion, overwork, depletion. I had lived on adrenaline for so long that I couldn't tell the difference between endurance and erosion. But this time, my body didn't whisper. It pulled the emergency brake.

That night, the hum of machines was the only sound. My body wasn't weak; it was wise. It didn't betray me. It protected me the only way it knew how: by shutting everything down.

Even my dreams had been warning me. Hallways with no doors. Staircases crumbling beneath me. Clocks with no hands, still ticking. Days looping without progress. I called them stress dreams, but they were messages.

After surgery, they shifted. Darkness became womb-like, still, protective. Water didn't drown me, it held me, floated me. Sometimes a presence appeared, grounded, watchful, teaching me without words that strength isn't force. It's stillness. It's breath.

I had mistaken limits for weakness. But that year, I learned my body was the only part of me still telling the truth. It wasn't failure that dropped me to the hospital floor. It was proof. Proof I wasn't meant to carry it all. Proof that stopping wasn't giving up, it was surviving.

2014 was the year I stopped pretending I was invincible. The year I stopped performing resilience. And in that pause, with hospital socks sliding across linoleum and my husband's hand steady on my shoulder, I remembered what peace felt like, fragile, human, and mine.

2015 – The Body Says No

Cards That Held the Year

- *Relative Tarot*
  Hermit (Karma) – I turned inward that year, pulling back to listen more closely to what was stirring inside.

- *Rider-Waite Tarot*
  9 of Pentacles – I stood on my own two feet, but it came with a mix of pride and resentment. Strength was built, but it was built alone.

  Temperance – Balance stopped being optional. Healing meant constant recalibration.

  High Priestess – My body spoke truths I couldn't yet prove. Intuition was asking me to trust it anyway.

- *Oracle of the 7 Energies*
  Quieting the Mind – Silence felt like medicine. Giving my thoughts a place to rest turned into its own ritual.

  A Merry Motive – I started shifting toward joy again, choosing it instead of living by obligation.

- *Animal Spirit*
  Fire Ant – Overwhelm lived in me that year. It didn't take much to tip me over, I was already carrying more than I could hold.

∞ ∞

It started in the arch of my foot, a burn sharp enough to make me wince, but never sharp enough to make me stop. I told myself it was just a strained muscle, maybe a shoe worn too long. I shifted my weight when I walked, rolling onto the outside edge of my foot, convincing myself I could outsmart the pain. I had things to do. A son to raise. A job to hold. Life didn't pause just because my body was asking me to.

For years I walked on it that way, ignoring the fracture I didn't know was there. It would flare, then fade. Hurt, then ease. I convinced myself this was strength: pressing forward, refusing to give pain more space than necessary. But the truth was, it never healed. It mended wrong, then broke again.

By the time the surgeon told me it needed to be repaired, I couldn't pretend anymore. This wasn't about toughness. This was inevitability. Surgery wasn't a choice. It was the only way forward.

The chair became my new world. Foot propped on pillows, ice packs sweating into towels, crutches leaning against the wall, their rubber grips pressing faint half-moons into my palms. Around me: stacks of books. Some finished, some half-read, some only cracked open on their way to the "someday" pile. I had collected words for years, promising myself time I never took. Now, in forced stillness, they surrounded me like quiet companions.

The chair was more than a place to heal. It was a mirror. I couldn't escape the truth it showed me: that I had been living on broken things, inside and out, for too long. The fracture in my foot was just the echo of the fractures I carried everywhere else, the way I brushed off exhaustion, silenced grief, and ignored the quiet warnings of my own body.

At first, I fought it. I kept telling myself I'd bounce back quickly, that I'd be back on my feet in no time. I tried to turn healing into another to-do list, another performance of endurance. But healing had its own clock, and I wasn't in charge.

Some days, the silence pressed heavy. Other days, it felt like permission. For the first time, I wasn't falling behind. I was catching up with myself.

One afternoon, restless and sore, I tried to make tea. I hobbled to the kitchen, set the kettle, dropped a bag in the mug, and then forgot about it for twenty minutes. When I finally took a sip, it was bitter, steeped into undrinkable blackness. I laughed out loud, startling the dog, because it felt absurd to still be expecting perfection from myself while stitched together and stuck in a chair. I poured it out, made another, and sat still while it cooled. That felt like progress.

The longer I stayed in that chair, the clearer it became: this wasn't about a foot. It was about a life lived in performance. Years of measuring my worth in output, proving I could endure. And now, I was being asked to do something radical, to stop. To rest. To exist without production.

I noticed it even in my sleep. The old dreams of staircases giving way, of endless unfinished to-do lists chasing me, were gone. Instead, I dreamed of lakes, calm and wide, of benches under trees, tall grass brushing my bare ankles. In one dream, I pulled off worn shoes with thin soles and set them aside, letting the earth cool my skin. In another, I sat beside a younger version of myself. She cradled her own foot tenderly in her lap, looking at me with steady eyes as if to say: Notice this. Don't ignore it this time.

And once, I dreamed of a vast library, shelves stretching past sight. Every book was blank until I touched it. When I opened one, the words appeared slowly, not stories of triumph, but of rest. Pages filled with ordinary days. Quiet mornings. Whole lives that were worthy simply because they existed.

That year, I finally understood: rest isn't the reward you earn after breaking yourself into pieces. It's the foundation. The baseline. The birthright.

My body hadn't betrayed me. It had told me the truth I refused to hear: you don't have to keep walking on broken things to prove you belong.

2015 was the year I didn't fall behind. I fell inward. And in that stillness, I discovered wholeness wasn't about what I carried. It was about what I finally set down.

2017 – Letting Go, Again

Cards That Held the Year

- *Relative Tarot*
  Justice (Karma) – Balance returned, but only because I learned to release. Letting go became its own form of alignment.

- *Rider-Waite Tarot*
  3 of Swords – Pain came back, familiar as ever, but this time I met it in a different way.

  6 of Swords – I crossed another bridge inside myself. It was quieter than the last crossing, but still carried weight.

  The Star – Even with the ache, a thin thread of hope stayed with me.

- *Oracle of the 7 Energies*
  Into Me I See – Looking inward wasn't indulgence. It was survival, and it was necessary.

  Bearing Fruit – What grew that year came less from effort and more from living honestly.

- *Animal Spirit*
  Octopus – I stretched myself too thin, reaching everywhere at once. Slowly, I started pulling my energy back where it belonged.

∞ ∞

2017 cracked me open in ways I didn't expect. Not with a single collapse, but through a series of quiet ruptures. Small fractures. Subtle goodbyes. It started with my son, my only living child, reaching the edge of boyhood. Every milestone felt like a countdown. Every celebration carried the shadow of departure. Pride lived in one lung, grief in the other. I watched him stretch taller, his back broadening, his voice dipping into that lower register that made me turn my head and blink. His future was unfolding in ways I had prayed for, yet still wasn't ready to face.

Somewhere between his growing up and my letting go, I realized how blurry everything had become, not just my vision, but my sense of who I was beyond him. My eyes were tired, my reflection softer at the edges, as though life had been slowly sanding me down. I had spent so many years focused on his becoming that I'd forgotten to see my own.

In March, I gave myself a different kind of gift: the gift of sight. An early fortieth birthday present. Lasik surgery. A promise kept to the little girl who once stood beneath a tree in 1985 and saw the world clearly for the first time. Both in spring. Both moments when the world sharpened and breathed in color again.

Back then, it was leaves that came into focus; in 2017, it was life. The morning after surgery, I woke to light pouring through the blinds, edges I hadn't known were missing, a crispness that felt almost holy. No more fumbling for glasses on the nightstand. No blur between what was and what could be. For a while, everything shimmered with impossible clarity, as if the universe had handed me back my own eyes. It felt symbolic, that seeing. After years of looking through layers of pain and perseverance, I could finally look at myself without distortion.

The clarity didn't last forever. My eyes, like everything else, softened again with time. The doctor said it was natural aging. I smiled. Maybe it was also a reminder: clarity isn't meant to be permanent. It's meant to be lived in, savored, then released when the world blurs again. Because sometimes, losing sight is just another invitation to see differently.

That April, I stood on a stage at a national law enforcement conference, a microphone cool in my hand, lights warming my face. The carpet was thick beneath my shoes, the silence of the room electric before I began. And there it was, the dream I'd had back in 2001. Me, standing on a stage, speaking with certainty. I had dismissed it as fantasy then, but it wasn't. It was a kind of prophecy, and now, I was living it.

By May, my son walked across his own stage, tassel swaying, cap crooked. We snapped a photo that still makes my chest ache: him holding his diploma, me holding the program for the day. Eleven years earlier, at my undergrad graduation, we had posed the opposite way, me in the gown, holding my degree, him just seven, grinning beside me, program in hand. In 2017, the roles reversed. Now it was him in cap and gown, me holding the program, both of us laughing, me through tears. A full-circle moment. Proof of what we had built together.

By June, he wore a uniform. And I walked away from mine, a role I had once fought tooth and nail to enter. The badge that had once felt like survival now felt like an old skin sliding off. Beneath it? Stillness. Uncertainty. Freedom I hadn't asked for but maybe always needed. My husband supported me, but he didn't fully understand it. He came from the old-school mindset that you stayed loyal to a job no matter what. He'd lived that creed until downsizing broke it for him, twice. But I've always followed intuition more than tradition. And I knew, it was time to go.

Letting go wasn't one act. It was a season. A slow dismantling of everything I thought was holding me together. Motherhood. Career. Identity. Each heavy as stones sinking in water. I tried to hold them all and felt myself drowning.

I whispered more than I spoke, to the universe, to my ancestors, to the children I had lost. Watch over him, I pleaded, again and again. Because I couldn't anymore.

One afternoon, while sorting through my closet, I found his first pair of baby tennis shoes, gray leather, black soles, small enough to fit in my palm. I sat on the floor, the carpet cool against my legs, holding one like a relic, remembering his arms stretched out like a wind-up toy as he toddled across the living room. I cried. Then I laughed. Because grief, I realized, is always wearing shoes two sizes too small and still trying to run.

My dreams turned heavy, braided with sorrow and memory. I packed boxes I couldn't close. Stood on train platforms, watching my son disappear into the distance, always waving, always proud. I walked down familiar hallways, the jail, the office, the classroom, each door shutting softly behind me. None opened again.

Yet I wasn't afraid. I was in mourning, yes, but I was also in motion. I dreamed of bridges suspended in fog. I couldn't see the end, but my feet stepped forward anyway. In one dream, I stood in a field holding two torches: one burning with everything I had lost, the other with everything I hadn't yet dared to claim. I stood frozen between grief and possibility while above me, the eagle traced wide circles in the sky, watching, widening my view, reminding me this wasn't failure. It was flight.

Release is rarely clean. It's not one doorway; it's a practice. A peeling back. A choosing, again and again.

That summer, I wept more than I admitted. Not just for my son, or my job, or the titles I was laying down, but for the self I was shedding. I had become so much, survived so much, and now I was being asked to become something else. Not bigger. Not better. Just true.

By autumn, the dreams softened. I stood barefoot in a clearing, pine needles cool beneath my feet, sunlight spilling through the trees like forgiveness, and the air smelled of resin and earth. The eagle returned, landing within reach—not as a threat, but as kin. And I heard myself whisper: I'm still here. Not with certainty, but with presence.

Walking away didn't mean I had failed. It meant I had made space for who I was still becoming.

Grief doesn't only follow loss. Sometimes it follows becoming. And release is rarely loud. It is a soft surrender, a peeling back of roles, identities, and expectations.

That year, I was in the tangle. And still, I moved. Even in the depths, something wiser circled above me. A knowing. A winged kind of grace. The eagle, watching, widening my view, reminding me again: this isn't failure. It's the sacred motion of release.

2018 – Relearning Myself

Cards That Held the Year

- *Relative Tarot*
  Hanged One (Karma) – My perspective shifted. Life slowed down so I could see more clearly.

- *Rider-Waite Tarot*
  Queen of Wands – I began to remember passion, and with it, my confidence started rising again.

  The Hermit – I chose to be alone. In the quiet, I gathered a small light inside myself.

  7 of Pentacles – Growth dragged its feet that year. I had to wait longer than I wanted, trusting that something was still happening underneath.

- *Oracle of the 7 Energies*
  The Storyteller – I began shifting my narrative. The more I spoke what was real, the more I felt myself change.

  Endless Possibilities – When I started rewriting my story, space opened up in ways I didn't plan for. Options showed up that I hadn't noticed before, and I wasn't sure yet what to do with them.

- *Animal Spirit*
  Fox – Reinvention didn't look graceful. I tripped more than once, but I learned to shift and keep moving anyway.

∞ ∞

This was the year I began to relearn myself, not in a dramatic reinvention, but in the quiet undoing of roles that had defined me for decades.

I had been so many things to so many people. A mother. A crisis-handler. A protector. A professional. I had carried others with both hands, always moving, always braced. But now my son was grown, living the very life I had fought to give him. And I had walked away from the badge, from the title I once thought I needed to be taken seriously.

Without the urgency, without the survival, the silence felt almost dangerous. Days stretched open like blank pages, and I didn't know how to fill them. No meetings. No paperwork. No deadlines. Just me. And a stillness I hadn't yet learned how to trust.

At first, rest felt foreign, suspicious. I'd lower myself into a chair, but my leg would bounce, my hands itching for something to do. My jaw clenched against the quiet. The body that had lived on high alert for so long couldn't tell the difference between peace and threat. But this time, I stayed. I let the stillness ache. I let it sit heavy in the room. I let myself not know what came next.

And slowly, something shifted. I realized I wasn't unraveling. I was unearthing. Beneath the restlessness lived a voice I had forgotten: You are more than what you produce. You are more than what you protect. You are allowed to simply be.

So I began practicing presence in small ways. I journaled without trying to sound wise. I read books without underlining them, letting words land where they would. I wandered neighborhoods without a destination, gravel crunching under tires, sunlight warm across my face. Some mornings, I sat on the porch and just let my skin remember the shape of warmth. The dog's weight pressed against my leg. A mug of coffee steamed in my hand. For once, there was no rush. It became a ritual I came to call *Coffee on the Porch with Pooches,* and it still roots my mornings, tails thumping happily at my side.

It wasn't boredom. It was a withdrawal from urgency. A lifetime of bracing takes time to unlearn. My body had carried every blow, every responsibility, every unshed tear, and now it was asking to rest. At first, stillness felt useless. Then it felt necessary. Then it began to feel sacred.

I wasn't healing from one wound. I was healing from the belief that I had to be wounded to matter. That exhaustion was proof of purpose. That perfection was the price of love. Now, purpose rose inside me like breath, quiet, steady, internal.

There were guilty days, lost days. But also, mornings when I caught myself laughing, surprised at the sound. Afternoons when I wrote without judgment. Evenings when I walked barefoot through grass, the blades damp and cool, grounding me back into my body.

My dreams softened too. One night, I dreamed I was walking through a library where the shelves weren't filled with stories yet. The books were plain, their covers blank, but when I ran my hand across them, I felt a pull, like they were waiting for me to decide what belonged inside. Another time, I dreamed of standing in a garden that hadn't been planted. The seeds in my hand felt small and rough, the way they stick to your skin when they've been sitting too long in a paper packet. And once, I found myself in front of a mirror that didn't exaggerate or soften anything. It just showed me, tired but steady, exactly as I was.

These weren't dreams of striving. They were rehearsals for returning. Returning to rhythm. To breath. To joy that didn't need to be earned.

I had always believed power came from presence in a room, from holding everything together for everyone else. But that year taught me another truth: power can also come from letting go, from softening, from saying, I am enough, even now. Even when I'm not producing. Even when I'm simply breathing.

That year, I didn't rebuild my life. I reclaimed it. Not through action, but through awareness. And in that awareness, I discovered something unexpected: I hadn't lost myself. I had simply been too busy surviving to recognize her.

2019 – Chasing Passion

Cards That Held the Year

- *Relative Tarot*
  Death (Karma) – Transformation didn't ask my permission. A part of me fell away to make space for what came next.

- *Rider-Waite Tarot*
  The Magician – My creative power flickered back on. I began remembering what I could shape with my own hands.

  3 of Wands – My vision stretched beyond the moment. I started looking toward what might be ahead.

  The Empress – Creation showed up in many forms, not just in flesh, but in how I lived and what I tended.

- *Oracle of the 7 Energies*
  Call of the Muse – Creativity wouldn't leave me alone. It kept knocking until I finally gave in.

  Awakening Genius – Genius didn't feel like pride. It felt like remembering something I'd carried all along.

- *Animal Spirit*
  Cobra – Wisdom stirred beneath the surface. I could feel a readiness building in me, even before I knew what to call it.

∞ ∞

2019 was the year I gave myself permission to create for no other reason than it felt good. After decades of caretaking, crisis management, and turning trauma into duty, I enrolled in pastry school. Not because I needed another credential, but because I wanted to remember how to shape something soft and strong at the same time. Not just food, but beauty. Not just sweetness, but structure.

I didn't walk into a sterile classroom with fluorescent lights. I walked into a space alive with heat and scent: butter hissing against a hot pan, flour dusting the air like snow, dough warming beneath my palms. Every fold, every rise felt like a small act of devotion.

At first, it felt almost rebellious to linger over sugar dissolving into cream, to pause and watch steam curl into morning light, to plate something not for applause but for joy. Each tart, each custard, each pastry became a quiet refusal of urgency. A declaration: I choose beauty. I choose joy. I choose to stay.

My Reiki practice slipped into the kitchen without effort. Energy moved through my hands as though the kitchen itself were a sanctuary. Cinnamon clung to the air. Citrus cut through the sweetness. Baking trays rattled softly as ovens released their warmth. I wasn't creating to prove anything. I was remembering what it felt like to come home to my senses.

At home, creation spilled across my countertops. The black and brown granite glistened under the kitchen light, warm against the sandstone backsplash and wood cabinets. My black professional series mixer, a gift from my husband who has always believed in me, became a kind of altar. Its steady hum blended with the scent of sugar and butter, filling the house with something richer than food, belonging.

Work smelled like bread coming out of the oven, cookies cooling on racks, and pastries lined up by the dozen. Cinnamon tangled with yeast, butter with herbs, chocolate softening into the air. It could be overwhelming at times, all those scents colliding, but it didn't drain me. It lifted me. The trays clattering, the low hum of the ovens, the simple rhythm of shaping dough, together it all became its own kind of song. In the middle of it, hands dusted with flour, I realized: this was my happy place.

That year, my body moved differently. Not from fear, but from desire. My jaw unclenched into laughter. My shoulders loosened. My hands reached for color and texture instead of bracing for defense. My body no longer felt like armor. It felt like a garden. And in that garden, I bloomed.

Even my dreams carried the fragrance of those days. Garlic, lemon, and sugar crusted on the rim of a spoon. I dreamed of kitchens alive with music, of women cooking beside me, our laughter rising like memory, maybe ancestors, maybe the versions of myself I had once kept waiting. In one dream, I wore an apron made of sunlight. In another, I stirred a pot that shimmered like magic. No one rushed. No one begged. No one broke. We just created.

At the edge of every dream, I felt a presence. Not looming. Not threatening. Just witnessing. Power, not the kind I once fought for, but the kind I had grown into. My dreams didn't try to save me anymore. They celebrated me. *Look*, they whispered. *Look what happens when you create from joy. No one's starving here anymore.*

That year, I wasn't escaping. I was arriving. I wasn't surviving. I was creating. Not because I had to, but because I wanted to. And for once, wanting was more than enough.

2020 – The World Paused

Cards That Held the Year

- *Relative Tarot*
  Hierophant (Karma) – The old structures came apart. I questioned traditions I'd leaned on, and in their place, I began to redefine spirit for myself.

- *Rider-Waite Tarot*
  The Hanged One – Circumstance forced surrender. I was handed a new lens and couldn't close it again.

  5 of Cups – I grieved both what I lost and what never had the chance to exist.

  The Fool – At the edge of everything familiar, I took a strange first step into what came next.

- *Oracle of the 7 Energies*
  Great and **Full** – Gratitude became something fragile I carried gently, even when nothing felt certain.

  The Land Between – I hung in the space between what was and what might be, suspended without answers.

- *Animal Spirit*
  Camel – My reserves ran deep, even when I didn't want to rely on them. They carried me through a desert I hadn't chosen.

∞ ∞

2020 began in grief. In January, my grandfather died, a man woven into the fabric of our family, quiet but foundational. We gathered in his church, shoulder to shoulder, hymns trembling in the rafters, the scent of old wood and winter coats heavy in the air. We hugged, we cried, we prayed. But a brutal Iowa blizzard made the graveside service impossible. The land stayed covered in ice, the ritual unfinished. Closure was postponed, and the grief felt suspended, like snow still waiting to fall.

By March, the whole world fractured. COVID-19 didn't crash in with a single blow; it unraveled us thread by thread. Routines dissolved. Certainty disappeared. Physical closeness vanished. At first came confusion, then fear, then a mourning without language. We lost normal. We lost each other. And amid it all, I lost my job. Not with ceremony, but with a rule that told me my breath wasn't worth protecting. Asthma and a doctor's note should have been enough. A mask should have been protection. Still, they said no. What would the customers think? It was a choice between breath and belonging. I chose breath.

The next morning, I stood in the kitchen, spooning peanut butter straight from the jar, pajama pants hanging loose from another decade. My husband asked if I was okay. I mumbled "yes," mouth too full to make sense, and we both burst out laughing. The sound startled the silence. My chest loosened. My body, so used to constriction, noticed the space that opened when I said: no more.

But grief doubled. In July, my sister was diagnosed with breast cancer. Pandemic rules meant she walked into treatment alone. No visitors. No comfort. Just her, the sterile hum of machines, and the ache of uncertainty. I couldn't fly to her. Couldn't wrap her in my arms. I felt helpless, tethered by distance and circumstance. So, I picked up yarn and a hook. A hat. A blanket. Every loop a whispered promise: *you are not alone.*

We talked on the phone, her voice thinner some days, stronger on others. We laughed about nothing, we cried about everything. She told me about the torturous procedures, the nurses, the quiet kindnesses, the fatigue that pressed down like lead. I listened. I whispered silent wishes. I stitched. My hands became the bridge my body could not. The yarn carried what my presence couldn't: warmth, care, solidarity.

The world had paused, and in that stillness, I began to notice what I had been too busy to feel: the exhaustion, the fear, the sacredness of saying no. I realized I had never really known peace, only distraction. Now silence echoed in my bones. No deadlines. No titles. No roles. Just me, in my body, holding more than I could name, my grandfather's absence, my sister's fight, the collective grief of a world on pause.

My dreams mirrored the stillness. Empty streets. Locked doors. Fogged windows from breath I didn't know I was holding. In one dream, I wandered a library where every book was blank, not ominous, but inviting, like a permission slip to write differently. In another, I stood in a field swallowed in fog, no horizon, just the feeling that something was coming. My grandfather came once, silent, extending his hand, his coat carrying the faint, familiar musk that lingered in memory. My sister came too, hair hidden beneath a scarf, eyes steady, smiling. She didn't speak, but her presence was unmistakable, strong, luminous, and enduring.

Sometimes I dreamed of crochet hooks glowing like embers, blankets stretching across time and space. Not just warmth, connection. Each stitch spoke what I could not, carrying what words could never hold.

In waking life, my body finally understood that care wasn't just something I gave away. It was something I could offer myself. I stood taller, not because life had grown lighter, but because I stopped apologizing for protecting my own breath.

The fire didn't rage that year. It flickered. But it never went out. I didn't blaze forward. I traveled inward. I carried what mattered across the vast unknown. Grief stayed, but it changed. It lived beside joy, beside gratitude, beside the kind of faith born only after falling, and still deciding to rise.

What the Body Carries

Power didn't arrive as a roar for me. It came in whispers, tucked inside the smallest choices: the way I set a mug down and let it stay where it landed, the pause before a no I didn't explain, the door I closed softly and didn't reopen.

For years, I believed strength looked like motion, proving, holding everything together for everyone else while I unraveled inside. I thought yes was the only language of worth. I mistook exhaustion for devotion and carrying too much for belonging.

My body disagreed. My spine ached from being the beam for everyone else. My jaw locked around words I swallowed. My shoulders burned under a weight that wasn't mine. My nervous system buzzed like a light left on too long: hypervigilance posing as loyalty, fatigue posing as focus, tension posing as toughness.

These years taught me something more radical than any roar: ease is power. Stillness is power. Saying no is sacred. My body had whispered this truth for years, in headaches, in sleepless nights, in shallow breath, but now it insisted. It didn't collapse; it clarified. It asked for rest, not as indulgence but as a right. For the first time, I stopped asking if I was allowed to slow down and began saying, *I will rest; I matter.*

Sovereignty didn't arrive with applause. It settled beside me in quiet rooms, yarn sliding across my fingers, the soft scrape of a hook anchoring my breath. Each loop became a sentence I didn't have to speak, each row a boundary I could touch. Each finished hat or blanket was a small sanctuary I could offer the world. My hands became a new kind of voice, carrying what I couldn't always say, warmth instead of noise, care stitched into form.

These years unraveled the old lie that boundaries are walls. They are not. They are devotion. A sacred return to what is mine to hold and what I must set down.

My power didn't need a stage. It lived in the pause between stitches, in the weight of a blanket across my lap, in the breath I reclaimed without bargaining. The body always knows when it is free, and for the first time, mine began to believe it. Not because I produced more or proved anything, but because I finally said, I choose me.

My body, relieved, understood: this ease, this breath, this quiet belonging, this was power.

Dreams That Told the Truth

During these years, my dreams shifted. They weren't frantic anymore, no longer chasing me through burning houses or swallowing stairwells whole. The edges softened, the pace slowed. They stopped mapping survival and began sketching the blueprints of the woman I was still gathering in daylight.

Sometimes I stood at cliffs in the night, cool air brushing my skin, open-palmed at the edge, not frozen, simply ready. Other nights, the fire glowed warm instead of consuming; I walked through flames without fear, their heat licking my arms like an invitation. Voices rose in the dark too, my own voice among them, steadier and certain, no longer waiting for permission.

The dreams stopped being escape hatches and became arrivals. I stepped into rooms with bare feet against stone, shoulders loose, lungs wide. Doorways swung open before I reached for the handle. Ancient hands pressed symbols into my palms, warm and weighty, not to bind me but to remind me of what had always been mine.

An old dream resurfaced as well, one I nearly forgot: I stood on a stage, lights warming my face, the hush of a crowd waiting, a microphone cool in my hand. Once I'd dismissed that scene as fantasy. Then, in 2017, I found myself in that posture in waking life, steady, rooted, speaking with a voice I finally recognized as my own.

It wasn't déjà vu so much as prophecy fulfilled. My dreams had seen her all along, the version of me who didn't flinch, who refused to wait to be chosen, who no longer asked permission to exist. She walked through rooms I once tiptoed through and stood at the edge to claim the view.

She remembered what I had been taught to forget: my voice, my worth, my power. When I woke, I no longer doubted her. I recognized her. She had always been there, waiting for the day I would stop asking if I was allowed and finally whisper back: I'm here.

Letter to the One Who Stood in Her Own Fire

Dear Me, in the years you stepped into your power,

I see you, under fluorescent ER lights, on podiums, in hospital socks that slapped against tile, standing at the edge of old identities with shaking hands but steady eyes. You were exhausted. You were unraveling. You were becoming. And still, you showed up. Not perfectly. Not painlessly. But fully.

This was the time when the old armor cracked. And for once, you didn't scramble to replace it. You let the air sting your wounds. You let the light pour in. You didn't need a crown. You needed rest. You needed relief. You needed to be seen without performing for it.

And when your body dropped you to your knees, in that emergency room, on those crutches, in the chair where yarn slid through your fingers, you finally listened. Those weren't interruptions. They were instructions. Your body wasn't betraying you. It was begging you to stop mistaking endurance for devotion.

And you did something radical in those years: you said no. No to pain as proof of love. No to expectations that asked for your silence. No to the cultural scripts that whispered, *your worth is in how much you carry.*

In that sacred no, you began to say yes. Yes to softness. Yes to stillness. Yes to sovereignty. Yes to self. You let go of roles that once defined you. You laid down the badge. You watched your son step into his own manhood, into his own life. And though your arms ached to hold on, your heart knew it was time to let go.

You stood at the threshold of who you had been and didn't run back. That took more strength than anyone could see. And then, you stepped into the light. Not for applause, but for truth. You spoke the words that once lived only in dreams. And in that moment, you remembered: I've been here before. Not in body, but in knowing.

Back in 2001, when you caught a flicker of your future self and thought, *that could never be me.* But it wasn't fiction. It was prophecy. You became her, the woman your younger self imagined. The one who speaks with clarity. The one who no longer apologizes for needing rest. The one who creates, not from fear, but from joy.

153

You became the woman who walks away, not because she's weak, but because she knows she's worth more than staying small. And I want to thank you for what you did in the quiet. For picking up yarn when the world said stay home. For stitching care into hats and blankets when presence wasn't possible. For loving your sister from afar. For choosing integrity over income. For holding the line when it felt like no one else could see it.

That is power. That is grace. That is you.

I know there were days you wondered if you were fading, if walking away from your job, if sitting with your thoughts, if staying still meant you were disappearing. But what was really happening was emergence. A reintroduction. A remembering. You weren't fading. You were re-forming. Learning to speak without shouting. To rise without explanation. To love without leaving yourself behind.

You became the fire, the altar, the home. The hands that hold yarn. The breath finally unbraced. The woman who knows her own space and dares to keep it.

So, if you forget again, and you will, because the world will still try to make you small, come back to this: You never needed permission. You only needed space. And now, you know how to make it.

With reverence,
Me

The Seeker's Lesson

Power was never handed to me. I had to take it back, piece by piece. Not in one grand moment, but in fragments. In ruptures. In rests. In hospital rooms with that cold, sterile air. In the hum of machines when I couldn't sleep. In the long recoveries, where my body whispered what my mind refused to hear.

For most of my life, I thought strength meant endurance. Survival meant pushing through. Being good meant staying quiet. But power taught me otherwise.

It showed up in moments that felt like endings: when my body collapsed, when I walked away from a job that once defined me, when my son stepped into the world without me at his side, and when the whole world itself was brought to its knees. Every time something unraveled, something wiser rose.

Each *no* I spoke out loud rewrote the script. Each *not anymore* brought me closer to who I was meant to be. Power wasn't loud. It wasn't showy. It lived in the way I chose softness while still holding boundaries. In the way I walked away when I could have stayed. In the way I trusted my body, even when everyone else doubted it.

It lived in the small choices: protecting my breath over a paycheck, choosing health over approval, setting down the mask of endurance, admitting, I can't carry this anymore.

Power came in letting go of roles, of identities, of dreams that had already done their work. And still, I didn't disappear. I stood.

I learned that power doesn't always look like forward motion. Sometimes it looks like stillness. A pause. A deep breath. Rest that doesn't apologize for itself. My shoulders finally dropped. My jaw unclenched. My hands found rhythm in crochet loops, soft and steady, a reminder that I could stop.

I'm not the woman I was in 2014. She carried weight in silence. She clung to titles for safety. She broke quietly. Now? I'm the woman who rose from that wreckage. Who spoke. Who chose herself. Who stopped begging to be seen and started seeing herself.

This whole dance of power was never about control. It was about return, return to body, to voice, to truth. I'm not just surviving anymore. I'm sovereign.

Reflective Journaling Prompt

Power doesn't just show up in force or control. Real power lives in presence. It shows up in the moments we choose ourselves, in the quiet boundary we hold without explanation, in the sacred *no* spoken with a steady voice and a soft heart.

For years, survival meant shrinking. Agreeing when we didn't. Nodding with a tight smile while our shoulders ached from the weight of silence. We hid the parts of us that felt too loud, too tender, too much.

But reclaiming our power isn't about inventing a new self. It's about remembering. Returning to the version of us that existed before silence felt safer than speech. Back then, before doubt had a say, there was already a kind of wisdom moving quietly through us. Our bodies knew it even when our minds pushed it aside; they knew when to rest, when to pause, when to whisper, *enough*.

So, ask yourself gently, the way you'd hold a warm mug in your hands and wait for the steam to rise before sipping:

- In what ways have you brushed off your own power, not because you were weak, but maybe out of habit, or the hope of fitting in?
- Where have you set your power down? In silence, in pleasing others, in fear, or simply from being worn out?
- What does power look like in your everyday choices? In the way you rest, the way you speak, the way you say *no* and mean it?
- How might you begin reclaiming your power back in everyday choices, little things that whisper to you, *See? You matter*.
- What happens in your body when you stand in your power, what sensations, warmth, grounding, or even trembling rise to meet you?
- When has someone else's power reminded you of your own, not through competition, but through reflection?

Let these questions be a mirror, showing you where your strength has been waiting, not outside you, but within, in your breath, in your boundaries, in the quiet choices that whisper: *I will not abandon myself again*.

You don't have to reach for your power. You only have to return to it. It's been here all along, steady as a heartbeat, asking only to be remembered.

And when the fire settles, when the applause fades, when performance falls away, what remains is presence. Not certainty. Not perfection. Just faith and the grounded truth that you are already whole.

Your Turn to Speak
Say it your way: words, sketches, fragments, arrows, messy lists. Let it out of your body and onto paper.

The Faith I Built in the Dark

"I did not find the sacred in the light. I found it in the shadows, in the silence, and in the moments when I was certain I'd been abandoned."

This part of my story is for the unseen. For the hopes whispered into pillows damp with tears. For the conversations I thought no one heard. For the nights I cursed the sky and the mornings I still whispered thanks, confused that both could live in the same breath.

Trust in something larger than me was never handed down. I built it, piece by piece. Out of darkness. Out of ordinary mercies. Out of moments too small to notice until later. A kettle steaming on mornings I swore I couldn't rise. The weight of a blanket when grief left me hollow. The unexpected kindness of a stranger's voice on a day I thought I had no strength left. Not grand gestures, but the quiet wonders only visible when everything else had been stripped away. Each time I thought I lost that trust, I began again.

It wasn't the certainty of pews or pulpits, not the scent of candle wax or varnished wood. It was raw. Personal. A quiet dialogue between soul and source. Sometimes it came as a flicker behind the veil, a knowing I couldn't explain, a presence that steadied me without words. Other times it was nothing more than a pause, one steady breath in a body that had forgotten how to breathe.

I learned that trust isn't a place you arrive at. It's not tidy or final. It's a return. A wrestle. A fragile flame you cup with both hands, even when the wind is howling.

There were signs, subtle and sure. Wisdom that only revealed itself in shadow. A transformation that demanded burning. Reminders that the unseen is no less real than what's right in front of us. That even joy, the small kind that sneaks in through the cracks, is holy too.

This was where I wrestled. Where I wandered. Where I wept. And still, I returned, again and again, to the possibility that maybe I wasn't alone after all.

I stopped looking for the sacred above me. I began to find it within me.

And in one of the quietest moments, barely a breath, I heard it:
I'm still here.

2021 – Between Belief and Burnout

Cards That Held the Year

- *Relative Tarot*
  Lovers (Karma) – Connection asked more of me that year. I had to choose when to stay and when to step back.

- *Rider-Waite Tarot*
  Hierophant – The old wisdom didn't fit anymore. I began pulling apart the beliefs I'd been handed.

  8 of Cups – I walked away, not in anger, but in a soul-tired kind of honesty.

  Justice – The scales tipped too far. I couldn't keep pretending the imbalance wasn't there.

- *Oracle of the 7 Energies*
  A Deep Breath – Slowing down became non-negotiable. I had to pause if I wanted to keep going.

  The Land Between – I hovered in the in-between, no longer who I'd been, not yet who I was becoming.

- *Animal Spirit*
  Gazelle – I stayed alert and tender, my body restless in the quiet. Slowly, I started learning how to remain still without running.

∞ ∞

This was the year I stopped pretending I didn't know who I was. For as long as I could remember, I had hidden my beliefs behind careful silence, the press of a pew under my legs, the scratch of questions scribbled in secret notebooks, the weight of answers that never came. As a child, curiosity wasn't welcomed. Whenever I asked about faith, it closed a doorway instead of opening one. My questions weren't met with guidance; they usually brought consequences. Wonder was corrected. So, I learned to perform belief like a script:

nodding in pews, folding my hands, bowing my head, while my real questions lived between the lines, whispered into the night sky.

My theology didn't grow from pulpits. It grew from ache, from honesty, from the unseen threads that felt more trustworthy than the doctrines I was told to swallow. But even as an adult, I camouflaged that part of me. It was easier to let people assume I belonged than to risk showing them the truth.

The shift didn't come as an explosion. It came as erosion. Slow, steady, undeniable. Not a crisis of faith, but a clarification. I wasn't walking away from the sacred. I was walking away from the fear of being seen with it differently.

By February, the truth landed in a way I couldn't ignore. I was riding in the passenger seat on a long stretch of highway, the cracked fabric of the seat rough under my fingertips, winter light slanting across the dashboard. My friend and I had been close for years. I thought we shared a language, about spirit, about healing, about the unseen threads that gave life its meaning.

I took a risk. I told her about the deck of cards my husband had bought me. How they felt like a new kind of conversation. I expected curiosity; maybe even delight. Instead, she wrinkled her nose and said, "You're creepy."

Her reaction confused me. She dabbled in tarot herself, and her mother even read for others. It wasn't the language of cards she rejected; it was this deck in particular. But for me, the details didn't matter. The judgment felt misplaced, and it cut deeper than she knew. After a lifetime of being told I was wrong for existing as I was, even this casual dismissal felt personal.

The words landed like stone. Casual for her. Crushing for me. My throat tightened. My palms dampened against my jeans. I turned to the window, fields blurring past, pretending I hadn't just flinched.

That one phrase didn't just bruise me; it thickened the wall I already carried. With her, it became impenetrable. And it cut so deeply because it reached back through time, back to when faith was dictated, back to when my wonder was dismissed as foolish or dangerous. Her judgment resurrected an old script: *You don't matter. You don't belong. You are wrong for existing as you are.*

The wall went up thick because it wasn't only her. It was every silenced part of me she echoed back. In that moment, I thought: *No one is safe.*

But then came the choice. Not all at once, but enough to shift the weight. I couldn't carry both silence and sovereignty anymore. Something had to give. And when I began to speak, tentatively, truthfully, my body noticed first. My breath lengthened. My spine loosened. My shoulders lowered, not in defense, but in dignity.

Letting go of the version of faith I had been told to carry didn't feel like failure. It felt like freedom.

And, as always, my dreams went ahead of me. They built the bridge while I was still standing at the edge. I dreamed of doorways with no locks, keys appearing in my hand, rooms that lit themselves as I entered. No sermons. No commands. Just presence.

I dreamed of my younger self sitting in a pew, silent and unseen, pulling books from invisible shelves, writing questions no one would answer. But this time, she wasn't erased. This time, she rose. Shoulders back. Eyes forward. No longer waiting for permission to wonder.

Every dream carried the same truth: the sacred doesn't live in rules. It lives in reverence. And reverence begins with honesty.

That year, I didn't argue for my truth. I didn't shout it into the room. I let it be seen. And in doing so, I let myself be seen.

It wasn't rebellion. It wasn't rejection. It was restoration. A homecoming. When one version of faith fell apart, grief opened the door to another, and I finally walked through.

2022 – Quiet Miracles

Cards That Held the Year

- *Relative Tarot*
  Chariot (Karma) – Progress picked up again, but this time it carried meaning instead of urgency.

- *Rider-Waite Tarot*
  The Star – Healing guided me forward. I felt a brightness inside I hadn't touched in a while.

  6 of Pentacles – I found better balance in giving and receiving. For once, it didn't all flow in one direction.

  Judgment – The call came again, louder and clearer, and this time I said yes.

- *Oracle of the 7 Energies*
  The Oracle's Gift – What I knew deep down revealed itself gently, in ways I almost missed at first.

  A Grand Symphony – I started noticing how my voice fit with the larger whole, not separate but part of it.

- *Animal Spirit*
  Whale – My emotions moved with depth again. From that deep place, a kind of peace began to rise.

∞ ∞

This was the year I lost my grandmother, my namesake, my anchor, the one who held the softest thread in my story. Forty-four years after she took me by train to meet my baby sister, I boarded a plane, rushing across the country to reach her bedside. I didn't make it. She passed while I was in the air, somewhere between departure and arrival, while I sat suspended in a layover in Washington, D.C.

When I landed and turned on my phone, the messages poured in, and I broke. The hollow didn't wait for privacy. It split me open there on the plane, among strangers. A woman reached from the row behind me, her hand steady on my shoulder, then wrapped me in an embrace that said, without words: *You are not alone.* I never learned her name, but her compassion became a thread I still hold, proof that even in devastation, kindness arrives.

The longest layover of my life stretched endless and cruel. I replayed the days before, wondering if I could have flown sooner, blaming the distance, grieving the silence where goodbye should have lived. And yet, I remembered our visit just two months earlier. The way we laughed. The way we talked about our crochet projects. The hug that lingered. Maybe that was her farewell. Maybe she wanted me to carry her in memory's light, not in hospital shadows.

Grief has its own texture. Not sharp. Not clean. More like water, slow and persistent, wearing down stone. My body knew before my phone did. Mid-flight, my chest tightened with a pressure no altitude could explain. By the time I landed, I was already unraveling.

And the loss wasn't only about death. It was about lineage. She was more than my grandmother. She was a living link to softness, to safety, to a maternal presence I rarely knew but always needed. Losing her felt like losing a foundation. And yet, in the stillness that followed, something else stirred. Not collapse. Remembrance.

I felt her in my hands when I crocheted, warmth threaded through yarn as though hers ran with mine. I felt her in the quiet of my chest, as if her spirit leaned against me in the silence. The ache didn't vanish, but I stopped fighting it. Instead, I carried her gently, reverently, as presence, not just pain. Love hadn't left. It had changed form.

Meaning returned in flickers. Not lightning bolts, but synchronicities, sudden pauses, dreams. She came often at night. Not as a ghost. Not to speak. Simply to be. I dreamed of her kitchen, warm and soft-lit, the smell of cinnamon rolls rising in the air. Her laughter moved through the walls. She didn't need words. Her eyes said everything: *I'm still here. You were always loved.*

Other nights, we crocheted together, yarn looping between us like time itself. Sometimes she was young again, vibrant, walking through golden fields I'd never seen but somehow recognized. Each dream was a thin place, where grief gave way to grace. Not messages. Music. A rhythm my bones remembered: love doesn't end, it transforms.

The goodbye I couldn't speak while awake had already been whispered in sleep. What echoed through those dreams wasn't judgment, but recognition. I was being too hard on myself for what I couldn't control. And my sweet grandmother, even in spirit, was reminding me to let go.

Hope returned softly that year. Not dazzling. Steady. A glimmer in the dark. A breath expanding gently after sorrow. Even kindness became sacred. Every act of grace a quiet wonder: a stranger's embrace, a dream filled with laughter, the sensation of yarn slipping through my fingers, the smell of cinnamon.

That year, life became a kind of symphony, every note belonging, the grief, the joy, the silence in between. I heard the sacred not in sermons, but in stillness. In crocheted rows. In golden fields. In the hum of presence that never truly left.

2023 – The Return to Devotion

Cards That Held the Year

- *Relative Tarot*
  Strength (Karma) – Devotion became its own kind of power. My presence grew softer, but it held steady.

- *Rider-Waite Tarot*
  Judgment – The call deepened. Purpose rose from inside me, not handed down from elsewhere.

  Queen of Cups – I let my feelings lead. Sometimes they were messy, but I stopped pushing them down.

  Ace of Swords – The fog lifted in sharp bursts. Truth landed hard, but it gave me air I hadn't had before.

- *Oracle of the 7 Energies*
  Call of the Muse – The desire to be creative stirred again, not heavy or demanding, just a quiet pull that felt good to answer.

  Sacred Reverence – Even the hard parts of life mattered. I didn't always like them, but I began to treat them as part of the whole.

- *Animal Spirit*
  Unicorn – The sacred in me returned slowly. It wasn't flashy or far away, it felt close, something I could hold in my daily life.

I was at the kitchen table when the call came. The light through the blinds slanted across the purple and cream tablecloth, my coffee gone cold, the house too quiet. My maternal grandfather had died in May. By then, dementia had hollowed him out. Not the soft kind that rounds edges, but the hard kind, the cruel kind. The kind that sharpens old wounds instead of softening them.

The truth is, he had never been easy. Not before dementia. Not after. He was abusive to my grandmother, to my mother, to his other children. A hard man to love, and a harder man to forget. I kept my distance, not out of pettiness, but preservation. I had done too much work to be pulled back into the knot of drama and trauma that lived on that side of the family.

And yet, when he died, I grieved. Not for him exactly. For the lineage. For the pain he passed down. For the cycle, he never stopped. His death felt less like a tragedy and more like a closing. My grandmother wept for him, of course, decades tethered will do that, but even in her sorrow, her body looked different. She would never admit it, but I saw it: she wasn't bracing the way she used to. As if some invisible storm had finally passed.

His children, my mother and her siblings, circled their unhealed wounds like smoke around a fire that had burned them all their lives. But I stood outside it. Watching. Holding my distance. The first granddaughter, the one he had always been good to. The exception in a history full of harm.

He told me one story over and over, every visit for over forty years. When I was a toddler, he had promised me a swing set and a sandbox. When I arrived and saw nothing there, I was upset, so he went out, got a swing set, dragged home an old tractor tire, and filled it with sand. He built it all on the spot, trying to patch a child's disappointment. I don't remember it, but he did. He clung to it as proof. He told it like it was redemption, as if one act of repair could outweigh the wreckage left in other rooms.

That was the story he polished like a talisman. The version of himself he needed more than I ever did. But kindness doesn't erase cruelty. A swing set doesn't rewrite violence. I can hold the memory of that gesture and still refuse to let it absolve the rest.

Because I've seen the legacy. His father was violent. He was violent. My mother was violent. And that's where it ends. My sisters and I made sure of it. We chose softness over rage. Boundaries over silence. Therapy over denial. Healing over inheritance. We are not the ones who will keep the fire burning.

At his funeral, the air smelled of lilies, too sweet, heavy in the throat. I spoke of the man he sometimes chose to be, the grandfather who could be gentle when he wanted to. Not the monster he became in the end. I let the swing set story live where it belonged, as a gesture of repair, not redemption.

And I let myself stand in what I have become: the ending of a lineage of harm. The silence that doesn't scream. The soft *no* that breaks the spell. The granddaughter who remembers everything, and still chooses peace.

My body carried this grief differently. In the past, loss had braced me, clenched me tight, left me gasping for air. But this time, my shoulders lowered. My breath didn't vanish; it deepened. My chest still ached, yes, but it wasn't panic. It was release. It was as if my body knew what my mind was still catching up to: this was not just death, this was closure. This was the kind of ending that clears space.

I felt him in my jaw when it finally loosened. I felt him in my spine, the part that had been taught to brace. And when that bracing softened, I knew the inheritance had shifted. The legacy stopped with him. My body didn't carry his violence forward. It carried the choice to end it.

That year, grief didn't crush me. It clarified me. My body wasn't just mourning a grandfather; it was exhaling a generational weight it had held too long. And in that breath, I remembered: I am the hinge in this story. The one who turns the lock. The one who lets the door finally close.

And still, even after I said those words, he followed me into sleep. One night, I dreamed of that swing set again, not in his yard, but in a wide-open field, tall grass brushing my legs, sky stretched endlessly above me. The chains were warm in my hands, the seat steady beneath me. No story to polish, no proof to cling to. Just me, swinging. Free.

It wasn't his redemption anymore. It was my release. A reminder that even in a lineage marked by fists and fire, joy had always been possible, and I was allowed to carry it forward.

2024 – The Mirror Isn't Always Yours

Cards That Held the Year

- *Relative Tarot*
  Hermit (Karma) – I pulled inward again, trying to sort out what was reflection and what was projection. Solitude sharpened my discernment.

- *Rider-Waite Tarot*
  The High Priestess – My intuition spoke the loudest in silence, and I finally trusted what it said.

  2 of Swords – I chose to pause rather than rush into the wrong choice. Waiting became its own boundary.

  The Moon – Shadows distorted things, but I began learning to separate what belonged to me from what I had been carrying for others.

- *Oracle of the 7 Energies*
  Seeing Beyond – I stayed open, even when things weren't clear. I didn't know where it was leading, but I kept paying attention.

  Spirit of Gratitude – Gratitude was small that year. Some days it showed up in ways I almost missed, but it was still there.

- *Animal Spirit*
  Cobra – Wisdom didn't push forward. It stayed quiet, and I had to learn patience while it unfolded in its own time.

I was at my desk when the first wave of unease began, not dramatic, just a small knot in my chest whenever her name appeared in my inbox. The light from the monitor cast long shadows across the room, my coffee cooling beside me, the steady rhythm of typing keys broken each time I hesitated before opening her messages. On the surface, the work itself fit me perfectly. Remote, structured, purposeful. Calendar boxes, tidy spreadsheets, small victories that gave a quiet sense of order. But her emails carried a different weight.

Others said, "She empowers women. She's all about helping them succeed." I didn't feel that. Not in the clipped lines of text. Not in the pit of my stomach before I clicked open. Not in the way I rehearsed apologies before hitting send. My throat tightened, my shoulders drew up, and somewhere inside me, an old question stirred: Why does this feel so familiar?

It wasn't about her. Not really. Though she made it harder, controlling every detail, micromanaging projects, withholding the information I needed to succeed. It wasn't just her habits that unsettled me. It was the way her silence echoed someone else. The way her shifting expectations mirrored another woman I had known all my life, my mother.

The resemblance was uncanny. Both women didn't just criticize; they withheld. Warmth. Approval. Enoughness. Their standards weren't only high, they were invisible, always moving, always just out of reach. I had lived this before, as a child, guessing the rules, chasing scraps of belonging. And here it was again, dressed up as professionalism.

By midyear, I was reassigned to another supervisor, and almost instantly, the dread dissolved. My breath deepened before I even noticed it had been shallow. The anxiety that felt carved into my bones vanished overnight. That's how I knew: it had never been about me. It had been the mirror all along.

This time, I didn't collapse under it. I listened. I noticed how my body reacted, the clench in my jaw, the relief that slid through my chest like water when the pressure lifted. I began to see the pattern clearly: I had spent decades trying to earn the approval of women who reflected back the hunger I was born into. The longing to be accepted not for what I produced, but simply because I existed.

Even my dreams carried the unraveling. I dreamed of doors that opened only when I stopped pushing. Of women with eyes like mine, handing me keys I didn't know I had lost. Of mirrors that didn't show my face but the tired face of my younger self, waiting to be chosen by me. Some nights, I found myself pulling at knots that never loosened, tangled strings tightening the more I tried to fix them, until finally I let go, and they unraveled on their own. And other nights, wings unfurled from my back, iridescent and fiery, stretching wide enough to scatter the weight I had carried for so long. I felt their lift in my chest even after waking, as if my body believed: *This is what release feels like.*

The dreams didn't give me answers. They offered invitations. To stop bracing. To stop carrying what was never mine. To return what never belonged to me. And when I woke, what lingered wasn't fear, but trust. Trust that what had burned away wasn't loss, it was liberation.

This year didn't end in resolution. It ended in recognition. And recognition felt like relief. Because sometimes the mirror isn't yours. Sometimes it never was. And walking away from it isn't abandonment, it's freedom.

I don't need to carry mirrors anymore. I need to carry myself.

What the Body Carries

After so much grief, faith began speaking to me in a quieter language. Not collapse. Not fire. But ease. My nervous system, long trained to brace, slowly began to remember it could be home again. The body doesn't only prepare for impact; it also remembers grace. This part of the journey was quieter, slower, but no less profound. My body, once conditioned to survive the loudest storms, had to learn to trust stillness. To believe that presence could arrive without pain. That connection didn't always demand proof.

Faith didn't return with fireworks. It came in micro-moments: a breath that didn't catch, a shoulder that didn't tighten, the simple ability to sit in a room without scanning for exits. My nervous system, once a battleground, began, slowly, tenderly, to feel like shelter. By 2023, that softness deepened. Not because life was suddenly easy, but because I stopped asking my body to only live in reaction. I let it lead instead.

Revelation didn't always come with rupture; sometimes it came with ease. A morning breath that stretched all the way down into my belly. A cup of tea warming my hands without hurry. A walk where my feet pressed steady against the earth, and for once, I wasn't rushing anywhere. My hands, once curled into fists of readiness, began to unfurl in reverence. My spine, no longer braced, remembered what it felt like to rise without apology.

There were days my body whispered, *We've been here before.* And this time, I listened. I moved slower, softer, not out of weakness, but respect. I no longer needed to perform worthiness. I allowed myself to simply be. Even the aches spoke differently. Not in screams, but in nudges: *This isn't yours to carry.* And sometimes, for the first time in my life, I set it down.

This wasn't about becoming invincible. It was about becoming honest. This was the season my body became sacred again, not just a site of pain, but a place of presence. Of deep knowing. Of steady, embodied trust. I used to think faith had to be earned. Now I know it can be lived. And when my body finally rested, my dreams kept teaching me what wholeness could feel like.

Dreams That Told the Truth

When I couldn't find faith in the daylight, I discovered it in the dark. I dreamed of temples with no walls, candle flames bending toward me, stars pulsing in rhythm as if they were sending messages, not shouted, but felt. These weren't visions of some far-off heaven; they were invitations to stay.

Kitchens appeared, full of memory and scent, warm bread, coffee rising in steam. Sacred altars surfaced, not ones I had built, but ones my bones seemed to recognize. I heard my grandmother's voice humming faintly through a closed window, soft as breath. Hands reached toward me, not to take, but to remind: *You are not alone. You never were.*

The dreams didn't hand me answers. They offered presence. Steady. Patient. Unyielding. They didn't dazzle. They stayed. I had once thought the sacred had to thunder. But my dreams showed me otherwise, that grace could arrive in the hush of breath, in silence that felt like sanctuary, in the way stillness wraps around you and says: *Stay here. You're held.*

Even when doubt pressed heavy against me, the dreams kept threading meaning through the dark. Not to prove anything. Just to remind me to listen. By 2023, they softened even more. No longer prophecy, just permission. I dreamed of ink rising through water, words etching themselves along my skin, messages I didn't need to decode. I dreamed of pulling cards beside ancestors I'd never met but somehow already knew. I dreamed of walking barefoot through sanctuaries that asked nothing of me, not piety, just presence.

Each dream moved like a pulse, a slow rhythm of remembering. Not of doctrine, but of the sacred that had always been here. And when I finally listened, I understood: faith had never left. It had only gone still, waiting in the shadows, woven through every dream, in the breath I had stopped noticing, in the silence that no longer ached. Not lost. Just waiting. Waiting for me to arrive.

Letter to the One Who Stopped Seeking Permission to Belong

Dear Me, in the days you grew tired of proving your worth,

I want you to remember: you don't have to earn your belonging. You already are it.

I know how tired you are from all the proving. Gentle enough. Strong enough. Worthy enough. I know how many years you've stood in front of mirrors other people held, bosses, systems, your mother, asking: *Is this who I'm supposed to be?*

You don't need those mirrors anymore. You never did. They weren't always lies, but they were never yours to live inside. You weren't born to contort yourself for someone else's comfort, or to shrink in exchange for approval.

That ache you feel in your chest, in your jaw, in your shoulders? It isn't weakness. It's memory. It's your body carrying truths your mind had to set aside to survive. And those truths don't need anyone's permission to rise.

You are not too much. You are not a problem to fix. You are not disqualified from divinity just because you found it in shadows instead of sunlight. The sacred has always spoken your language, dreams, cards, threads, breath, firelight. You were never faithless. You just hadn't yet allowed yourself to believe in your way. Now you do.

Here's what I want you to hold onto: devotion doesn't require perfection. It asks only for presence. And presence is something you carry in abundance. You walk with ancestors beside you. You carry the sacred inside you. You don't have to perform to be loved. You don't have to shrink to be safe. You are your own sanctuary now.

The woman I am today is softer, yes. But also steadier. Wilder, too, in the ways that matter most. She rests without guilt. She rises without apology. She listens inward first. She no longer chases worth. She lives it.

So, if you forget again, and you will, because the world will keep holding up its false mirrors, come back to this: you are sacred. You are sovereign. And your belonging? It was never up for debate.

With love, and unshakable faith,
Me - the woman you were always becoming.

The Seeker's Lesson

Faith was never about certainty. It was about returning, sometimes crawling, sometimes limping, again and again to the quiet. To breathe. To the mystery that never explained itself, but never left either.

I didn't meet the Divine in stained glass or in carefully rehearsed prayers. I met her in the steam rising from a chipped coffee mug at my kitchen table, in the silence after an argument, in the ache that bent me double in hospital rooms, in laughter that escaped sharp and surprising when I thought I had none left. The sacred showed up sideways, in odd signs, in uncanny timing, in the way a song or dream slipped into my day like it had been waiting for me to notice.

It was never about earning worth. Never about putting on the right face so I'd be allowed in. It was about remembering: the holy had always been here, stitched into breath itself. In the drop of my shoulders after years of clenching. In the ordinary choice to be present instead of perfect.

The Divine hadn't abandoned me. I had been running too hard to notice her hand at my back.

Somewhere between burnout and awakening, I started recognizing the pattern. The boss in 2011. The boss in 2024. Different faces, same shadows: the sharpness, the impossible standards, the way my body braced and my voice shrank. They weren't just supervisors. They were echoes, mirrors of the first woman I had spent a lifetime trying to please: my mother.

That recognition didn't undo me. Oddly, it steadied me. I saw the loop I'd been running, the hunger to be "enough" for women who had already decided I wasn't. But this time, I didn't run after their approval. I let the mirror crack. I said, out loud and inward: *That reflection isn't mine.*

The roles I carried for so long, perfection, obedience, and invisibility, had shaped me. I learned early to measure love by performance, to earn my place by being useful. Even as an adult. Even in rooms where I should have belonged without question.

The ache still rose sometimes: *Am I enough?*

But faith began to answer what the ache never could.

Worthiness isn't earned. It's inherent.

Sometimes everything has to burn, roles, fears, expectations, so what's real can walk forward from the ashes. Faith taught me to honor pauses. To stop gripping the steering wheel of control. To let mystery do its quiet work. To let questions sit unanswered and still be holy.

The Divine never left. I just had to stop running long enough to hear the steady pulse beneath it all: I had always been part of the conversation.

Now I don't measure myself against distorted mirrors or borrowed definitions. I know which voice to trust, the one that had been waiting all along under the noise, under the fear, under the doubt.

And that, more than certainty, more than perfection, is devotion.

Reflective Journaling Prompt

Faith doesn't always arrive steady. More often it slips in messily, in the middle of not knowing, when silence presses heavy and answers refuse to come. And doubt? It isn't the opposite of belief. Sometimes it's part of the path. The right questions don't always resolve; they pull you deeper.

The sacred within doesn't only speak through thunder or fire. Sometimes she leans in as a quiet pull, a soft nudge, the faint sense that even surrender is teaching you something new.

If you're ready, let these questions guide you, not toward polished solutions, but toward the wisdom already humming beneath your skin. No rush. No performance. Just listening.

Just trust what rises:

- Where has doubt cracked something open and led you closer to truth?
- What stories about your worth were handed to you, and which ones are you ready to set down?
- What quiet wisdom have you always known, even before you could name it?
- Where has the sacred within met you? Not in certainty, but in silence, synchronicity, or surrender?
- What would it look like to trust your own reflection, fully and finally, without apology?
- What patterns keep circling back, pointing to an old wound that still longs to be seen?

Let this reflection be a pause. Sacred. Unhurried. You don't have to defend belief or unbelief. Both have a place. What matters is the listening.

The sacred within doesn't demand clarity. Only presence. You are allowed to be unfinished. You are allowed to be whole, even inside the mystery.

Faith didn't hand me certainty. It handed me surrender. And from that surrender, something unexpected emerged: a quiet readiness to begin again. Not from scratch, but from wisdom. From wholeness.

This is the chapter where everything I've lived begins to braid together. Where I stop asking if I am healed, and start living as though I already am.

Your Turn to Speak

Say it your way: words, sketches, fragments, arrows, messy lists. Let it out of your body and onto paper.

Where the Story Becomes the Gift

"I didn't become someone new. I just returned to the part of me that survived beneath the silence, the part that never stopped burning."

This isn't an ending. It's a remembering, a gathering of every truth, every scar, every insight that carried me back to myself.

Rebirth doesn't erase what came before. It gathers it, holds it gently, and says, *You, too, belong.*

Integration is the sacred work: the weaving of scattered pieces into one whole. It is the moment you stand in the mirror not to correct, but to witness, and say, *Yes. All of this is me.*

The rhythm here was different. Not collapse. Not fire. But the stillness after the wave, the moment the body unclenches, shoulders lower, breath moves without catching, and something quiet rises in the space that used to be all tension.

Here, purpose began to root itself. Not in doing, not in roles, but in presence. In simply being. A pulse whispered: *You've always known the path.*

The fire hadn't gone out; it had changed. Less about survival, more about warmth, a steady flame that lights paths and keeps me company. It warmed without consuming; it offered a steady light I could trust to guide me forward.

There was movement too, not frantic, but like a wheel turning steadily onward. A rhythm that said, *You are ready now.* Forward motion without hurry, a steady insistence that the next right thing would arrive when I was ready to receive it.

And I understood: transformation isn't a single event. It is a lifelong unfolding. Even the hardest steps, the ones that left me in pieces, moved me forward. The fractures were not failures but doorways, each one letting in a light I could not have imagined before it opened.

This is where the seeker begins to guide, where the story stops being a wound and starts becoming a gift. Healing no longer consumes all my energy because now I offer it outward: small rituals, soft practices, the permission to rest that once felt like rebellion.

The life I lived becomes the wisdom I extend, to others, and to the younger versions of myself who still wait for reminders.

You've made it. Not to the end, but to the beginning of something deeply true, a life shaped by presence, not by the pressure to prove.

2025 – The Seeker Becomes the Guide

Cards That Held the Year (Partially)

- *Relative Tarot*
  Wheel of Fortune (Karma) – The cycle shifted again, but this time I was the one turning the wheel.

- *Rider-Waite Tarot*
  The World – A circle closed. I could finally see the shape of the walk I'd taken.

  King of Wands – Leadership lit up in me. Vision didn't stay an idea, it became movement.

  9 of Pentacles – Self-trust came slow but steady. I stood on ground I had built myself.

- *Oracle of the 7 Energies*
  The Time Machine – I saw the old patterns for what they were. I honored them, then chose to rewrite them.

  The Power of Purpose – Purpose carried me forward. I didn't have to drag it anymore.

- *Animal Spirit*
  Butterfly – Transformation showed its final form. What had been released made room for beauty.

∞ ∞

I used to think healing had a finish line. That if I just did enough work, asked enough questions, and weathered enough storms, I'd arrive at some mythical place called wholeness.

But this spring, I was placed on a project under my old supervisor, the same one whose silence and shifting standards had once left me unraveling. Within a month, seven of my teeth cracked from clenching. Four trips to the dentist, a new guard molded for my mouth, sometimes worn even during the day. My body carried the weight I thought I had laid down.

At first, I felt betrayed by my own reaction. Hadn't I already learned this lesson? But then I saw it clearly. She wasn't my mother. She only wore the same shadows. Same sharpness. Same impossible expectations. But she was not me, and I did not have to keep carrying her in my jaw or my chest.

The truth settled in slowly: I can't control her, but I can choose how much of me she gets to occupy. And she doesn't get much anymore. Now, she's only an afterthought. Just a name on an email, a task on a list. Not a reflection. Not a mirror. Certainly not a measure of my worth.

When I let that truth root, the clenching eased. My body softened. My chest lifted as if it had been waiting for me to notice. That's how I knew I had taken my power back. Not by escaping her. Not by defeating her. But by refusing to confuse her reflection with my own.

Now, sitting across from my husband at the kitchen table, candle flickering between us, coffee steaming gently in my mug, I see wholeness differently. It isn't a destination. It's this: the ability to hold my entire story without flinching. To trace the scars, the laughter, the lessons, and see them not as contradictions but as threads in the same tapestry, like the pale line across my foot that still aches when the air turns cold, or the laugh lines etched deeper every time I buy a new journal to fill its pages, knowing that one day I'll burn it like all the journals before. I release my stories back to the universe because I finally understand: I don't have to carry them alone.

Nothing needed erasing. Everything belonged.

What once looked like endless circles now reveals itself as a spiral path, each return a deepening, each step a remembering. Clarity no longer feels like certainty. It feels like direction. Not a spotlight blazing for others, but a steady fire I follow from within.

And peace? It isn't quiet because it's empty. It's quiet because it's rooted.

These small rituals, lighting a candle before coffee, blessing my morning toast with a whispered laugh, remind me I don't have to earn gentleness. They are my devotion, stitched into the ordinary.

It still stings sometimes, how tightly the elders in my family cling to their rigid religion, how foreign this softer, wilder reverence would seem to them. But I no longer measure my faith against theirs.

I once believed transformation was a season. Now I know it is my nature. I will always evolve, but with reverence, not resistance.

I am no longer only the seeker. I am the guide.

Not because I hold all the answers. But because I finally trust the questions.

Because I can see now that the stumbles, the long nights, and clumsy recoveries were nudges back toward myself.

It kept nudging me home, in small, stubborn ways.

And *home* keeps unfolding.

What the Body Carries

My body was the first to know when something wasn't right. Long before I had words, it spoke in migraines, in shortness of breath, in that tightness that crept into my shoulders and jaw when I couldn't name the ache.

Years later, deep into healing, it spoke again, this time through my teeth. In one month, seven of my teeth fractured. Not from neglect. Not from failure. But because I had finally stopped pretending, because I was no longer numbing the strain I'd carried for decades.

It startled me at first. Why now? Why after so much work? And then, in conversation with my sister, the truth surfaced: I had stepped back into a familiar space, into a dynamic with someone whose presence once made me question my worth. My nervous system remembered long before I did.

It wasn't punishment. It was a message.

The cracks weren't weakness. They were a revelation. My body had been quiet for years, but now it spoke again, through clenched jaws, through enamel splitting under pressure I didn't even realize I was still holding.

The mouthguards I wear each night aren't just protection. They are a small, stubborn border I will not cross for anyone, physical reminders of a vow: *I'm not holding this anymore.*

Because healing isn't linear. The past resurfaces not to undo us, but to be fully processed, fully honored, fully released.

Now my bones carry wisdom, not only memory. They hold the imprint of every time my body said yes when my heart meant no, every silence I offered to keep the peace, every breath I stifled to make space for someone else.

But not anymore.

Now, I breathe. I listen. I trust what rises. This time, I answer when the body speaks.

Dreams That Told the Truth

The dreams changed when I did. The staircases no longer collapsed beneath me. The silence no longer swallowed my voice. The old nightmares of running, searching, and escaping began to fade.

In their place came something quieter. Unfamiliar at first, but unmistakable once I recognized it: safety.

I dreamed of gardens in full bloom, soil rich beneath my feet, golden light spilling through windows I didn't have to force open. I was invited in.

I dreamed of rooms without locks, thresholds I didn't have to earn, skies so wide they softened my breath.

Often, I saw younger versions of myself. Not afraid. Not lost. Simply waiting. And in those dreams, I didn't rescue her. I sat beside her. I held her hand. I whispered what I now know with my whole body: *We are whole.*

There was no urgency, no chase, no desperate push to wake myself up. I stayed. It felt like returning, not to a place, but to myself.

These dreams no longer carried me away. They reflected something grounded. Not just the ache to survive, but the possibility of belonging, not longing. A rootedness that steadies.

The message had shifted. I wasn't just preparing anymore. I was living it.

For years, my dreams echoed the ache. Now, they mirror my peace. My dreams are no longer about survival. *I dream because I've arrived.* Home isn't somewhere out there; it's here, in me.

Final Letter – The One Who Always Was

> "You weren't becoming someone new.
> You were remembering who you've always been."

Dear One,

You were never lost.
Even when the world told you your softness was weakness. Even when you were asked to perform for love, to shrink for safety, to stay quiet so others could stay comfortable.

You were never broken. You were becoming. Even in the chaos, the silence, the searching, you were becoming.

I see you now. The child who asked too many questions. The teenager who carried too much. The woman who stood her ground with shaking hands and a steady soul.

I see all of you. And I want you to know this: you don't have to earn peace. You don't have to prove your worth. You never did.

Every storm you survived, every truth you whispered in the dark, every time you kept going when it would've been easier to disappear, none of it was for nothing.

You didn't just survive the wreckage; you shaped it into meaning. Not because it was beautiful, but because you were willing to tell the truth about it. That's what makes it sacred.

You're not a symbol. You're the evidence that healing can happen. That love can feel safe. That softness was never the opposite of strength. They were always companions.

I wish I could reach back through time and hold you when you felt invisible. I wish I could whisper, *You make it*. But more than that, I wish you could see what I see now:

You weren't just surviving. You were seeding a future, one where your joy, your voice, your rest, your presence, all of it, would be yours to keep.

And now?
You stand rooted. Whole. Unapologetically luminous. No longer running. No longer asking. Just being. And that is everything.

With reverence, gratitude, and a heart full of awe,
I love you. I always have. I always will.

Me

The Seeker's Lesson

I spent so long trying to fix myself, not realizing I was never broken, only scattered by survival, shaped by stories that were never mine to hold.

Rebirth wasn't about becoming someone new. It was about returning, again and again, to the one who had always lived beneath the armor. I found my voice. My wisdom. My light.

Integration isn't a goalpost or a breakthrough. It's the soft moment when the old pain no longer defines you. It's a breath you didn't know you were holding, finally released. The ease of taking up space without apology. The quiet knowing that you are allowed to be here, fully.

This part of the journey reminded me: healing isn't the destination. Wholeness was never lost.

It was always about weaving every version of me, every ache, every rising, into something whole. Something sacred. And walking forward with her, not in spite of her, but with her.

Now, I don't just carry my story. I embody it. With grace. With purpose. With the quiet strength of someone who has learned that living her truth is its own light.

And that is enough. It always was.

Reflective Journaling Prompt - The Sacred Work of Wholeness

Change doesn't always arrive with a sign. Sometimes it comes in the way your shoulders soften, in the tone you use when you speak to yourself after a mistake, in the quiet recognition that you belong to yourself again. That's transformation, too.

Integration isn't an endpoint. It's a weaving, a remembering, a lifelong practice of gathering yourself home. This is the sacred work of wholeness: gathering the scattered parts, not to polish them into perfection, but to welcome them back. To be able to say: *Yes, this belongs, too.*

- Where have you noticed your own transformation, not just in what you've endured, but in the ways you now feel safer, more at ease, or more at home in your body?
- Which parts of yourself have quietly come back, showing up in moments of ease, in trust you once thought impossible, or in joy you didn't expect to feel again?
- Imagine sitting beside your younger self, or someone still carrying the same kind of weight. What simple truth would you want to hand them about healing, about being known, about belonging?

Let this be a moment of reverence.

You haven't been remade into someone else. You've come back to the self who was always waiting beneath the noise, steady and true.

Every step has brought you here. And *here* is enough. Enough to rest. Enough to rise. Enough to be.

Your Turn to Speak
Say it your way: words, sketches, fragments, arrows, messy lists. Let it out of your body and onto paper.

Breaking the Inheritance

The rebuilding that happens without reconciliation is its own kind of sacred labor. Not every wound is meant to be stitched closed in the presence of the one who made it. Sometimes healing means walking away from the fire without waiting for an apology. Sometimes the most radical act of love is leaving the door shut and locking it from the inside.

My relationship with my mother will never be what people picture when they say "mother–daughter bond." It was never a place of soft landings. For most of my life, it was a landscape of volatility, yelling that shook the walls, followed by silences that cut just as deep. Tension. Confusion. Fear. The kind of fear that teaches you to read a room before you learn to read a book. The kind that makes love feel like a transaction you have to earn again and again.

Even when clarity came, when the fog of survival finally began to lift, it took her decades to name it. I was in my early forties when she asked, carefully, "When you were little, did you love me because I was your mom, or because you were afraid not to?" My answer hurt her, and I knew it would. But it was the first time she'd asked the right question.

"I was afraid of the consequences if I didn't," I told her. That truth had lived in my throat for over thirty years. When it came out, it didn't carry rage. It carried relief. And grief, not because I hadn't said it before, but because it had never been received. Grief that it had taken so long. Grief that it didn't change much. Grief that I had lived a lifetime inside that tension, smiling on the outside while my nervous system screamed.

These days, we have some contact, a few phone calls a year, scattered texts, and rare visits. Still, there's a frayed thread. She is heavy with guilt, trying to compensate for years she can't rewrite. My brothers, still caught in their addictions, lean on that guilt like currency. For years, it fell to us, her daughters, to tell her: their choices aren't yours to fix. They're grown. They will live with what they decide. You can't mother them back into safety.

I don't live inside regret. I never have. Regret, to me, is wasted air. I've been through horrors, but I learned from every single one. I wouldn't be who I am without them, and I wouldn't change it, because I like where I am.

That's part of why I can hold space for some kind of relationship with her while still refusing to carry what was never mine. I don't chase a version of bond we never had. I don't perform daughterhood for tradition's sake. I answer when I can. I hold the line when I need to. I've stopped trying to fix something built on fault lines I didn't create.

And I've done more than release my mother. I've released the entire stage. I rarely show up at gatherings on that side of the family. I don't attend the drama or the revisionist memories. No one stepped in then, and I won't sit quietly among them now. This isn't cruelty. It's protection. It's discernment. It's self-trust, hard-earned.

There is peace in finally knowing it isn't my job to carry the pain that made me. Peace in refusing to bend myself into someone else's wound. Peace in loving myself more than I ever loved the idea of being loved by them.

The truth is: I don't need reconciliation to find redemption. I don't need restoration to feel release. I don't need approval to feel whole.

I haven't abandoned my family. I've stopped abandoning myself for them. Maybe that's the most sacred rebuilding of all, the choice to carry forward what is life-giving and to leave behind an inheritance that was never mine to bear.

Integration: The Sacred Weaving

You've walked through memory and meaning, silence and fire, the ache of becoming and the grace of arrival. You've sat with the cards, the symbols, the dreams, and most of all, with yourself. This journey was never meant to hand you answers. It was meant to help you trust the questions.

Because integration is not an arrival. It is a returning. Returning to the parts of you that were buried beneath roles, beneath silence, beneath fear. Before the world taught you to forget, your body remembered. There was always a quiet center inside you, the one that still knows how to guide you back.

Let this be a pause, not a finish. A breath before the next becoming. A moment where all that you've unearthed can settle and breathe. A place where the wisdom of your past, the presence of your now, and the hope of your becoming can sit side by side.

You do not have to be healed to be whole. You do not have to be certain to be faithful. You do not have to be loud to be powerful. You are allowed to carry it all, the joy, the grief, the clarity, the questions. You are allowed to begin again, any time, any day, in any breath.

The cards may change. The stories may evolve. But the seeker within you remains. Not lost. Not broken. Not behind. Just becoming. Still becoming. Always becoming.

Welcome home.

Realization: Where the Body and Dreams Meet

For years, I thought the dreams were distractions, the odd, private cinema that rolled through my nights while the real work happened in daylight. But the longer I listened, the clearer the pattern became: my dreams were not separate from my healing. They were the language my body used to say what words couldn't hold.

Those barefoot dreams kept coming back, me walking with no shoes, grass cool against the soles of my feet, soil giving way softly under my step. At first, I mistook them for nostalgia or whimsy. Then one morning, mid-sip of coffee sitting on my porch, it clicked: the feet were a map. Bare feet in dreams were always about connection, to ground, to safety, to an allowance to be unprotected and still okay.

The body had been carrying a curriculum long before my mind enrolled. Hypervigilance taught me to read rooms, to brace my spine, to hold my jaw like a hinge waiting to snap. I learned to make myself small so others would not hit me with their storms. I learned to measure belonging against answering: *yes*. The teeth that cracked in the spring were not random; they were a late, blunt sentence from a nervous system that had been making the same argument for decades: *I am still holding this.*

Dreams, though, offered a different reply. When staircases stopped collapsing and kitchens smelled like warm bread, my inner system began to test what safety might feel like. When I sat beside younger versions of myself and simply held her hand, my body practiced being steady without rescuing. Those barefoot steps were rehearsal, my body relearning how to trust the earth would catch me, and that I could put weight down without being swept away.

That realization shifted everything. The mouthguards I wear became less about damage control and more about boundary practice. The journals I would one day burn became less proof of failure and more testimony: I have lived through these pages and come out with hands that can hold, not only fight. The grief that once lived like a stone in my chest softened into a place I could visit and leave.

Understanding this, that the effects of trauma threaded through my life physically, and that the dreams were offering corrective movements, gave me a new grammar for my days. When my shoulders wanted to climb into my ears, I asked: *What is my body showing me now?* When a dream offered a barefoot path, I tried walking slower the next day, letting my feet feel the floor instead of rushing over it. Small experiments. Tiny proofs.

The final, quieter lesson: healing is not an erasure of harm but a reeducation of sensation. The body does not forget; it re-learns. And the dreams? They are the drills, the secret practice sessions where my nervous system experiments with safety until it believes it enough to trust in waking life.

If you want to name this new knowing, call it permission: permission to be felt, permission to plant your feet and stay, permission to answer when your body speaks.

I want you to try something.

What the Body Carries - Try this:
Close your eyes. Scan from the crown of your head to the soles of your feet. Where does your body still brace? Breathe into that place for three slow counts. Notice one small, safe movement you can make right now (shift your weight, soften your jaw, plant both feet). Do it. Notice what changes.

Dream Reflection: Think of the most repeated image from your dreams (bare feet, doors, rooms, gardens). What is it asking you to practice? Write a single sentence, there is room below, or say it aloud to yourself, that answers it. For example, *"I am allowed to feel the ground."* Repeat it for a week and note the changes.

Integration Reflection: The Sacred Weaving

We carry more than we know. In our muscles live the memories we never meant to memorize. In our breath sit the pauses between what we said and what we silenced. In our dreams lie the truths we weren't ready to speak by day, but still found a way to whisper.

This book was never just about what happened. It was about what remained, what returned, what rose when the world went quiet. The body held what the mind couldn't. The voice rose when the body began to trust again. The dreams spoke when both had gone still.

And now? Now they move in unison. My body no longer braces for what has already passed. My voice no longer waits for permission. My dreams no longer run. They rest. They reveal. Maybe you've noticed moments like that, too, the subtle shifts that tell you something has changed, even before you had words for it.

This is the sacred weaving: the parts that once fought to survive are now learning how to live. Not in spite of the story, but through it. Not as a single voice, but as a symphony, body, breath, soul, sound, silence, dream.

This is what wholeness feels like. Not perfect. Not polished. Present. Still becoming. Still arriving. Still free.

Reflective Journaling Prompt – *The Way Forward*

What you hold now isn't only the stories that shaped you. It's the strength it took to live them. It isn't only the wounds; it's the way those wounds have become wisdom. You've held space for your becoming, and now you stand at the threshold of what's next.

Integration isn't a finish line. You're not starting over. You're returning, with more truth, more clarity, more trust in who you've become.

This beginning isn't loud. It's grounded. It's yours.

Think of this last reflection as a pause: a chance to gather up everything you've found along the way and decide what comes with you. Give yourself permission to carry forward what still feels true.

- Which pieces of truth from this journey do you want to bring with you?
- What no longer fits, and can be laid down with grace?
- How has your understanding of healing, identity, or purpose shifted?
- What sacred promise are you ready to make to yourself?
- What does moving forward look like now, in your own words?

This is your becoming. It may be quiet. It may be wild. It may unfold slowly, like a morning.

Trust that you are already on the path, and that the path is yours to walk, softly, fiercely, freely.

The seeker pauses. The path continues.

Your Turn to Speak
Say it your way: words, sketches, fragments, arrows, messy lists. Let it out of your body and onto paper.

Interlude: There Is Always a Light

The summers saved me. For six weeks every year, my sister and I left the chaos behind and headed west to our father's house. He would drive all the way to the Midwest to pick us up. Then he'd turn around and drive us back across the country in his van, just him, the two of us, and the wide-open road.

Somehow, he made it fun. We stopped at quirky roadside attractions. Camped in the van when he grew too tired to drive. Wound our way through the mountains with the windows down, the air rushing in like freedom. We giggled at the trucker chatter on the CB radio until Dad quickly shut it off, protecting us from the words we weren't meant to hear.

My younger sister didn't always get the jokes. But he and I would share glances, stifled laughter, the quiet joy of belonging to a secret moment. One summer drive, she must've been four or five. We were both sitting in the front seat so we could see out the window (it was the early '80s, so tuck your judgments away, seatbelt laws weren't really enforced yet). We passed a field of cattle, and right there in the open, a bull mounted a cow. Without missing a beat, my sister shouted, "OH LOOK! Those two are trying to play leapfrog!"

My dad and I absolutely lost it. I don't remember anything else about that day, just the laughter, hysterical, soul-healing in a way only a child's innocence can be.

Once we arrived, the adventures continued. Camping. Hiking. Playing in the dirt without a care in the world. At night, Dad would bring out his guitar. He strummed the same chords again and again, making up ridiculous lyrics about burnt marshmallows, hairy legs, or muddy feet. It wasn't about perfection. It was about presence. About joy.

Even when the world felt uncertain, those moments held steady. That old guitar lives with me now. When my husband plays it, something soft echoes through the room, a sound that carries me back to childhood, legs swinging off picnic benches, nights by the fire, a time before everything grew complicated. Not all inheritance is painful. Some of it sings.

On those trips, Dad taught us the "pine needle trick," scraping needles under the tent to soften the ground. But it wasn't given as a chore. It was an invitation. "Hey, you two, why don't you gather up some pine needles so we'll have a comfortable place to sleep, and I'll unload the van. Sound fair?" And it always did. We weren't being bossed. We were part of a team. With him, being helpful didn't cost me my childhood; it celebrated it.

Years later, he admitted the truth: the pine needles were just a clever way to keep us busy while he set up camp. We cracked up all over again. But what stayed wasn't the trick. It was how I felt: useful, safe, connected, seen.

He cooked simple meals that became staples in my life. I didn't realize then that they were inexpensive. I only knew they tasted like love. Like safety. Like home.

Those summers didn't erase the darkness I returned to. But they reminded my body what it felt like to be safe. To laugh freely. To belong without condition. I didn't know it then, but those memories planted something I would return to again and again: a blueprint for softness, for belonging, for the kind of love that welcomed me as I was.

When life grew heavy, when survival became my only language, these memories whispered: *Light isn't something you earn. It's something you remember.* And that lantern became mine to carry.

Years later, the light came in another form. In January of 2014, a seven-month-old black Lab mix arrived in our lives, wearing a white Tasmanian Devil t-shirt, carrying his own kind of storm. Brody had been rescued in a drug raid, abused, overlooked, and held too long by people who never saw him. But one look at his photo and I knew: he was ours. I didn't ask permission. I didn't need to. I simply said, "He's coming home with me."

My husband, still grieving his miniature schnauzer Angel, wasn't thrilled. But the next morning, Brody curled into his chest like he belonged there, and he never really left. That dog rewired something in us. He was loyal, protective, endlessly sweet, but also scarred. He knew how to read danger in a room. When certain energies entered, his whole body shifted. We never questioned it. We moved him. Calmed his breath. Reminded him he was safe. Pain had taught him much. But love taught him more. He wasn't just our dog. He was our shadow. Our sentinel. Our soul-companion.

He left us on October 14, 2024. Something in me left with him. I still feel the last breath he drew in, the one he never let out. The quiet surrender in his eyes. That day is etched into my marrow. Brody will always be a missing piece of my heart, a space I do not want to fill. Because that emptiness belongs to him. I will carry it, gladly, until we meet again.

And then there is Charlie. Born in December 2015, he arrived in our home in February 2016, a tiny, soft-eared puppy already at the edge of death. The woman who gave him to us knew. She asked about vets, then shut off her phone the moment we tried to call her back. But Charlie didn't disappear. He fought. Parvo. Worms. Fleas. Days in the hospital. Heat lamps. Fluids. Conversations with the Universe. And he lived.

He didn't just survive. He chose me. My son had picked him out, but Charlie imprinted on me. When my son left for the Army, Charlie stayed by my side. He became my constant. When Brody passed, Charlie broke with us. He howled in the silence. Sat in the empty doorway Brody once guarded. Waited at the front door like he expected him to return. He stopped playing. Stopped eating. Stared into spaces only he could see. We watched him grieve. We watched him wait.

Even now, nearly ten years old, he still doesn't like to be alone. Back then, every time we left the house, whether for five minutes or five hours, our security cameras would capture the same scene: Charlie, sitting in that empty space, howling. Not barking. Howling. A sound between longing and despair. A sound that makes your ribs ache. I knew he needed a companion. But I wasn't ready. Not yet.

Until Farrah. Ten months into our grieving, she came to us by what felt like fate. We had gone to see a litter of little male puppies, but she trotted right up to us, a fluffy, bright-eyed corgi. Her owner said, almost as an afterthought, "I just decided yesterday I was ready to part with her. She wasn't even listed for adoption." And we knew. We weren't waiting for another puppy. We had been waiting for her.

Since the day she came home, Charlie has not howled once. Not once. Farrah imprinted on me too, this sweet, mischievous little shadow who follows me everywhere, to bed, to the bathroom, to the desk where I write. She is glue and laughter and light. She is healing in fur.

She will be one year old on October 6th. Already spoiled. Already beloved. Already part of the story. Every moment with her is a promise that joy still finds its way in, even after loss.

Because these dogs didn't just fill our home. They made it one. They didn't erase the pain. They witnessed it. Softened it. Stood guard beside it. Their love wasn't transactional. It was devotional. Like summer air. Like laughter spilling from another room, or music on an old guitar string that still hums, even after the hand lets go.

They weren't the light at the end of the tunnel. They were the small, steady flames that lit the way through it. They never asked for anything but our presence in return. That is the most sacred love I've ever known.

And with that light in hand, I began shaping what had once lived only inside me into something others could hold.

Epilogue: The Deck I Built

Just as the cards evolved, so did I. Not in a single blaze of certainty, but slowly, breath by breath, choice by choice.

The migraines I've carried since childhood still come, but they no longer rule me. My breath, once stolen by asthma, by fear, by the constant bracing for the next blow, moves softer now. Steady. My body no longer flinches at silence. It doesn't brace for storms that aren't coming.

There was a time I thought healing meant feeling nothing, that it would make me untouchable. But now I know healing isn't the absence of pain. It's the ability to sit with it without being swallowed. To stay present. To remain myself.

This book began with cards, archetypes, symbols, a conversation with something greater, or maybe just with myself. I thought I was pulling cards to understand my life. But somewhere along the way, I realized I wasn't only reading the deck. I was building it.

I am The Fool's leap and The World's completion. I am the Tower's collapse and the Star's quiet hope. I am Death's transformation, Justice's balance, the High Priestess's knowing, the Chariot's will. I am every cycle I thought I wouldn't survive, and every rebirth I didn't see coming. And so are you.

You don't have to be healed to be whole. You don't have to be fearless to be free. You don't need anyone else to decide when you are worthy. You only need to keep choosing truth, love, integration, and light.

Because the sacred was never found in perfection. It lives in presence. In picking up the pieces and realizing they were never broken at all, just waiting for you to arrange them into something beautiful.

Thank you for walking with me through these lessons. If you've seen yourself in these pages, know it was never an accident. It was a remembering.

And when you close this book, I hope you remember too: the next chapter has always been in your hands.

But before you set it down completely, come sit with me once more. In *My Interpretation of the Tarot*, I'll show you the language beneath these stories, the way the cards helped me make sense of it all. Maybe they'll help you make sense of your own.

My Interpretation of The Tarot

A quick note before we dive in.

If you've made it here after walking through my story, good. Think of this section as the compass, the way to see how the path, the cards, and the memories all line up. Tarot isn't an afterthought in my life. It's woven into how I survived, how I made meaning, and how I tell it now.

And if you've flipped here first, welcome. This is the lens I use to see the world. Without it, some chapters might feel thinner than they are. With it, you'll catch the echoes running beneath every card and every story.

A Brief History of Tarot
(Just in case you thought it started with witches and crystal balls)

Pop culture would have you believe tarot came straight from a velvet-draped tent, someone whispering, "I see your future…" under candlelight.

In reality, it began in the 1400s as a card game called *tarocchi*, played by European nobility. Think old-school Uno, hand-painted cards, fewer family arguments.

By the 18th century, the game had shifted. People began noticing the archetypes in the deck, symbols of change, wisdom, risk, loss, and hope. Tarot became less about winning a game and more about asking questions like: Who am I? What's shifting? What's possible?

The "tarot is evil" myth came later, born mostly out of fear and misunderstanding. Historically, institutions haven't loved the idea of people trusting their own inner compass. And that's what tarot really does: it hands you back to yourself.

Today, tarot wears a lot of hats. For some, it's a spiritual practice. For others, it's like journaling or therapy in card form. Some people just love the artwork. For me, tarot has been a teacher, a mirror, and sometimes a megaphone shouting truths I wasn't ready to admit.

And here's the thing: you don't have to believe the cards are "magical" to use them. You only need to be willing to notice the symbols, the stories, the way something in the image stirs something in you. That's where the conversation begins.

What follows isn't a dictionary of meanings. It's a lived conversation. Personal, not prescriptive. Born out of walking with these cards through joy and grief, silence and clarity, and learning to trust the language they speak.

Whether you've read tarot for decades or are meeting it here for the first time, let this section meet you where you are. The wisdom isn't in the card alone. It's in what rises in you when you turn one over, in the seeker who shows up to listen.

The Major Arcana

0 – The Fool

"She wasn't running away. She was running toward something. She just didn't know what it was yet."

The Card, As They Say:

The Fool marks a beginning. Not the polished kind you read about in stories. People call it a leap of faith, the first step into adventure, the courage to walk into the unknown. They like to imagine her playful, a flower in hand, face turned toward the sun. A blank slate. A bright door opening. But that's the postcard version. The real Fool shows up at the edge of what you've known, when you're standing with your stomach tight and your heart beating too hard, and you move anyway. It's not whimsy, it's risk. It's hope tangled with fear. It's realizing that standing still costs more than stumbling forward.

The Card, As I Lived It:

I didn't meet The Fool in some shining moment. I met her as a teenage girl gripping a torn black garbage bag stuffed with clothes, notebooks, and everything she could carry, stepping through a door she didn't think she could come back through. There was no map. No guide. Just the sharp edge of survival and the deep knowing that leaving, even without a plan, was less dangerous than staying. I remember the pull of that bag against my shoulder, how the sky felt too big, how the silence pressed in, daring me to take another step. What I carried wasn't hope, not yet. It was instinct. It was the voice that had whispered for years, *You don't belong in this pain*, and for once, I believed it enough to move. That step wasn't pretty. It wasn't fearless. But it was mine. And that's where the journey began.

I – The Magician

"I didn't need rescuing. What I needed was to remember I already had what it took."

The Card, As They Say:

The Magician is often described as the one who makes things happen, the card of turning ideas into something you can touch. But here's what gets overlooked: it doesn't hand you anything new. It simply gestures at what's already sitting on your table, the tools you've picked up along the way, the ones you've doubted or dismissed. And here's the trick: half the time, you still look at your own skills and wonder if they "count." I do. That's the Magician too, showing up again and again to remind you that the table is already yours.

The question isn't whether you're allowed to use it. The question is whether you'll stop acting like you're not ready.

The Card, As I Lived It:
The Magician didn't storm in. She slipped into the edges of my life on nights when the house was dim, my toddler breathing steady in the next room, and fear pressed so heavy on my chest I thought I might crack. The bills on the counter kept piling. The fridge looked bare. The future was nothing but fog. And inside that fog, the same voice I'd known for years whispered: *You can't do this. You're not enough.*

But then I did. Not because the fear lifted. Not because anyone swooped in to save me. But because I realized, finally, that no one was coming. And instead of undoing me, that truth sparked something awake.

I began using what was already in reach: a mind sharpened by survival, a backbone built from carrying others when I was running on empty, a voice that still spoke truth even when it shook, a will that refused to let go of possibility no matter how thin it seemed.

That's when I felt The Magician's presence. Not flashy, not loud, just steady, as if she'd been there all along, arms crossed, waiting for me to notice myself. It wasn't spells or miracles. It was the slow alchemy of realizing what I carried was already enough to begin. I didn't need rescuing. I needed to trust what was in my own hands.

II – The High Priestess
"I didn't need evidence. I needed to trust what I already felt."

The Card, As They Say:
The High Priestess carries the weight of intuition and mystery. Her wisdom doesn't shout to be heard. It shows up as a tug in your stomach, a sudden tightening in your chest, a sense you can't shake even when nothing on the surface looks wrong. People like to describe her as silence or secrecy, but that flattens her. She isn't quiet because she's weak or uncertain. She's quiet because she doesn't need anyone else's approval to trust what she already knows.

The Card, As I Lived It:
I didn't stumble across The High Priestess in ceremony or stillness. I found her in tension, in those uneasy pauses when everything around me looked fine, but my body carried a different story. She was there the summer I was sent far from home, told to smile, to say

thank you, to act grateful. They said I was safe. My body said otherwise. My chest tightened every time I entered a room. My skin itched with the knowing that my boundaries would not be honored, that "no" would not hold if I ever needed it to.

There was no neat evidence. No clear moment I could hold up to prove what I felt. But the unease was real. The discomfort was real. The High Priestess was there too, whispering, *You don't need proof. You need trust. Yours.*

Back then, I didn't know what that meant. I thought intuition needed defending, that it had to be explained, rationalized, made acceptable to someone else before it could be valid. I didn't know I was allowed to say "no" simply because something felt wrong. I didn't know my nervous system was wiser than the rules I'd been taught.

Now I do. I know that The High Priestess doesn't speak in bullet points or evidence. She speaks in the quiver in your stomach, the sudden chill at the base of your spine, the inner voice that whispers before the red flag is even visible. Her lesson is this: your knowing is sacred. It doesn't have to be proven to be honored.

III – The Empress
"Sometimes You Have to Mother Yourself First"

The Card, As They Say:
The Empress carries creation, nurture, abundance, and the fertile energy of growth. She's the archetypal mother, the earth's embrace, the place you land when the world has been too much. When this card appears, people often say it's a call to receive, to create, to care or be cared for. And yes, that sounds beautiful. But what if nurture wasn't something you received? What if The Empress didn't come with open arms at all, but as a mirror reflecting what you longed for and would have to become yourself?

The Card, As I Lived It:
The Empress didn't arrive for me in lullabies or soft embraces. She didn't show herself in maternal tenderness. She appeared the moment I looked into my newborn son's face and said, *It ends with me.* I wasn't raised in nurture. I was raised in survival. I knew how to earn affection, how to step carefully around emotional landmines, how to mistake silence for safety. But when my child was laid in my arms, something primal rose, fierce, unyielding.

The Empress wasn't soft then. She was fire. She was clarity. She was a vow. I became a mother that day, not only to my son, but eventually to the parts of myself that had never been tended. I learned that care doesn't have to be inherited to be real. That gentleness can be a choice. That nurture can be an act of defiance.

I didn't know how to do it perfectly. I still don't. But I knew this much: love in my home would not be conditional. Safety would not be a privilege, but a right. Softness would not be a risk, but a refuge.

The Empress didn't just teach me to birth children. She taught me to birth belonging. To believe that legacy doesn't only live in lineage, but begins in how I choose to love on purpose.

IV – The Emperor
"I didn't grow up with a steady foundation. I had to learn, brick by brick, how to build one of my own."

The Card, As They Say:
The Emperor doesn't make a grand entrance. No fireworks, no spotlight, just the steady kind of presence that makes things feel real under your feet. He brings a kind of structure, a steadiness you can actually stand on. He reminds us that some things need shape, that boundaries can be protective instead of punishing. At his best, he doesn't confine you. He steadies the ground so you can stand without bracing for collapse. But let's be honest. Sometimes, The Emperor doesn't show up as strength. Sometimes he's the voice of rigidity, the press of expectations you never asked for but still ended up carrying.

The Card, As I Lived It:
The first Emperor in my life was my father. He was there, and then he wasn't, and when he did appear again, it was only in pieces, fragments left over from choices my mother made.

The next Emperor who stepped in wasn't safe. He wasn't warm. He was a voice that said, *Don't question me.* I met him in authority handed to people who hadn't earned my trust, in rules that silenced instead of protected, in the expectation that I would comply before I even had words to ask why. So, I learned to equate structure with control. Boundaries with punishment. Order with fear.

Much later, and only on my own terms, I met a different Emperor. Not one who demanded submission or proved power by breaking others, but one I had to become when no one else was steady enough to lean on. Because when no one gives you a foundation, you build your own. Maybe uneven, but strong in the ways that matter.

I found him in the quiet hours, sitting alone, sketching the next step, not for applause, not to prove anything, but because I was tired of chaos being my only default. I wanted peace. I wanted purpose. And I was willing to build them from scratch. This Emperor showed up when I created structure where there had been none. When I set boundaries, even when they made others uncomfortable. When I realized discipline didn't have to be a cage. It could be self-respect in action. Not restriction, but scaffolding.

This Emperor wasn't the voice that told me to shrink. He was the presence within me that said, *You've got this. Let's build something real.*

V – The Hierophant
"When You Realize the Rulebook Wasn't Written for You"

The Card, As They Say:
For me, The Hierophant showed up in tradition, in the rules I was told to trust, the systems I was told to stay inside, and the old lessons people passed along without pausing to think about them. Most often, he speaks through institutions: religion, education, family expectations, or the weight of society itself. For some, The Hierophant feels like comfort, clear rules, and clear roles. For others, like me, it felt like a cage dressed up as wisdom. Because The Hierophant doesn't ask, "What do you believe?" It says, "Here's what you're supposed to believe."

The Card, As I Lived It:
I met The Hierophant in hushed sanctuaries, in family expectations, and in every stiff nod that signaled, "We don't ask that here." I met him in the stiff collars and sermon tones that told me certainty was more important than understanding. In the way tradition wrapped itself around my shoulders like a heavy cloak, one that didn't fit, but I wore anyway, out of fear, out of habit, out of survival.

As a child, belief wasn't a journey. It was a script. Any attempt to deviate, to question, to explore, was treated like betrayal. So, I learned the choreography of obedience. I memorized the lines. I bowed my head when I wanted to lift it toward the stars. But even then, something inside me was gathering light. Late-night wonderings turned into sacred rituals. Books tucked beneath blankets became portals. And behind the walls of dogma, I was slowly, quietly, building my own theology.

It took years, decades, even, for me to understand that The Hierophant didn't only speak in the voice of the gatekeeper. He could also speak through discernment, through the steady hand that sorts through what's been passed down and says, *This part still serves me. This part doesn't.*

I used to be terrified that leaving behind the old rules meant I'd be lost. But I wasn't lost. I was liberating myself from a story that was never mine. Now, when I meet The Hierophant, I don't see just institutions and inherited truths. I see a wise guide standing beside me, offering the tools to choose for myself what to carry forward, what to release, and how to create meaning without surrendering my voice.

VI – The Lovers
"The Hardest Choice Is Choosing Yourself First"

The Card, As They Say:
The Lovers, it's the card everyone gets excited about. "Ooooh, love is coming!" they say. Soulmates, romance, passion. But here's the thing no one tells you: The Lovers isn't just about who you fall for. It's about the choices you make when it comes to who you are, in relationship to yourself, to others, and to your values. It's alignment. It's standing at a crossroads and asking, does this connection, this path, this version of love honor who I really am? Sometimes, The Lovers is soft and sweet. But sometimes? It's the most painful kind of love, the one where you realize you've been abandoning yourself just to feel chosen.

The Card, As I Lived It:
I didn't meet The Lovers in a whirlwind romance or some sweeping gesture. I met them in the quiet reckoning that followed a thousand small betrayals of myself. I had a long history of shrinking myself just to keep the peace. Biting my tongue, smoothing things over, convincing myself it was safer that way. Over time, I twisted into shapes I barely recognized, all in the hope that affection, even when it came with conditions, might feel like real love.

For years, I mistook devotion for endurance. I thought love was something you proved by staying quiet, by over-giving, by holding on even when every part of you ached to let go. The Lovers didn't appear to me with hearts and harmony. They showed up like a mirror and a crossroads. They asked me, not gently, *Who are you becoming to be loved? And is that version of you still whole?*

The turning point wasn't dramatic. It wasn't a breakup or a cinematic revelation. It was a quiet moment, standing in front of my own reflection, when I finally said: *I want love that lets me stay intact.* And from there, everything shifted. Because once I stopped reaching for connections that required my disappearance, I began to make room for relationships that actually saw me, held me, and honored who I was.

The Lovers wasn't about finding "the one." It was about remembering that I was already worthy, and letting that truth shape every bond that followed.

VII – The Chariot
"You Don't Have to Like the Road, You Just Have to Keep Driving"

The Card, As They Say:
The Chariot is all about willpower, determination, victory through discipline, and moving forward no matter what obstacles are in the way. It's the "take the reins" card, control, focus, momentum. People like to paint it as triumphant, charging ahead, confident, and unstoppable. But here's the truth they don't tell you. The Chariot isn't always about chasing glory. Sometimes, it's just about not letting life pin you in place. It's not flashy. It's survival on wheels.

The Card, As I Lived It:
I didn't step into The Chariot with a polished plan or a cheering crowd. I climbed into it because I had to. Because life didn't give me a map, just a moment where I knew *I can't stay here any longer.* The Chariot met me on back roads and borrowed time, in rusted-out cars and gut decisions. It was the voice that said, *You don't need to have it all figured out. You just need to keep moving.*

I was the one changing tires on the shoulder at midnight. The one driving cross-country with everything I owned stuffed in garbage bags and plastic bins. The one who kept going, not because I knew what came next, but because I couldn't afford to stay still. People think The Chariot is about confidence. About control. But for me, it was about motion in the face of fear. About stubborn hope. About refusing to believe that the road ended just because I couldn't see the next turn.

The truth is, I wasn't always brave. But I was always in motion. And that mattered more than knowing the destination. Because sometimes victory doesn't look like a finish line. Sometimes, it's just the moment you say, *I'm not turning back.* And you don't.

VIII – Strength
"Soft Doesn't Mean Weak, and Survival Isn't Always Loud"

The Card, As They Say:
Strength is often shown as a serene figure gently closing a lion's mouth, calm, composed, in control. It isn't about muscle. It's the quieter stuff, patience, resilience, learning how to face hard things without bulldozing your way through. But let's be honest, when life hits hard, who really feels graceful? Strength isn't always peaceful. Sometimes, it's standing in the wreckage, shaking, and still saying, *Not today.*

The Card, As I Lived It:
I didn't learn Strength by roaring. I learned it in the silence, when no one saw what I was holding, and I carried it anyway. Strength showed up in childhood kitchens filled with tension, in school mornings that started after sleepless nights, in the way I learned to steady my voice so my siblings wouldn't hear the fear behind it. I didn't have the luxury of falling apart. So, I wore calm like armor. I made myself useful, dependable, invisible if I had to be. Because survival meant staying strong, even if it meant disappearing under the weight.

But that kind of strength? It's costly. It turns into chronic tightness in the chest, a jaw that never unclenches, a belief that rest is weakness, and softness is unsafe. And yet, years later, in therapy rooms and quiet moments, Strength began to look different. It looked like putting the weight down. It looked like asking for help. It looked like sobbing without apology, and finally, finally, exhaling without bracing for impact.

Strength, I realized, isn't about holding it all together. It's about knowing when to stop pretending you have to. It's not just about being tough. It's about learning to be tender, with yourself, with your story, and with the parts of you that are still healing.

IX – The Hermit
"Sometimes pulling back isn't running away. Sometimes it's the only way to find your way home."

The Card, As They Say:
For me, The Hermit is that moment you walk out of the noise with nothing but a lantern, hoping to hear yourself again. It isn't really about hiding. It's about carving out a pocket of quiet, not to escape life, but to be able to hear yourself again. The kind of wisdom this card points to doesn't drop in from the outside world; it stirs up from within. Some

describe The Hermit as serene: a mountaintop retreat, the bliss of stillness. But stillness isn't always chosen. Sometimes you step back because the world feels jagged, too loud, too unsafe, and solitude stops being about peace; it becomes survival.

The Card, As I Lived It:
I never chased solitude because I thought it would make me wise. I pulled back because being seen felt dangerous. As a kid, I figured out that silence could work like a shield, that if I stayed quiet, I might slip under the radar, and sometimes that was the only way to stay safe. I wasn't shutting people out for the sake of it. I was trying to protect the parts of me that had nowhere soft to land. Being seen meant being exposed, and I couldn't afford that.

So in the beginning, Hermit energy looked like locked doors, scribbled notebooks, the practiced smile that said, "I'm fine," when the truth was anything but. Over time, though, the quiet I once hid inside started to feel different. The silence softened. And tucked inside that stillness was a voice I didn't recognize at first, my own. Raw. Honest. Free from everyone else's demands.

The Hermit stopped being about disappearing. What began as escape turned into a slow return, not to safety outside me, but to the person I'd tucked away inside. I began to see that withdrawing isn't the same as giving up. Sometimes it's the first honest step toward healing. Time alone doesn't always mean abandonment. It can heal. It can clarify. It can hold the space between who I've been and who I'm still learning to become.

In that hush, I didn't just stumble into peace. I found a kind of strength that only shows up when the noise is gone. Maybe that's the Hermit's quiet gift, showing that the roads that feel the loneliest are often the ones that carry you back home to yourself.

X – The Wheel of Fortune
"When Life Spins You Sideways, And You Learn to Steer Anyway"

The Card, As They Say:
The Wheel of Fortune is fate, cycles, sudden shifts, the reminder that nothing stays the same forever. Sometimes you're on top, sometimes you're underneath it, but the one guarantee? The wheel always turns. People love to frame this card as "good luck," a sign that fortune is finally coming your way. But if you've lived enough life, you know The Wheel doesn't always feel like winning the lottery. Sometimes, it feels like the rug getting ripped out from under you.

The Card, As I Lived It:

The Wheel of Fortune didn't knock politely or wait for an invitation. It spun, sudden, sharp, and unapologetic, whenever I thought I finally had my footing. I met The Wheel in moments that felt like betrayal, standing in a sheriff's office, hearing the words, "We've already met our quota of women," and realizing that merit wouldn't be enough to move forward. I met it again when I sat at a kitchen table, rage simmering beneath the surface, and applied to grad school out of sheer defiance, still grieving one dream while chasing another. I met it when love arrived not as lightning, but as calm. When grief cracked my foundation. When a new opportunity rerouted my entire future in a single phone call.

The Wheel didn't ask for permission. It just turned. I learned, again and again, that stability was never a guarantee, only the invitation to adapt. But that's where the magic began. The Wheel didn't just spin me into chaos; it spun me into new truths, into better fits, into lives and versions of myself that I wouldn't have chosen on purpose but wouldn't trade for anything.

Eventually, I stopped cursing the spin. I stopped bracing every time I felt momentum shift. Instead, I started asking: *What is this redirecting me toward? What have I outgrown that life is trying to free me from?* The Wheel of Fortune isn't just about fate. It's about learning to meet change with presence, not panic. And knowing that even when the ride feels wild, you're not lost; you're being moved.

XI – Justice

"When No One Stands Up for You, So You Do It Yourself"

The Card, As They Say:

Justice is about truth, fairness, accountability, and consequences, cause and effect in motion. It's the sword and the scales, the promise that what's right will prevail. But anyone who's lived in the real world knows Justice doesn't always show up when it should. And it definitely doesn't always wear a robe or sit behind a bench. Sometimes, Justice isn't handed down. Sometimes, you have to claim it yourself.

The Card, As I Lived It:

Justice didn't arrive in a robe or with a gavel. It arrived quietly. In the weight in my chest after being told to stay silent. In the moments I watered myself down so I wouldn't be labeled "difficult." In the internal negotiations where I gave everyone else the benefit of the doubt... except me.

I met Justice not in courtrooms, but in conversations I didn't have, the ones where I bit my tongue to keep the peace, the ones where I convinced myself that being agreeable was safer than being honest. For a long time, I thought fairness meant waiting my turn. I believed if I just worked hard enough, stayed patient, and proved myself over and over again, then the scale would eventually tip in my favor. But it didn't. Because Justice doesn't show up for the quiet ones who never speak. It shows up for those who claim it.

And that's what changed. I stopped performing politeness to avoid making others uncomfortable. I found myself saying the things I used to swallow back, even if my voice trembled when the words came out. And afterward, I couldn't help but wonder: *Why had I spent so long treating their comfort as if it mattered more than my truth?*

What I came to see is this: staying quiet doesn't make anything fairer. It only drags out the moment when balance finally demands to be faced. And the most radical thing I ever did? Believe that my peace mattered too. That my discomfort counted. That holding everyone else together while I unraveled was not a badge of honor; it was a wound.

Justice didn't demand rage. It demanded clarity. And the courage to speak it.

XII – The Hanged One
"When You're Stuck, But Your Perspective Sets You Free"

The Card, As They Say:
The Hanged One is all about surrender, pause, and seeing life from a new perspective. It's the cosmic timeout, the moment when forward motion stops, not because you failed, but because you need to look at things differently. People talk about The Hanged One like it's peaceful enlightenment. But let's be honest, hanging upside down rarely feels serene. It feels like being stuck, suspended, waiting for something, anything, to shift.

The Card, As I Lived It:
I didn't choose The Hanged One. It chose me in the seasons where life halted mid-sentence and refused to hand me the next page. Where the harder I pushed, the more everything held still. Not as punishment, but as an invitation I didn't yet know how to accept. I wasn't moving forward. But I wasn't crashing either. I was just… hanging there. Between chapters. Between identities. Between the person I had been and the one I wasn't ready to become.

And in that suspended space, I was confronted by truths I couldn't outrun: that clinging to what's broken doesn't heal it. That over-efforting won't earn peace. That sometimes the most courageous thing you can do is surrender. Not the kind of surrender that means giving up, but the kind that says, "I release what's not mine to hold."

The Hanged One wasn't serene at first. It was tense, uncertain, maddening. But in the hush of that stillness, something else stirred, the sound of my own knowing, steady and insistent, rising above the noise. I had called it suspension. I had called it stuck. Yet over time, that space became something different. It opened me. It shifted my perspective. And when I finally unclenched my grip on control, I could see a way forward I hadn't been able to before.

XIII – Death
"The Version of You That Had to End So You Could Begin"

The Card, As They Say:
Death, cue the panic. People see this card and immediately think doom, loss, devastation. But anyone who's walked through real transformation knows death isn't about endings for the sake of pain. It's about release. It's the clearing of what's dead weight, so something true can finally grow. Death doesn't knock politely. It takes. And what it leaves behind is space, raw, uncomfortable, but necessary.

The Card, As I Lived It:
I didn't just meet Death. I've walked with it, again and again, through doorways I didn't want to open, into versions of myself I didn't want to lose, but couldn't carry any further. It wasn't always about loss in the traditional sense. More often, it was the quiet, relentless shedding of identities I'd outgrown, of roles I never chose, of survival masks that once protected me but had become too heavy to wear.

Death met me in a teenage girl clutching a garbage bag of clothes, stepping into the unknown with more grit than guidance. It found me in the woman who finally admitted that staying in a marriage meant abandoning herself. It stood beside the daughter who sat in a courtroom and let the truth fracture the illusion of family. And it came for me through a body that finally said, *Enough*. And meant it.

Every time, I resisted. Every time, it hurt. And every time, I was sure I wouldn't survive the letting go. But I did. And with each ending, I met a version of myself I never could have imagined on the other side. Not lighter, always, but truer. Less willing to carry what wasn't mine. More willing to burn the script and start again.

Death didn't come to destroy me. It came to strip away what was never meant to last. To clear the ground. To give me back to myself.

XIV – Temperance
"You Don't Have to Swing Between Survival and Burnout"

The Card, As They Say:
To me, Temperance has always carried the spirit of an alchemist, mixing fire with water, weaving shadow into light, letting past and present touch until something unexpected begins to take shape. It leans in and whispers, *easy now*. But if you've lived a life of extremes, of all-or-nothing survival, Temperance doesn't feel natural. It feels like a language you have to relearn after years of only knowing how to sprint or collapse.

The Card, As I Lived It:
I didn't stumble into balance. I collapsed into it. Temperance didn't greet me with serenity. It arrived after the crash. After the burnout. After my body said, *We're done.*

I had spent years moving at breakneck speed, juggling roles, chasing safety, trying to prove I was strong enough to carry it all. And I did carry it. Until I couldn't. Until my muscles, my spirit, and my will whispered, *No more.* That's when Temperance came. Not as a soft whisper, but as a reckoning.

It wasn't self-care Sundays and bubble baths. It was rebuilding my life from the ashes of overextension. It was learning that real healing is subtle, sustainable, and often invisible to anyone but you.

What Temperance taught me is that peace doesn't arrive all at once. Peace is found in the space between effort and ease, in learning how to pause before the spiral, in choosing the middle path not because it's flashy, but because it's kind. I didn't stop being strong. I just stopped needing to prove it through suffering. And in that shift, I discovered a deeper kind of power, the power to pace myself, to pour without emptying, to become whole without burning everything down to get there.

XV – The Devil
"The Chains Were Never as Tight as You Thought"

The Card, As They Say:
The Devil gets a bad rap, fear, addiction, temptation, and being trapped by unhealthy patterns or attachments. It's the card that makes people nervous. But here's the truth most don't realize: The Devil doesn't force you to stay stuck. It convinces you that you can't leave. It feeds on the lies you've been taught to believe: "You're not strong enough." "This is just how life is." "Better the devil you know…" It's not chains. It's conditioning.

The Card, As I Lived It:
I didn't meet The Devil as some sinister figure in the dark. I met it in bright rooms filled with smiles that didn't reach the eyes. I met it in habits that numbed rather than nourished, in the quiet agreements I made with myself to stay small, to stay quiet, to just survive. The Devil crept in through coping mechanisms I called "normal." It sat beside me in relationships where love was conditional, where I convinced myself that walking on eggshells was safer than walking away.

I met The Devil in the lie that said: *This is the best you'll get. Be grateful it's not worse.* And for a long time, I believed that voice, because I didn't know I had the right to question it. Over time, that shifted. I stopped mistaking comfort for safety. I stopped confusing loyalty with self-abandonment. I looked down at the chains I thought were welded shut and realized they were loose. They always had been.

The Devil didn't disappear in a blaze of glory. It faded slowly, with every no I said, with every boundary I honored, with every moment I chose discomfort in freedom over comfort in captivity. I realized I wasn't powerless. I had just been taught to fear my own liberation.

XVI – The Tower
"When It All Falls Apart, And You Realize You Can Stand Without It"

The Card, As They Say:
The Tower doesn't come with a whisper. It comes loud, unavoidable. It comes with shocks, with truth, with the collapse of things you thought were unshakable. It's the lightning strike, the "before and after" moment where nothing looks the same. People fear The Tower because it doesn't ask, it takes. It tears through the false foundations, the comfort zones, the illusions you didn't even realize you'd been living inside. The fall isn't

about punishment. It's about showing you what was never steady in the first place. It falls because it was never safe to begin with.

The Card, As I Lived It:
I've lived through so many Towers, I stopped keeping score. Not because the moments got easier, but because I finally understood what they came to do. I met The Tower every time the ground gave out beneath me, when my mother left and the shape of "family" shattered overnight, when I stood in court telling truths that scorched the earth of my childhood, when my body gave out after years of pushing through pain and I had no choice but to rebuild from stillness, when every version of stability I had fought for dissolved, leaving behind nothing but questions and rubble.

At first, it always felt like destruction. And in many ways, it was. But not of me, of the illusions I had built to survive. What the Tower really does is strip away what won't last, the facades, the roles, the old stories we never thought to question. It doesn't ask for permission. It just comes, loud, uninvited, and necessary.

And yet, every time the walls fell, something fierce and honest emerged. Not polished. Not pretty. But real. I learned that collapse is not the enemy. Denial is. Because once The Tower has done its work, you're left with the most sacred thing of all: a clear view of what truly matters. The illusions drop. The roles slip. What's left is just you. Just the solid truth of who you are, and the raw, powerful freedom of building again, this time on your own terms.

XVII – The Star
"Hope Isn't Loud, It's the Light You Refuse to Let Go Of"

The Card, As They Say:
I've always felt The Star as a kind of healing, a quiet renewal, the calm that follows after the storm has passed. People think The Star feels magical, like sudden inspiration or a wave of peace washing over you. But real hope? It isn't a floodlight. It's a flicker you learn to protect with everything you have.

The Card, As I Lived It:
The Star didn't arrive with a bang. It crept in quietly, through the cracks left by The Tower. It didn't look like salvation. It looked like a breath, shaky but real. Like the moment I looked at the wreckage of everything I'd lost and thought, *Maybe... I can still build something beautiful from this.*

I met The Star not in triumph, but in the in-between. When I let myself want again, even after disappointment had taught me not to. When I found meaning in a cup of coffee, a book I didn't want to end, a slow walk under a sky I once forgot to look at. When I whispered hopes I wasn't sure I believed in, not because I needed answers, but because I needed to remember how to reach.

The Star didn't promise everything would be okay. It didn't offer proof. But it offered something better: possibility. It reminded me that healing isn't loud. It happens in the soft places, in the quiet decision to keep showing up for life, even when it hasn't been kind.

The Star taught me that hope isn't blind. It sees the ruins and dares to glow anyway. It's the part of me that refused to be snuffed out. That said, I don't know what's next, but I want to find out. That's not weakness. That's a kind of strength only the broken know how to hold.

XVIII – The Moon
"When You Can't See the Truth, But You Feel It Anyway"

The Card, As They Say:
The Moon is uncertainty, illusion, intuition, and the shadows we fear to name. It's the card of not knowing, of walking through a landscape where things aren't what they seem, and clarity feels just out of reach. People pull The Moon and ask, "What's being hidden from me?" But sometimes, it's not about deception from others; it's about learning to navigate when life itself is unclear.

The Card, As I Lived It:
The Moon and I met in the moments when everything looked fine, but nothing felt safe. In the spaces where the truth was too dangerous to name, so it was buried under smiles, silence, and "You're overreacting." The Moon was the hum beneath the noise, when love came with conditions and control but wore the mask of care. When family secrets were kept polished while wounds festered just out of view. When my gut screamed *This isn't okay,* but I was the only one who heard it. When I had learned to second-guess myself so thoroughly, I no longer trusted my own knowing.

As a child, I thought the discomfort was mine to fix. As an adult, I realized I'd been trained to mistrust the truth just because it wasn't convenient for others. The Moon didn't hand me answers. It handed me questions, and slowly, I began to understand that clarity doesn't always come in daylight. Sometimes it arrives through instinct, sensation, a quiet unease that refuses to be ignored.

The Moon taught me that intuition isn't irrational. It's ancient. It's wise. It's the inner compass we learn to muffle to keep the peace, until one day, we stop apologizing for reading the signs no one else wants to see. I stopped waiting for proof. I started listening to what my body, my dreams, and my discomfort were already telling me.

And that's when the shadows started to part. Not because the truth became easy, but because I was no longer afraid to walk through the dark to find it.

XIX – The Sun
"When You Realize It's Safe to Stand in the Light"

The Card, As They Say:
The Sun is joy, clarity, success, and that radiant feeling of being fully seen, with nothing to hide and nothing to fear. It's freedom. It's warmth. It's the light after a long night. People see The Sun and think, "Finally! Everything's good!" But if you've lived in survival mode, The Sun doesn't always feel safe at first. Sometimes, light feels exposing. Sometimes, joy feels suspicious, like you're waiting for the other shoe to drop.

The Card, As I Lived It:
I didn't step into The Sun like a hero crossing a finish line. I eased into it, one unguarded breath at a time, skeptical that warmth this steady could actually be real. For years, I'd been taught that joy was a trapdoor, that ease was just the setup before the fall, that if I let myself be happy, I'd be punished for the audacity. So, when peace arrived, I didn't dance. I flinched. I waited for the catch.

But The Sun didn't burn me. It stayed. It stayed when I laughed without apology, and no one scolded me for being "too much." It stayed when I looked around at a quiet, ordinary day and realized I didn't want to escape it. It stayed when I stopped chasing validation and simply allowed myself to be, unhidden, unedited, unafraid.

The Sun wasn't a climax. It was a return to myself, to safety, to a lightness I thought I'd lost forever. It taught me that joy doesn't have to be earned in blood and burnout. That softness isn't fragile; it's resilient. And that choosing happiness isn't naïve, it's radical, especially after a life that told you it wasn't for you.

I stopped holding my breath. I stopped rehearsing disaster. And in that exhale, I found it: freedom, brightness, belonging. The kind I didn't have to fight for. Just the kind I finally stopped turning away from.

XX – Judgment
"The Moment You Stop Waiting for Permission to Rise"

The Card, As They Say:
Traditionally, Judgment points to awakening, reckoning, and rebirth, the call to step into truth and leave old disguises behind. People think Judgment is external, someone else deciding your fate. But real Judgment? It's the moment you decide. To stop shrinking. To stop hiding behind old stories. To become who you were always meant to be.

The Card, As I Lived It:
I didn't meet Judgment in a blaze of glory. I met it in the quiet tension of choice, over and over again. Do I swallow the words to keep surface peace, or speak them and face what follows? Do I keep contorting myself into someone else's comfort zone, or claim the version of me that no longer asks for permission? Do I stay small because it's safe, or rise, knowing that rising will cost me the comfort of who I used to be?

Judgment wasn't a single moment. It was a series of them, strung together like a lifeline I had to choose to grab hold of. It was sitting in that courtroom, heart pounding, telling truths that cracked the family mythology wide open. It was walking away from relationships that no longer recognized the woman I was becoming. It was looking into my own eyes in the mirror and hearing a voice, not cruel, not angry, but steady, say: *You know better now. It's time to live like it.*

Judgment asked for something sacred and terrifying: a reckoning. Not with anyone else, but with myself. It asked me to rise, even when I wasn't sure I was ready. To shed the skin of who I'd been, even when parts of it still felt familiar. To answer the call of my own becoming, even when I knew it would disappoint the people who preferred me small, quiet, and convenient.

Because once you hear that call, the deep, clear knowing that you're meant for more, you can't unhear it. You either rise, or you shrink. You either evolve, or you echo your past. I chose to rise. And yes, it cost me things. But what I gained was me.

XXI – The World
"You Were Never Broken, You Were Becoming"

The Card, As They Say:
The World is often seen as completion and fulfillment, not the kind that's about crossing something off, but the kind where you look back and know every stumble and every rise brought you to this place. People often see this card and think: achievement, success, the big win. But that's not what real completion looks like. It's not a trophy. It's more subtle than that, a quiet moment when you realize you've brought your scattered parts back to yourself.

The Card, As I Lived It:
I didn't arrive at The World with my arms in the air or streamers falling from the ceiling. There was no finish line. Just a feeling, like something that had always been broken inside me had finally come back together. There was no drumroll, no declaration. Just me, sitting at the kitchen table, a warm mug in hand, my husband across from me, and a quiet realization settling into my bones: I'm not surviving anymore. I'm living.

For years, I measured my worth by how much I could endure, by how well I kept going when everything said I shouldn't. I chased approval. I braced for storms. I kept trying to prove that I was enough, that I had made it, that I was safe now. But The World didn't arrive with applause. It arrived in stillness. In the moment I stopped trying to become and simply was, and realized: this version of me includes them all.

The seeker who longed for something more. The survivor who learned to notice light slipping through the breaks. The silenced girl who watched everything, remembered everything. The woman who rose anyway, despite it all.

The World wasn't about closure. It was about integration, the stitching together of every chapter, every scar, every triumph and mess and milestone into a tapestry I could finally wrap around myself and call home. I didn't escape my story. I reclaimed it. And in doing so, I stopped asking what needed to be fixed. I started saying: *This is me. All of me. And I wouldn't change a thing.*

The Minor Arcana

Wands

Ace of Wands
"That Flicker of 'What If' When the World Told You No"

The Card, As They Say:
The Ace of Wands comes across like a spark in the dark, a quiet tug that makes you lean forward and wonder what else could be. It's that spark of desire that makes you catch yourself thinking, *I want this.* It doesn't arrive with a plan or hand you step-by-step directions. What it offers instead is possibility, the opening to strike a match if you're willing.

The Card, As I Lived It:
I felt this card before I ever saw it in a deck. It was that pull in the background when nothing around me fit, though I couldn't explain why. There wasn't a vision yet. No plan on paper. Just the knowing that the life I'd been handed wasn't the one I wanted to keep.

So, I started imagining something else. Something more honest. Even without a name for it, I could feel it building, the tension, the stretch, the spark that refused to vanish no matter how many times I was told to shrink.

I didn't need certainty; what I needed was permission. And somehow, deep inside, I gave it to myself.

For me, the Ace of Wands never showed up as a map. It arrived as a nudge, a whisper. It wasn't about clarity so much as about keeping a thread of curiosity alive, even when the dark was thick around me. It was about trusting that something could catch fire, even if I had to be the one to strike the flame.

Two of Wands
"When You Know There's More, But 'More' Scares You"

The Card, As They Say:
The Two of Wands is about potential. It's the space between knowing you've outgrown something and deciding what to do about it. You're holding the map, looking out past

what's familiar, asking: *Could I really go further than this?* But here's the thing, this card isn't about movement yet. It's the pause. The deep breath before the leap. That place where anticipation and fear start bumping into each other.

The Card, As I Lived It:
I met the Two of Wands every time I saw a door opening and felt both thrilled and terrified. The idea of change lit something in me, but so did the fear of letting go. I remember standing on the edge of decisions: jobs, relationships, entire ways of living that no longer fit. They made me feel small. But they were also what I knew.

I'd start to plan. I'd make lists, dream big, picture what could be next. And then I'd freeze, caught between what I longed for and what I was afraid to lose.

The Two of Wands became a mirror. It asked me to name what I really wanted, and then asked if I was willing to risk the known to go after it. It didn't demand action. But it didn't let me look away, either.

Three of Wands
"When You Finally Step Out, And Realize There's No Turning"

The Card, As They Say:
The Three of Wands is progress, the moment after you've dared to step beyond your comfort zone. It's not the spark of inspiration, that was the Ace. This is the follow-through. You've already said yes to more, and now you're standing at the edge, watching the horizon, trusting that what you've set in motion is working, even if you can't see the full results yet.

It's about expansion, foresight, and that mix of anticipation, hope, and deep breaths while the universe catches up to your courage. It's hopeful, but it's also a little scary. Because once you take that step forward, you know, there's no turning back.

The Card, As I Lived It:
I met the Three of Wands every time I took a leap, and then had to sit in the uncomfortable quiet that followed. It was the space after the choice, but before the outcome. The moment when you've left what no longer fits but haven't yet arrived at what will.

I felt it when I walked away from the familiar with no backup plan, only a deep knowing that I couldn't stay. I felt it again when I applied to grad school after life had slammed doors I thought were mine to walk through, hoping someone, somewhere, would believe in what I had to offer. I felt it in my gut and in my bank account, as I made decisions that felt aligned but came with no guarantee.

The Three of Wands isn't about movement. It's about trust. It's standing still, facing the wide unknown, knowing you've done what you could and now the rest is out of your hands. It's not being stuck, but it's not being in control either.

The old life is behind you. The new life is calling. And your work is to hold your ground with grace, to resist the pull of fear that tries to drag you back into what you've already outgrown.

Four of Wands
"When You Realize You Deserve to Exhale, and Even Celebrate"

The Card, As They Say:
The Four of Wands is a card of homecoming, stability, and joyful pause. It's about celebration, not because you've finished everything, but because it's worth honoring how far you've already come. It marks those rare moments when you let yourself feel safe, supported, and connected.

But here's what isn't always said: for people who've lived in survival mode, joy can feel foreign. Rest can feel suspicious. And celebration? Almost guilty.

The Card, As I Lived It:
I met the Four of Wands in small, fleeting moments, ones I nearly dismissed because I was too conditioned to keep bracing for impact.

Like the first evening I sat in my tiny apartment, watching my son play, and realized it was simply peaceful. No chaos. No fear. Just quiet safety.

Or the laughter that bubbled up with people who didn't expect anything from me, no performance, no proof, just presence.

Or the warmth of a simple gathering, where I felt a belonging I hadn't grown up with, but was slowly learning to trust.

At first, I doubted it all. The stillness felt suspicious. The joy felt temporary. But the Four of Wands kept whispering, *It's okay. You can exhale here.*

And that was the lesson: life doesn't have to be perfect to be celebrated. There are places, moments, and people that give you permission to breathe. To rest. To feel at home in your body and in your story, even if only for an evening. And those moments? They're sacred.

Five of Wands
"When Everyone's Swinging, and You Have to Decide If It's Worth It"

The Card, As They Say:
The Five of Wands is tension, conflict, competition, the chaos of too many voices, too many agendas, and not enough clarity. It's that feeling of being pulled into battles that aren't always yours to fight.

Sometimes it's harmless friction. Other times, it's a daily struggle to be heard, seen, or valued in spaces where everyone's swinging sticks just to prove they belong.

The Card, As I Lived It:
I first felt the Five of Wands at home. In the kind of family tension where you never knew what might set someone off. Later in life, at work in breakrooms, boardrooms, classrooms, and courtrooms, where I had to work twice as hard to be taken seriously, especially as a woman in spaces dominated by men. And I met it in myself, in the relentless comparisons, the inner voice that told me I had to prove my worth just to justify taking up space.

The Five of Wands wasn't about one grand battle; it was the cumulative weariness of constant friction. And the hardest truth it offered me? Not every fight is worth my energy.

I started to learn the difference between standing my ground and wasting my strength. That walking away isn't weakness, it's wisdom. I didn't have to pick up every stick handed to me. I didn't have to engage just because someone else wanted a sparring partner.

Peace wasn't going to be handed to me. I had to choose it. I had to protect it. And that meant being brave enough to leave the noise behind and walk my path without needing to prove a thing.

Six of Wands

"When They Finally See You, But You Know You've Been Winning All Along"

The Card, As They Say:

The Six of Wands is victory, recognition, success after struggle. It is the moment when people finally applaud you for what you've accomplished. When you're seen, celebrated, maybe even admired.

But here's the thing. If you've spent your life fighting unseen battles, recognition feels complicated. Because by the time they notice you're winning, you've already survived things they'll never understand.

The Card, As I Lived It:

I met the Six of Wands in moments like getting the promotion after years of showing up, doing the work, and staying late when no one was watching. In compliments like "I don't know how you do it," spoken by people who weren't there when I had no choice. In praise for my resilience, when I would've much rather had a life that didn't require so much of it.

And don't get me wrong, it felt good to be seen. It felt good to be recognized. But there was always this quiet voice beneath the applause whispering, *You're celebrating me now? Where were you when I was drowning?*

That's when I understood. The Six of Wands isn't really about the audience. It's about owning your victory for yourself.

Because I had already won long before the recognition. I won when I kept going without applause. I won when I chose peace over proving. I won when I decided my worth wasn't waiting at the finish line, it had been with me the whole time.

Seven of Wands

"Sometimes you're too far up the hill to waste time arguing with people at the bottom."

The Card, As They Say:

Seven of Wands energy shows up when you're asked to defend your place, when eyes turn critical, or when others try to pull you down a notch. It's about staying steady under pressure and choosing which battles are worth your strength.

But no one really talks about this part: it's not always about defending your ground. Sometimes it's knowing when to plant your feet, and when to let the noise roll past without grabbing it. Because when you've climbed this far, you don't need to explain the view to people still at the bottom.

The Card, As I Lived It:
I met the Seven of Wands every time I earned something, whether it was a title, a little peace, or the right to speak freely, and suddenly, the questions rolled in. Not always direct, but loud enough to sting.

I heard it in the whispers behind closed doors after I got promoted. In the passive-aggressive remarks when I set boundaries people weren't used to. In the coldness from those who seemed fine with me, until I stopped playing small.

At first, I bent over backward trying to explain myself. I toned things down. I made sure no one felt threatened by my growth. I thought if I stayed soft enough, it wouldn't rattle anyone.

But the Seven of Wands showed me another kind of strength, the kind that doesn't dim just because someone else is uncomfortable. It reminded me: I don't need to explain what I've earned.

Holding your ground doesn't always mean being combative. Sometimes it's quiet. Just staying rooted. Letting your presence speak for itself, and knowing that not every invitation to defend yourself is worth answering.

Eight of Wands
"When Everything Starts Moving, and You Realize You're Ready"

The Card, As They Say:
The Eight of Wands is momentum, swift movement, progress without obstacles. It's when delays lift and everything you've been working toward suddenly takes off.

It does sound exciting, fast movement, momentum, things finally clicking into place. But honestly? If you've spent most of your life pushing through hard seasons, ease can feel strange. You get so used to tension that when something flows, your body kind of braces.

I used to think, *Is this real? What's about to go wrong?* It took time to learn that not everything good was a setup for pain.

The Card, As I Lived It:
I met the Eight of Wands in those rare, almost surreal seasons when everything moved with startling clarity and speed. Opportunities appeared before I had time to second-guess them. The right people showed up. Problems unraveled without me needing to grip them to death.

Life felt, dare I say, easy. And that's what made me pause. After years of surviving chaos, the sudden flow felt suspicious. I found myself scanning for the catch, bracing for the backlash, or even manufacturing problems just to feel something familiar. I didn't know how to simply receive.

But the Eight of Wands reminded me: not every season demands hustle, proving, or repair. Sometimes things align because you've already done the work behind the scenes. The energy is ready. The path is clear.

Your only task is to keep your heart open, your feet steady, and let the momentum carry you forward without apology.

Nine of Wands
"When You've Been Knocked Down, But You're the One Still Holding the Line"

The Card, As They Say:
The Nine of Wands is resilience. It's the warrior who's been through hell but refuses to quit. It's that moment when you're battle-worn, leaning on your staff for support, but your eyes are sharp, scanning for the next hit, because experience has taught you it's probably coming.

This is not about thriving; it's about enduring. And knowing that survival is its own kind of victory.

The Card, As I Lived It:
I am the Nine of Wands. Not just because I've been knocked down and stood back up, but because I've done it more times than I can count.

I met this card every time life tested me, and I kept going anyway. When I showed up exhausted, bones aching, soul worn thin, but still did the thing, for my son, for my survival, for the stubborn belief that I wasn't finished yet.

I wore my scars like armor. Not to prove how much I could endure, but because each one reminded me: *You're still here.*

The Nine of Wands was waking up with nothing left to give and whispering, *Not today. You don't get to break me today.* It was finding just enough strength to take the next step, even on the days when forward looked more like dragging myself than walking.

But here's what I've come to understand: this card isn't just about endurance. It's also about discernment, knowing when to fight, and when to rest. Knowing that vigilance can become a cage if you never put the walls down.

The Nine taught me that strength isn't only in the standing. It's in the pausing. In letting yourself soften without falling apart. In remembering that you are more than what tried to break you; you are what held it all together.

Ten of Wands
"When Carrying It All Stops Feeling Like a Badge of Honor"

The Card, As They Say:
The Ten of Wands has always felt like being loaded down with more than your share, the responsibilities, the exhaustion, the pieces you didn't ask for but picked up all the same. It's the image of someone hunched over, carrying too much, not because they want to, but because it's what they've always done. Pushing forward out of habit, or because no one else was going to.

This card doesn't just point to overwhelm. It asks you to stop and ask yourself: *Is all of this weight really mine?*

The Card, As I Lived It:
I crossed paths with the Ten of Wands every time I confused exhaustion with strength, when I thought being overwhelmed meant I was doing something right.

I felt it while juggling single motherhood, work, school, and the invisible weight of everyone else's expectations, convinced that if I didn't carry it all, it would collapse. I felt it

236

when I smiled and said, *I'm fine,* while my body whispered, *Please stop.* And when I absorbed other people's messes, emotions, and responsibilities, not because I had to, but because I was so used to being the strong one that I didn't know how to be anything else.

At first, I wore it like a badge of honor: *Look how capable I am. Look how much I can hold.* But eventually, the ache grew louder than the applause.

The Ten of Wands taught me something I didn't want to learn: no one is coming to take the weight from your hands. If you want to breathe, you have to choose to set it down. Not because you're weak, but because you're wise enough to know that peace doesn't come from martyrdom.

It comes from boundaries. From release. From finally saying, *This is no longer mine to carry.*

And from there? You walk lighter. Not because the road got easier, but because you chose yourself.

Page of Wands
"When You Finally Ask, 'What If This Gets to Be Fun?'"

The Card, As They Say:
The Page of Wands is youthful energy, curiosity, exploration, and the excitement of new beginnings. It's that playful spark, the part of you that looks at an open road and thinks, *Ooooh, what's possible?*

This is not about mastery. It is about being willing to try, to wander, to get excited about what's next without needing a detailed plan.

The Card, As I Lived It:
I met the Page of Wands every time it hit me that life couldn't just be about surviving or serving or grinding through the next box to check. It could be about wonder, too.

It was after I laid down the weight I had carried for too long, and in the stillness that followed, a new voice emerged: *What if joy was a compass?*

It came in moments that felt almost reckless in their freedom. It came in simple moments. When I said yes just because something felt fun. When I started a project not to finish it, but because it made me feel alive. When I let excitement steer for once, instead of fear.

237

The Page of Wands wasn't loud. It sounded more like the younger version of me, the one who asked questions before learning to expect disappointment. The one who could begin without needing the whole map.

That energy reminded me: you don't have to know how it ends to get started. Sometimes all you need is a flicker of curiosity and a little space to follow it.

Knight of Wands
"When You're Fueled by Passion, and Patience Is Nowhere in Sight"

The Card, As They Say:
The Knight of Wands doesn't wait at the door, it bursts through, wild-eyed and ready to run. This is the restless surge in your chest that says *now* before you've had time to weigh the cost. It's intoxicating, like striking a match in a dark room, but I know how quickly that flame can leave blisters if you don't learn when to let it burn low.

The Card, As I Lived It:
I met this Knight every time my gut told me to go, and I obeyed, even when the map was blank. It was me throwing boxes into the back of a car, moving states with no plan but the certainty that staying put would be worse.

It was the part of me that leapt into jobs, projects, or obsessions simply because they made my blood run hotter, not because they looked neat on paper. I can still picture her as that younger self, quick to nod *yes* before the question was even finished, convinced that momentum itself would draw the road ahead.

The Knight of Wands was like an electric current, no pause, no brake. I moved fast. Too fast, sometimes. I burned through energy, through people, through chances that might have grown if I'd tended them more slowly. I learned, in ways that left ash in my mouth, that some sparks are only meant to flash, not to devour everything they touch.

And still, I can't regret it. For all the chaos, that headlong rush left me with something permanent: the taste of freedom. It's still there in me, humming under the surface, reminding me that movement, even messy movement, has always been its own kind of grace.

Queen of Wands
"When You Finally Realize, You Are the Damn Spark"

The Card, As They Say:
The Queen of Wands doesn't chase. She carries herself in a way that draws others in, not because she's trying, but because her presence is its own kind of gravity. She is sure of what she brings, sure of her fire, and unafraid to let it burn where it needs to.

She knows how to stand in a crowd and light up a room, and she also knows how to stand alone without apology. Her passion is steady, not frantic; her drive doesn't ask permission.

The Card, As I Lived It:
I didn't step into this Queen all at once. She arrived slowly, almost shy at first, each time I stopped asking someone else to tell me I was allowed to take up space.

She came through as I peeled away the old stories that told me to sand down my edges so I'd be easier to hold. She was there when I walked into rooms where I didn't look like anyone, didn't sound like anyone, and still chose to plant my feet.

She stood with me when I stopped cushioning my truths for comfort, when I let the versions I had twisted myself into finally unravel. The Queen of Wands didn't show up with trumpets. She showed up with heat.

She appeared the day I began chasing what set me alight, not to prove I could pull it off, but because I had come to believe I was worthy of wanting it in the first place.

She reminded me that confidence isn't about how loud you are. It's about the steadiness that settles into your body after years of shrinking, when you finally decide: *no more*.

This Queen doesn't need applause. Her power is quiet and undeniable, in her spine, in her clarity, in her refusal to dim the colors of who she is.

Once I let her in, I stopped confusing visibility with danger. And what once felt like exposure began to feel like freedom.

King of Wands
"When You Realize You're Not Just Walking the Path, You're Lighting It for Others"

The Card, As They Say:
The King of Wands isn't a crown-and-throne figure to me. His energy feels more like someone pointing at the horizon and saying, *I'll go first, come with me if you want.*

He doesn't wait for a clear trail. He moves anyway, even if the ground is uneven, even if the way forward hasn't been walked yet.

The Card, As I Lived It:
I felt this energy take root once I stopped making choices only for myself. It hit me that even the smallest choice, saying yes or saying no, was shaping the kind of space other people could step into.

At first, it was small things: letting my team run with their own ideas instead of trying to control every step. Speaking out when my voice wobbled but saying the thing anyway. Taking chances that didn't make sense on paper but felt solid in my gut.

The King of Wands didn't show up with a title. He came the day I trusted what I knew without overexplaining. That's when I noticed something shift. What I carried forward, the risks I took, the fire that kept me moving, wasn't just about me anymore.

It was about the light it left behind for the people walking after me.

Cups

Ace of Cups
"When You Realize You're Allowed to Receive, Not Just Give"

The Card, As They Say:
The Ace of Cups is said to be the beginning of renewal, an open heart, healing, and connection. The overflowing cup. The invitation to love, and to let yourself be loved. To stop bottling up what was meant to move through you. But if you grew up learning to guard your heart, the invitation doesn't always feel simple. Sometimes it feels like a risk.

The Card, As I Lived It:
Not every beginning arrives loud. Some slip in quiet, so quiet you almost miss them at

first, like a hand reaching out that makes you pause, or the ache in your chest when you realize how long you've been holding yourself tight without even knowing it. I didn't exactly greet the Ace of Cups with arms flung wide. I came to it slowly, almost sideways, like meeting a creature that lingers near the edge of your palm, curious but not sure it can trust you. That was me. Suspicious of softness. Cautious with touch. Wanting connection, but bracing against it at the same time.

It showed up in the cracks: when someone offered kindness, and I waited for the catch. When I reached out to give love, I tripped on the part where I was supposed to let it in. And the gentlest things undid me, a hug I didn't expect, a word spoken gently, a quiet moment where no one needed anything from me. I cried then, not because I was falling apart, but because my body finally believed it was safe enough to soften.

The Ace of Cups was my slow thaw. It whispered that emotions weren't meant to be rationed. That crying isn't proof that something is wrong, it can be a release. That real connection doesn't have to feel dangerous. Love, I learned, doesn't always demand bravery or performance. Sometimes it asks only presence. This card didn't insist I tear my defenses down overnight. It asked for something smaller, a crack in the armor, a door left open just enough for light to slip in. To believe, even for a breath, that my heart wasn't only a thing to defend. It could be a home. A place worthy of rest.

Two of Cups
"When You Let Someone See You, and Stay Soft Anyway"

The Card, As They Say:
The Two of Cups is union, connection, and emotional reciprocity. It's the card of love, yes, but deeper than that, it's about meeting. Two people, both bringing their whole selves to the table, offering not just affection, but truth, tenderness, and trust. It's not about fantasy. It's about being seen, and still being held.

The Card, As I Lived It:
I met the Two of Cups not in some cinematic rush of romance, but in quiet, human moments, the ones where I let someone in a little further than I usually would, and held my breath to see what they'd do with that closeness. It was when I shared something raw and they didn't flinch. Didn't look away. Didn't run. It was when I stopped performing love as a transaction and let it be offered freely, without conditions.

It was when I realized that real connection doesn't always come like a spark in the dark; sometimes it's a steady flame, not burning but warming. But I didn't come to this easily. After years of abandonment, betrayal, and being valued more for what I could do than who I was, the idea of a mutual, tender connection felt... foreign. Like waiting for the floor to drop beneath me, only to find it never does.

So, when it finally came, the soft presence of someone who saw me and stayed, it felt like a miracle. Not the loud, showy kind. The quiet kind that changes everything. And in that quiet, I began to learn, slowly, how to receive it.

Three of Cups
"When You Find the People Who Don't Just Take, They Pour Back In"

The Card, As They Say:
The Three of Cups is celebration, friendship, and emotional support. It's the card of finding your people, the ones who cheer for you, cry with you, and hold space for all your versions. It's laughter that feels healing, presence that feels grounding, and connection that doesn't come with a scorecard.

The Card, As I Lived It:
For a long time, I was the giver in every room. The strong one. The one who steadied others. The listener who didn't ask to be heard. And don't get me wrong, I carried that role well. But it hollowed me out. There's a particular kind of loneliness in that, being leaned on, but never leaning back.

The Three of Cups didn't arrive as wild celebrations or lifelong soul sisters. It showed up in smaller, sacred moments: when someone poured into me without being asked, when a friend sat beside me without needing me to perform, when laughter bubbled up not as a mask, but as release. It was in the people who didn't just want to sit by my fire; they brought kindling. They helped tend it.

And slowly, I learned that connection doesn't have to come at the cost of myself. That I didn't have to trade usefulness for belonging. That being celebrated wasn't indulgent. It was necessary.

Four of Cups
"When You're Offered Good Things, But You're Too Tired to Reach for Them"

The Card, As They Say:
The Four of Cups is disconnection, emotional fatigue, and apathy. It's the figure under the tree, surrounded by blessings, but too worn down, too guarded, or too unsure to open their hands and take them. It isn't about being ungrateful. It's about being tired of hoping.

The Card, As I Lived It:
I crossed paths with the Four of Cups in those odd stretches when life looked fine enough on the surface, the milestones were there, the smiles in their place, everything that should have added up to joy. But inside, it felt heavy. A kind of weight I couldn't explain or shake off.

When love or support was offered, I did what I knew: smiled, nodded, and said the right words. And underneath it, nothing. Just that dull blankness where feeling should've been. When I finally reached something I'd worked so hard for, only to sit in the stillness after and wonder: Why doesn't this feel like enough?

And when joy came close, like it was waiting at my door, I couldn't open it. Not because I didn't want to. But because I didn't trust it. The Four of Cups wasn't about rejection. It was about hesitation. About not knowing if I had the energy to try again, to hope again, to believe that maybe, just maybe, things could be different.

Because when you've lived years braced for impact, even peace feels suspicious. You learn to scan the horizon for storms, even with the sun blazing overhead. Sometimes the thing you've been longing for shows up, and that's exactly when it feels the hardest to reach for.

Five of Cups
"When You Mourn What's Gone, and Forget There's More Waiting Behind You"

The Card, As They Say:
The Five of Cups is grief, regret, sorrow. It's the card of standing over what's been spilled, loss you can't undo, relationships you can't repair, dreams that didn't survive. But here's the part we often miss: there are still two cups standing behind you. There is still something left to build from. You just have to turn around.

The Card, As I Lived It:
I met the Five of Cups every time life knocked something precious out of my hands. When I gave everything I had to people who left anyway. When the dreams I clung to slipped through my fingers all the same. When I sat in the ashes of what I thought my future would be, a family, a home, and whispered, *What was the point of hoping at all?*

The grief was sharp. The disappointment, consuming. And for a long time, all I could see was what I had lost. But eventually, quietly, gradually, I began to lift my head. Not to forget, not to diminish it, but just to notice what was still there: a friend who stayed, a spark that refused to go out, a part of me still reaching toward the light.

The Five of Cups didn't rush my mourning. It sat with me in it. But it also nudged me, gently, toward the cups still standing. Because grief isn't a dead end. It's a crossing, sacred, painful, but a way through. And on the other side, life waits. Changed, yes. But still here.

Six of Cups
"When You Visit the Past, Not to Stay, But to Understand"

The Card, As They Say:
The Six of Cups is nostalgia, memory, childhood innocence. It's the card of revisiting where you came from, not to live there, but to gather pieces of yourself you might have left behind. It's bittersweet. A reminder of simpler joys, and of wounds still waiting to be seen.

The Card, As I Lived It:
I met the Six of Cups every time a scent, a song, or a worn photograph pulled me back into a version of myself I hadn't seen in years. The child who believed love was unconditional, before she learned it came with terms. The teenager holding her dreams like fragile glass, daring herself to believe in more. The young woman who looked around at a life that didn't fit and thought, *Maybe I don't have to settle.*

Sometimes those memories ached like bruises I didn't know were still there. Other times they wrapped around me like warm light. The Six of Cups didn't ask me to hide in the past. It showed me the past wasn't just about going back, but about gathering what I'd left behind and carrying it forward. That I could still pick up the pieces I dropped in my rush to grow up, to survive, to move on. Wonder. Laughter. Boldness. Softness. They didn't vanish. They were waiting.

And now, I carry them with me. Not as burdens, but as pieces of home I could finally return to.

Seven of Cups
"When Every Door Looks Open, But Not All of Them Lead Home"

The Card, As They Say:
The Seven of Cups is imagination, opportunity, fantasy, and confusion. It's standing in front of a sea of options, dreams, or desires, each one sparkling with possibility. But some are illusions or traps. Others are soul calls. The hard part? Choosing wisely.

The Card, As I Lived It:
I met the Seven of Cups in seasons where I finally had options. Unfortunately, I almost immediately felt like I was drowning in them. After years of scraping by without much choice, suddenly everything opened at once. It was thrilling, yes, but also too much, almost dizzying. I wanted to chase everything, say yes to it all, make up for the time I had spent believing there was no other way.

I learned fast, just because a door is open doesn't mean it's the one that leads you home. There were opportunities that looked perfect on paper, but my body pulled back, even as my mind tried to bargain me forward. There were relationships where I felt seen, but only when I twisted myself to match someone else's version of me. And there were dreams I carried too long, not because they still lit me up, but because once, they kept me alive.

The Seven of Cups reminded me that discernment is a kind of love, too. That not everything that shines is sacred. Some choices are distractions. Loud, insistent, testing whether I remember who I am. Some are illusions, designed to tempt the wounds I haven't fully healed. And a few, the rare ones, are soul calls. Quiet. Resonant. True.

I learned that clarity doesn't come from frenzy. It comes from stillness. It shifted when I stopped asking what I should choose, and began asking instead: What honors who I'm becoming? That's when the real path started to show itself.

Eight of Cups
"When You Leave Behind What You Once Prayed For"

The Card, As They Say:
The Eight of Cups is walking away, emotional closure, a soul-led departure. It's the hard decision to leave behind what once mattered, because it no longer feeds your spirit. It's not about rejection. It's about honoring growth.

The Card, As I Lived It:

I met the Eight of Cups every time I looked around at a life I had built; sometimes with care, sometimes in desperation, and realized it no longer felt like home. I clung to certain jobs as if they were lifelines, even when they stopped feeding me and started to confine me. Some relationships made me feel visible at first. But slowly, I felt myself disappearing inside them.

And there were dreams I once needed, desperately, dreams that carried me through hard seasons. But in time, I had to face that they'd already run their course, even if I wasn't ready to admit it. And even then, even knowing the truth, leaving was never easy. There's a strange kind of grief that comes with growth, especially when you've fought hard to earn something. It feels like betrayal to whisper, *This isn't enough anymore*, when you once prayed for the very thing you're now walking away from.

But the Eight of Cups taught me that soul-honesty matters more than comfort. That loyalty to the past should never cost you your future. You're allowed to outgrow what once fit. You're allowed to walk away from something you still love. You're allowed to disappoint others, if it means you finally stop abandoning yourself.

And leaving? It isn't failure. It's listening. It's trusting the part of you that knows it's time for something deeper, wilder, truer. Because staying might feel easier in the moment. But leaving, that's where your next life begins.

Nine of Cups

"When You Realize You Are What You've Been Wishing For"

The Card, As They Say:

The Nine of Cups is contentment, satisfaction, emotional independence. It's often called the "wish card," the moment when what you longed for is no longer something outside yourself. It's about being with yourself and knowing, *I'm okay. Just like this. Not flawless or finished. But full, and fully worthy.*

The Card, As I Lived It:

I didn't stumble on the Nine of Cups in achievements or applause. It showed up in the quieter places, the ones no one else was watching. Moments where I made peace with myself. Times that felt like home. Like sitting in my own space, quiet, safe, mine, and realizing I wasn't lonely. I was at peace.

Like laughing at my own jokes in the kitchen, not because anyone else was there to hear, but because joy had finally rooted itself in me. Like looking around at the life I pieced together from scraps and stubborn willpower, and feeling not pride for the fight, but deep gratitude for the woman who kept going.

By then, it wasn't about a wish list. It wasn't about chasing some finish line. The Nine of Cups showed me that fulfillment isn't flashy. It was a return, softer than I expected. A knowing, deep down, that wholeness had never lived in someone else's hands. It's when you stop performing happiness and begin living it, in a quiet house, in a small laugh, in the way your soul finally exhales and whispers, *This is enough.*

Ten of Cups
"When You Build a Life That Feels Like Home, From the Inside Out"

The Card, As They Say:
The Ten of Cups is emotional fulfillment, soul-deep happiness, lasting love. It's about wholeness, not because everything is perfect, but because the foundation is real, nurtured, and yours. It's not a fantasy. It's the earned peace.

The Card, As I Lived It:
I didn't get to the Ten of Cups through some magical movie moment. It wasn't one big thing. It was smaller things, ordinary things, that snuck up on me. Like laughing with my family and realizing no one was tense. Or seeing my kid steady in his own skin and thinking, *he's safe, he doesn't have to unlearn what I did.* Or just having people around who weren't trying to take anything from me.

We showed up for each other. We stayed, even when it wasn't shiny. There was no dramatic arrival. No grand climax. Just mornings where I woke up without dread. Someone passing me the salt and me not bracing for the fallout. Laughter that felt real, laughter I could join in, not just sit outside of. It wasn't perfect. Sometimes it was messy. But I trusted it. And maybe that was the point all along.

Page of Cups
"When Your Heart Whispers, *'Maybe... Just Maybe'*"

The Card, As They Say:
The Page of Cups is youthful emotion, sensitivity, creative wonder, and the first stirrings of emotional vulnerability. It's the dreamer, the soft-hearted, open-souled part of you that

247

hasn't been fully shut down by the world yet. It's the maybe. The what if. The could I trust again?

The Card, As I Lived It:
I met the Page of Cups in every moment something tender stirred after a long, hard season of emotional shutdown. She showed up when a kind word caught me off guard, when my eyes stung before I even knew why. When I started to believe, quietly, cautiously, that maybe love didn't have to mean loss. When I found myself writing journal entries no one would read, poems I never planned to share, whispering hopes to the ceiling just to keep them alive.

The Page of Cups wasn't polished or confident. She was raw, tentative, wide-eyed, offering fragile feelings with shaky hands. Not always knowing what to do with her emotions, but refusing to numb them. She let them rise. She felt, even when it hurt. Even when the world told her feeling was dangerous. She was the part of me that softened again, even after I'd learned to go hard. The part that reached out, trusted a little, loved a little, believed a little, without demanding guarantees.

And looking back, I've learned to thank her. Because every risk I've taken that led to something real, every moment of connection, creativity, and courage, began with her quiet, brave heart saying: *Feel it anyway.*

Knight of Cups
"When You Carry Your Heart Forward, Even When It's Still Healing"

The Card, As They Say:
The Knight of Cups? He's the emotional one. The romantic. The one who chases feelings, not facts. He's got a dream in one hand and a heart in the other,
and he's not great at reading road signs. But he means well. He moves toward whatever stirs something inside him, even if it doesn't always make sense on paper.

Moving with the Knight of Cups never looked practical. It wasn't careful or calculated. It was bold, emotional movement, driven by hope, by longing, by that fragile belief that something good might still be waiting.

The Card, As I Lived It:
He came to me in the times I chose hope, shaky as it was, over the pull of fear, while

reason hovered close, warning, *Be careful*. Honestly, that's been most of my life. I like safety. I like knowing the plan. And yet, keep leaping anyway.

He showed up when I dared to say I love you first, heart racing, but honest. He was there when I packed my life into boxes and followed a gut feeling, not a plan. I didn't know how it would work out; only that I couldn't stay where I was.

He showed up every time I jumped into something new with no safety net. Just hope. And a heart that still wanted to believe.

The Knight of Cups wasn't always strategic. Sometimes he mistook fantasy for fate. He chased people, places, and promises that couldn't hold what he had to offer. But he never stopped believing. And that's what I came to love about him.

He taught me that courage doesn't always look like armor and battle plans. Sometimes it looks like raw vulnerability, trembling hands, and a voice that says, *I'm going anyway*. He taught me it's better to move with emotion and risk heartbreak than to stay sealed behind walls built from old pain.

Messy, earnest, open-hearted motion, that's where real life begins.

Queen of Cups
"When You Realize Your Sensitivity Was Always Your Superpower"

The Card, As They Say:
The Queen of Cups is emotional maturity, intuition, compassion, and deep inner knowing. She feels everything. But she isn't ruled by it. She holds space for it all, sorrow, joy, hope, fear. Not perfectly. But steadily, like a vessel that knows how to hold. She became a kind of grace, even when the heat of emotion was all around her.

The Card, As I Lived It:
I didn't step into her energy by going numb. I became her when I stopped apologizing for how deeply I feel. She came through in the quiet,
in the moments I could sit with someone else's grief and stay grounded in my own skin. When I finally understood I could hold boundaries and still lead with empathy.

That sensitivity didn't make me weak. It made me honest. This Queen showed me emotions don't need to be shoved down or explained away. They need room. They need respect.

She helped me see that intuition isn't some floaty magic trick. It's a body skill. A survival instinct. A way I've always known what was true, even when I couldn't prove it. She helped me stop making my softness a liability.

And in that shift, in the space where I held compassion for others and for myself, I found something I hadn't expected: A strength I didn't have to earn or perform. It was already there.

King of Cups
"When You Can Hold the Storm, Without Letting It Sink You"

The Card, As They Say:
The King of Cups is someone who's been through it, emotionally, spiritually, and figured out how to hold it all without shutting down. He's steady. He feels things deeply, but he doesn't get knocked over by them. He knows how to stay present in chaos, offer real care, and not absorb every feeling like it's his job to fix it.

The Card, As I Lived It:
I didn't wake up one day suddenly calm, suddenly wise. It came slower than that. This version of me showed up slowly. In the middle of hard conversations. In painful moments, in quiet breakdowns, times I didn't run, didn't shut off. It wasn't about being detached. It was about being grounded.

I've always been a feeler. A crier. I'll cry with you. I have cried with you. But I've learned that I can cry and still be the steady one in the room. I can feel everything and still hold space like it's solid ground. I used to think I had to fix people's pain. That I had to hold it all for them. But now? I just show up. I listen. I stay. Not because it's easy. But because I finally trust myself not to get lost in the weight of it.

The King of Cups isn't about being above it all. It's about being in it, heart open, without letting the waves drag you under. He taught me that emotions don't make you weak. Feeling with people. Staying steady through the tears. That's strength.

Swords

Ace of Swords
"When You Finally Name Your Truth, and Everything Changes"

The Card, As They Say:
The Ace of Swords shows up when the fog clears, when something that used to feel tangled finally sharpens. It's the card of truth. Of clarity. That moment when something in you just clicks, and you know. It cuts through the noise, the excuses, the 'maybe-later' stories we tell ourselves. It doesn't always feel good. But it's real.

The Card, As I Lived It:
For me, the Ace of Swords came when I hit a wall. Not with other people. With myself. When I couldn't pretend anymore. When something inside me said, *No more*. And I had to listen.

I've felt it in hard conversations, the ones where I finally said what I'd been holding back. I've felt it late at night, when I told myself a truth I didn't want to admit, and realized I couldn't go back to how things were.

That kind of clarity isn't gentle. It slices in, sharp and undeniable. But it also brings a strange kind of peace. Because once you say the thing, the real thing, everything starts to shift.

I learned with the Ace of Swords that truth doesn't always tie things up neatly. Sometimes it just comes with honesty. And that's enough. Because staying in illusion might feel safe… but it costs you something. And I know now, I don't want to pay that price anymore.

Two of Swords
"When You Know What's True, But Can't Bring Yourself to Choose"

The Card, As They Say:
The Two of Swords is stalemate, inner conflict, and the tension of knowing you need to decide, but feeling stuck between head and heart. It's the figure blindfolded, swords crossed, guarding a tender center, unwilling or afraid to see clearly. It's not ignorance. It's self-protection.

The Card, As I Lived It:
I met the Two of Swords in seasons where I stood at a crossroads. My truth was there, clear enough to burn. But fear had its grip on me too. I knew certain jobs or relationships didn't fit anymore. But I stayed. Loyalty. Guilt. All the what ifs. They kept me rooted in place.

My heart pulled one way, my head pulled another. And for a long while, I just stood there, hoping the decision would somehow make itself. But it never did. It only pressed in harder. This wasn't confusion. It was the ache of knowing that either choice meant something would be lost. So, I stayed, gripping both swords, eyes shut tight, because stillness felt safer. Safer than loss.

Three of Swords
"When the Truth Cuts Deep, And You Learn to Breathe Through the Blade"

The Card, As They Say:
The Three of Swords is heartbreak. Betrayal. That gut-punch kind of pain that knocks the air out of you. It's the moment when something finally clicks, or breaks, and you know, deep down, things can't go back to how they were. It shows you what's been hidden. And it hurts. But sometimes that pain is what finally helps you let go of what was never really safe to hold.

The Card, As I Lived It:
I've lived this card more than once. It showed up when I told the truth, and everything changed. When I testified in court. When I named what happened in my family, and watched relationships fall apart. When I found out things I didn't want to know, and had to sit with it anyway.

It showed up in sharp, sudden moments that dragged back old wounds, the ones I thought I'd buried deep enough to forget. That kind of pain hits hard. It knocks the wind out of you. Leaves you staring at walls, replaying moments, wondering how you didn't see it sooner. The silence after was loud. It filled my body, made everything feel too still. I didn't have words for it at first. Just heaviness. Just ache.

Eventually, I started to understand: Pain doesn't always mean you're broken. It's the part where truth finally lands. Not because it feels good, it rarely does. But because it clears space. And in that space, something new can start.

Four of Swords
"When You Step Out of the Fray, And Learn That Rest Is Resistance"

The Card, As They Say:
The Four of Swords is sanctuary, recuperation, and the vital pause before you continue the battle. It's an image of someone lying quietly, the swords beside them, as if even they need a pause. A reminder that sometimes courage means stepping back long enough to heal. It's not surrender. It's strategic rest.

The Card, As I Lived It:
I met the Four of Swords after every furious storm of emotion, when the adrenaline wore off and the weight of it all caught up to me. After court hearings where my mind spun so loudly I couldn't sleep, until I finally allowed myself to drift. On weekends when I forced myself to retreat, even though some part of me still itched to fight, to do, to fix. In quiet rituals: a hot bath, a silent walk, a few stolen moments of breath before sunrise, when the world screamed keep going, and I chose not to listen.

At first, rest felt like weakness to me, like a luxury I had no right to claim. But over time, the Four of Swords showed me something gentler. Rest isn't surrender. It's strategy. It's where the wounds begin to knit. Where clarity rises not in noise, but in stillness. It's how strength is reclaimed, not through pushing, but through pausing. I didn't stop because I had nothing left. I stopped because I was learning to preserve what remained. And maybe that's the bravest kind of endurance.

Five of Swords
"When Victory Tastes Like Ash, And You Wonder What You Gave Up to Win"

The Card, As They Say:
The Five of Swords is conflict, hollow victory, and the cost of winning. It's the image of someone standing over defeated foes, swords in hand. But the real question lingers: what did it cost? It's not about skill. It's about integrity.

The Card, As I Lived It:
I didn't meet this card in grand ways. It slipped in sideways, through small choices. Sharp words. Little wins that didn't feel like winning. Moments where I pushed too hard, spoke too sharp, or proved my point without noticing what it cost. Like when I kept winning praise at work. And felt my team slowly pull away. Or when I won an argument with

someone I loved, and realized we'd both lost something in the silence that followed. Or those times I needed to be right more than I needed to be kind.

I didn't go looking for those battles, not really. And they weren't victories that brought peace. But they did bring a question I couldn't ignore: *Was it worth it?* The Five of Swords showed me that not every win really feels like one. Some leave you standing alone. Some cost more than you thought you'd have to pay. And sometimes, the strongest move isn't drawing your sword. It's knowing when to lay it down.

Six of Swords
"When You Board a Boat to Somewhere New, Even If Your Past Follows Close Behind"

The Card, As They Say:
The Six of Swords is a transition. It's choosing to move on. Not because it feels simple, but because staying isn't an option anymore. It's that small, overloaded boat pushing forward through uncertain waters, carrying just enough hope to keep going. It's not an escape. It's an attempt. A shift toward something better.

The Card, As I Lived It:
I've found myself inside this card more than a few times. Like when I packed up and left home, still carrying more pain than peace, but knowing I had to find a different kind of safety. Or the time I drove across state lines in a sputtering car, fear sitting in my throat, bills in the glove box, and a shaky sense that maybe, just maybe, there was something more waiting for me.

I've walked away from jobs, relationships, and entire ways of thinking that had kept me stuck. I didn't leave because I had some new plan. I left because staying had started to feel like suffocation. I didn't leave my past behind. Not really. It came with me, quiet and heavy, strapped in like baggage I wasn't ready to unpack. But alongside it was something else: a small, persistent belief that healing was possible. That it lived somewhere just ahead.

The Six of Swords reminded me that forward doesn't have to be fast, or tidy, or certain. It just has to be honest. And it has to be yours.

Seven of Swords
"When You Learn That Sometimes the Best Move Is to Slip Away, Not to Fight"

The Card, As They Say:
This one gets labeled as sneaky, deception, trickery, all that. But honestly? That's not always what's going on. Sometimes the Seven of Swords is about strategy. About discernment. Knowing when to speak up and when to slip out the back quietly to keep yourself safe. It's that figure walking away with what they can carry, not to harm, but because staying would've meant self-abandonment. It's not running. It's recognizing the cost of staying where you're not seen. It wasn't cowardice. It was clarity.

The Card, As I Lived It:
There were times I didn't have a clear explanation, just a gut feeling. That clench in my chest. That subtle shift in the room. The way someone's tone turned sharp or the air got heavy. So, I said less. Sometimes nothing. Not because I didn't have words, but because I knew they wouldn't land. I could feel the edge in the conversation, and I knew what would happen if I kept going.

There were moments I held my truth close, not to deceive anyone, but to keep myself whole. Sometimes I stayed quiet. Sometimes I left. Not loudly. Not with a grand exit. Just… stopped showing up where it felt like I had to perform. The Seven of Swords reminded me that's not weakness. That's instinct. And it's okay. Not everyone gets access to the soft parts of you, especially not when you're still trying to hold them together.

This card taught me that pulling back isn't giving up. It's choosing your peace. And honestly? Sometimes walking away is the brave thing. Sometimes the strongest move isn't standing your ground. It's choosing another path, quietly, and walking away without asking permission.

Eight of Swords
"When You Realize You've Been Guarding a Prison You Built Yourself"

The Card, As They Say:
The Eight of Swords is that stuck place, mentally, emotionally. You feel trapped, boxed in by fear or old patterns that won't let go. The hard part is realizing it's not always someone else holding you there. Sometimes, it's you. Not because you're broken. Because you learned to survive that way.

The Card, As I Lived It:

I didn't walk into a cage. I built one. Slowly. Out of fear. Out of habit. Out of all the times being too much, too loud, too honest had cost me. At some point, I stopped reaching. Told myself I was fine. I stayed in jobs that drained me, relationships that dulled me, routines that numbed everything sharp or wild inside me, because it felt safer that way.

And then, when life got loud, when pressure hit, I'd freeze. My chest would tighten. I couldn't breathe. Couldn't move. My body panicked before my brain caught up. That's when I knew: I wasn't stuck in reality. I was stuck in fear. The walls weren't real, but I'd memorized them. Even when the door was wide open, I didn't trust it.

This card didn't tell me to smash the cage. That felt impossible. It told me to name it. To see it. To start where I was. And so, I did. Not in some big, brave leap, just little cracks. A breath. A choice. One truth whispered instead of swallowed. Not the escape. But the slow, clumsy steps back toward yourself.

Nine of Swords
"When the Night Whispers Every Fear, And You Learn to Nurture Your Light"

The Card, As They Say:

The Nine of Swords is anxiety. Sleeplessness. That awful mental loop that only gets louder after dark. You're not in danger, not exactly, but it feels like you are. Every 'what if' becomes a siren. Every quiet moment turns into a battleground. People call it weakness. But it isn't. It means you've lived through things your body still remembers, even when your mind wants to rest.

The Card, As I Lived It:

I've known those nights. The ones where sleep wouldn't come, no matter how tired I was. When my son was in the hospital and I couldn't stop checking if he was still breathing, even when I knew he was okay. When migraines pounded so hard, I didn't trust what would happen if I let go and fell asleep. When the house was quiet, and the clock ticked steady, but my mind was louder, whispering: *You're not doing enough. You're messing it all up. You're too much and still not enough.*

I didn't sleep. I braced. I cried quietly so no one would hear. I sat with the ache of everything I couldn't fix. And still, the night passed. Eventually. Not because I found answers, but because I made it through. One breath at a time. One reminder at a time. I started keeping soft things nearby: a blanket, a sound, a memory that helped. I wrote notes to myself on the bathroom mirror. I stopped expecting peace to look perfect.

The Nine of Swords showed me that even in those brutal hours, there's a light to tend. Not to fix everything. Just to remind you: You're still here. You made it to morning. And that counts.

Ten of Swords
"When Everything Falls Apart, And You Learn to Rise Anew"

The Card, As They Say:
The Ten of Swords is collapse. The bottom. It's when the weight is too much and something finally gives out beneath you. Ten swords. One figure. Face down. The image feels like the end, except there's always a thin light on the horizon. Even when you're gutted, something is still trying to rise. It's not the end. It's the moment when pretending is no longer an option.

The Card, As I Lived It:
I've stood in those moments where everything went quiet and blunt at once. Smiling through graduation photos while my mother sat behind bars. Trying to make sense of a future that had no obvious next step. Holding the pieces of a career I thought I could count on, only to watch it fall apart overnight. Lying awake with pain so big I wasn't sure my body could hold it anymore.

It felt like betrayal, by the world, by people, by life. And sometimes, worst of all, by my own body. I didn't feel strong. I didn't have answers. I just kept breathing. Kept showing up. Kept asking, *Now what?* And then, slowly, something shifted. Not all at once. Not tidy. But in the quiet, change came.

The Ten of Swords didn't save me. It cleared the illusion that I had to keep holding everything together. It gave me permission to stop. To fall apart. To feel it all. And from there, I started again. Not polished. Not certain. But real.

Page of Swords
"When You Dare to Ask the Questions You've Been Afraid to Voice"

The Card, As They Say:
They call the Page of Swords the curious one, the question-asker, the quiet observer who

notices what others miss. Not loud. Not polished. Just… sharp. A little restless. Hungry to understand. It's the energy of wait that doesn't add up. Not to argue. Just to know. To poke at the silence and see what falls out. It's not defiance. It's instinct.

The Card, As I Lived It:
I didn't come out swinging a sword. I came in sideways. Quiet. Watching. Trying to make sense of what I'd been told versus what I was starting to feel. At first, it was just thoughts I couldn't shake. Little questions that clung. Why was it always my fault? Why did love feel like a test I kept failing? Why did silence feel safer than speaking?

I wrote them down before I ever said them out loud. Filled notebooks with thoughts I didn't yet have the courage to claim. It was messy, uncertain, but it was mine. Eventually, I started saying the things. Sometimes in therapy. Sometimes, to people who didn't want to hear it. My voice didn't come out smooth. It cracked. I backpedaled. Apologized. But I still said it.

That's the Page. Not brave in the flashy way. But persistent. Asking anyway. Even when your hands shake. Even when your voice wavers. This card showed up when I stopped pretending I didn't care. When I realized curiosity isn't rebellion, it's how we wake up. And how we take our truth back, awkward, shaky, one question at a time.

Knight of Swords
"When Conviction Sends You Flying, and You Learn How to Steer"

The Card, As They Say:
This Knight moves quick, cutting through with conviction before anyone else has finished their sentence. So sure, so focused, he cuts through chaos like it's the only way forward. But that kind of speed? It doesn't leave much room to look around. To notice who else is in the room. To ask: is my truth the only one here? It's not exactly recklessness. But it isn't awareness either. It's purpose, yes, but with no brake pedal in sight.

The Card, As I Lived It:
I've known this Knight well. He showed up in the part of me that moved fast because slowing down felt like danger. When I was younger, I mistook urgency for wisdom. If I could move fast, decide fast, act fast, maybe I could stay ahead of the pain. Maybe then I wouldn't have to feel the doubt creeping close.

I jumped into jobs, relationships, arguments, sword drawn, heart racing, because I believed I had to be sure, to be strong, to be first. And sometimes, that clarity helped me. I advocated when no one else would. I pushed for change. I chased truth like it was oxygen. But sometimes, I bulldozed. I missed details. I spoke when I should've listened. I acted without checking whether the people around me were actually the enemy, or just scared too.

That's the thing about this card. It isn't only the battle cry. It's learning to slow down enough to see what might be getting crushed under your conviction. The Knight taught me that fire is good, necessary even. But if you don't pair it with clarity, it burns more than it builds. I didn't need to lose my momentum. I just had to learn how to steer it. To know when to aim it, and when to hold it like a lantern instead of a weapon.

Now, I still ride toward what I believe in. But I ask more questions. I breathe before I speak. And I've learned, not every battle needs to be fought at full speed. Some truths don't need to arrive shouting. Sometimes they land clearer, in quiet.

Queen of Swords
"When You Realize Compassion Doesn't Require You to Hide Your Truth"

The Card, As They Say:
People like to say she's cold. But that's not it. She doesn't wrap truth in lace. Her words don't always land soft. But they're offered clean, because clarity matters more than comfort. She's lived enough to know: avoiding the hard things doesn't make them disappear. She still feels everything. She's just learned how to speak through it.

The Card, As I Lived It:
I didn't wake up one day and claim this part of me. It happened slowly, over years. After years of biting my tongue, hard enough it may as well have bled. After nodding when I should've said no. After keeping peace, even when it cost me my voice.

The Queen showed up in pieces. In the conversations I didn't dodge. In the time I said, that's not okay, and meant it. In the boundary that shook but held. I learned that care and truth can live in the same sentence. That saying what's real doesn't make me cruel. It makes me whole.

King of Swords
"When You Lead with Both Your Mind and Your Heart, And Strike with Purpose"

The Card, As They Say:
The King of Swords is the one with the clear voice. The one who speaks steady in the middle of the storm. He thinks fast, speaks the truth, and doesn't waste words. People talk like he's all logic, like the heart doesn't factor in. But that's not it. He feels. He just doesn't always lead with it.

He's learned that sometimes clarity has to lead. Not because emotion isn't important, but because when everything is loud, someone has to stay clear. It's not detachment. It's anchoring. Not cold, just careful. Rooted in something solid.

The Card, As I Lived It:
I didn't step into this energy all at once. I didn't arrive saying, *Here I am*. It took time. It took messing up, holding back when I should've spoken, speaking when I should've listened. Honestly, I wasn't even trying. I just got tired of the way things were, of watching decisions get made that hurt people who couldn't speak up.

So, I spoke. Even when my hands shook. Even when I knew it would cost me something. I stood in rooms full of tension and said the uncomfortable thing. I listened when others couldn't find the words yet. I didn't always get it right. But I showed up with all I had.

This wasn't about being in charge. It was about being accountable. About knowing I couldn't ask others to live by values I wasn't willing to live by myself. There were moments when I felt alone at the table. Moments I had to choose between being liked and being honest. But I knew what I stood for. And I knew that mattered more.

The King of Swords didn't teach me to be fearless. He taught me to pause. To speak when it counted. To lead not with ego, but with steadiness, a hand that doesn't shake, and a heart that stays clear. Sometimes power isn't in volume. It's in the choice to stay, even when it would be easier to fold.

Pentacles

Ace of Pentacles
"When Opportunity Drops into Your Hands, And You Finally Believe You Deserve It"

The Card, As They Say:
This is the card of new beginnings, the kind you can touch. A check in the mail. A job offer. A quiet yes from life when you were expecting another not yet. It's fresh starts in the material world, career, money, habits, home. But it's not luck dropping something shiny into your lap. It's a door opening because of everything you've already survived. And now? You get to decide how to walk through it.

The Card, As I Lived It:
I didn't meet this card in one sweeping moment. I met it in envelopes, in emails, in small things that landed like thunder anyway. A scholarship after years of scraping by, and for the first time, I felt seen. Not just helped, but acknowledged. A job that didn't just cover rent, it felt like it fit. I realized I wasn't asking for too much by wanting work that aligned with my values.

I started doing things for myself, a single therapy session, a good meal, a soft blanket, and I didn't explain it to anyone. It wasn't some grand reward. It was the slow realization that maybe I didn't have to keep proving my worth to be supported. The Ace of Pentacles wasn't about the money. It was about the shift inside me, the moment I stopped bracing for things to fall apart and started thinking: maybe this could grow. Not just survive. But take root.

Two of Pentacles
"When You're Juggling Everything, And Discover Grace in the Rhythm"

The Card, As They Say:
This is the card of balancing acts. The kind that aren't always pretty, but somehow keep everything moving. It's that moment when you've got a lot in the air, and you're doing your best not to let it all crash. People talk like balance is calm, centered, serene. But sometimes? It's messy. It's loud. It's nonstop. It's not about mastering the chaos. It's about learning to ride it.

The Card, As I Lived It:
I met this card during a season when I was working full-time, raising a child, and pushing

through an undergraduate program, all while trying to hold onto my sanity. I was tired. Most days, I couldn't even name what I was running on. There wasn't some perfect system. No magical routine. There was just me, tired, determined, sometimes late, sometimes crying in the car, but still showing up.

I learned trade-offs. Sometimes dinner was cereal. Sometimes "balance" looked like letting something drop and hoping it didn't shatter. Every yes carried a cost. And sometimes the only way through was a no, even to things I cared about. The Two of Pentacles didn't arrive to praise my juggling. It came to remind me that I could bend without breaking. That balance doesn't always feel good, but it can still be good for you. That rhythm isn't about perfection. It's about presence. One foot in front of the other. One thing at a time. Even when it feels like it's all happening at once.

Three of Pentacles
"When Collaboration Transforms Skill into Mastery"

The Card, As They Say:
This isn't the card of working alone. It's the card that says: You don't have to do this by yourself. It's about building side by side with others, even when you're used to carrying it all. Not to prove. Not to be the expert. But to take part in something shared.

The Card, As I Lived It:
For a long time, I thought I had to hold it all. If I did the work alone, no one could ruin it. No one could let me down. But that got heavy. And lonely. Eventually, I realized: maybe letting people in wasn't weakness. Maybe it was the very thing that made the work better.

I met this card when I joined a team rebuilding programs that mattered. None of us had all the answers. But we listened. We argued sometimes. And we still kept building. What came out of it wasn't just efficient. It was meaningful. Solid. I saw it again in writing circles, when feedback sharpened my words instead of dimming them. I saw it in support groups, where healing didn't just happen in silence. It happened when stories echoed back, reminding us we weren't the only ones.

These weren't just projects. They were reminders. That some things are meant to be made together. The Three of Pentacles taught me that mastery doesn't have to be solo or flawless. Sometimes it looks like learning out loud, creating alongside people who see what you can't, and letting that make the work deeper.

Four of Pentacles
"When You Hold Tight to What You Have, And Question If It's Ever Enough"

The Card, As They Say:
This card often carries the weight of control. Holding back. Clinging to what you've earned because you're afraid of losing it. It's the image of someone clutching what they've got, protected, yes, but also cut off. It's not greed. It's fear dressed up as caution.

The Card, As I Lived It:
I know this one in my bones. It showed up in the seasons I stayed with the same routines, the same roles, not because they fit, but because they felt safe. I turned down opportunities that might've helped me grow because a small voice kept saying, *What if it all disappears?* Even joy felt risky.

I saved every penny like the sky might fall. Skipped therapy. Skipped rest. Skipped anything that didn't feel like a necessity. And my time? I guarded it like armor. Told myself I was protecting my peace, but really, I was scared to let anything shift.

Eventually, I started to see the pattern. This wasn't caution. It was a cage. I wasn't only holding things. I was holding myself in. The Four of Pentacles reminded me that security isn't about the tightest grip. It's about trust. That I can loosen my hand and still be okay. That I can spend time, money, energy, and trust that what matters most will stay. It isn't about throwing it all away. It's about softening the fist just enough to let something new take root.

Five of Pentacles
"When You Feel Left Out in the Cold, And Learn Where to Find Warmth"

The Card, As They Say:
The Five of Pentacles speaks to loss, scarcity, and the ache of being shut out, sometimes from resources, sometimes from belonging. It's often pictured as two people outside a warm building, walking through snow. You can feel the chill. It's not a life sentence. It's a moment that asks: Where is comfort still possible? And who might walk beside you to find it?

The Card, As I Lived It:
I met the Five of Pentacles during seasons where I felt on the edge of relief, close enough to see it, too far to reach. When my son was in the hospital and the nights blurred into

each other, I could feel the pressure mounting: bills, worry, sleep deprivation. Every small thing felt enormous.

It came again when my job was cut during a round of layoffs. I felt like I'd lost not only income, but footing. Even my sense of self felt distant, like I was watching life from outside the window. But the card didn't leave me there. Because alongside that isolation, small lights started to flicker. A friend dropping off coffee. A neighbor checking in. A resource I hadn't counted on, arriving without conditions.

And slowly, I began to understand: resilience doesn't always look like standing tall. Sometimes it's quieter than that, a leaning in, a whisper of I need help, and the willingness to let someone answer. Healing doesn't happen in a vacuum. And warmth, real warmth, isn't always in grand gestures. Sometimes it's in the quiet company of those who stay.

Six of Pentacles
"When You Give and Receive as Equals, And Find Dignity in Both"

The Card, As They Say:
The Six of Pentacles is about generosity, but not in a top-down, savior kind of way. It's reciprocity. Fair exchange. The image of someone offering coins with one hand and holding scales in the other. Not out of superiority, but with the quiet understanding that things grow stronger when shared. It's not about giving to feel important. It's about remembering that we all need each other.

The Card, As I Lived It:
I met the Six of Pentacles in that tender space where giving and receiving blur together, when you realize that both can be acts of love. It showed up the night my son was stuck 2,500 miles from home, caught in a blizzard. I couldn't get to him. I felt helpless. But then people stepped in. Friends, family, even strangers, they helped. Without hesitation. Without fanfare. And for maybe the first time in a long time, I let myself receive. Fully. Gratefully.

And later, I saw the same energy in the work I did with others. Little things, a ride, a phone call, a kind word, could shift someone's whole day. I stopped thinking of giving as something big and dramatic. It could be small. Quiet. Offered with open hands. Eventually, I got to give back. To mentor. To guide. Not because I had everything figured out, but because someone once showed up for me, and I remembered how much it mattered.

That's the heart of this card. Not pity. Not performance. It's less about the act itself and more about the spirit behind it, meeting each other with respect, showing up with presence, offering what care we can.

Seven of Pentacles
"When You Pause to See Your Progress, And Choose Where to Cultivate Next"

The Card, As They Say:
The Seven of Pentacles is that moment when you step back and take stock. It's patience. Reassessment. Looking at what's been growing and asking, Is this still where I want to put my time and energy? It's the card of the gardener, not harvesting yet, not starting over, just standing in the middle of things and checking in. It isn't about being finished. It's about making the next part count.

The Card, As I Lived It:
I've felt this card in the pauses I finally allowed myself. Not because everything was wrapped up, but because I was far enough in to look around and ask, *What's really working here?* I flipped through old projects, revisited choices, and saw that every messy step had planted something. Some things were thriving. Some were barely holding on. Some needed to be pulled up at the root.

I saw it in my calendar too, the habits I kept saying yes to without thinking, the projects that left me drained, the ones that sparked energy and joy. I had to ask: What's worth watering? What am I tending out of fear, not love? And sometimes the realization came mid-project. Not at the end, but in the middle, when I was tired, uncertain, tempted to quit. That's when the card whispered: *check the soil. Name what's already growing.*

The Seven of Pentacles reminded me that growth isn't always hustle or momentum. Sometimes it's slow. Subtle. Almost invisible. And that the pause itself, the breath, the looking back, is part of the work too.

Eight of Pentacles
"When Patience Turns Effort into Something Real"

The Card, As They Say:
This one doesn't arrive with flash or fanfare. It's not about some overnight success story. It speaks to the hours when you're bent over your work, half-tired, half-determined, doing

the same small thing again and again. A stitch that holds. A sentence reshaped until it finally rings true. Numbers scratched out, erased, and written once more.

On their own, these moments look ordinary, even forgettable. But over time, they stack, and you begin to notice how steady it feels to keep going. It was never about perfection. It was about staying present long enough for the work itself to teach you something.

The Card, As I Lived It:
I met this card in the hours no one noticed. The late nights when I kept writing, drafts awkward and heavy, until, slowly, almost clumsily, they bent into words that felt like mine. Not perfect. Just real enough to keep going.

I met it again in the therapy room, listening not only to words but to the cracks between them. The way someone's tone shifted, or the way silence carried its own meaning. I felt it in the mornings I pulled a card, not hunting for quick answers, but letting the rhythm of journaling, the quiet return to the page, shape me over time.

This card never gave me sudden mastery. No neat finish lines. No moment where I could say, I've arrived. Instead, it asked me to show up, again and again, trusting that the small, repeated motions were adding up to something deeper than I could yet see. Those little efforts don't look like much at first. You barely notice them. But over time, they start to take hold, slowly, quietly, almost behind your back, until you look around and realize growth has been happening all along.

Nine of Pentacles
"When You Walk Through Your Garden, And Recognize Your Own Prosperity"

The Card, As They Say:
The Nine of Pentacles speaks of self-made peace. Not luck, not shortcuts, but the kind of stability that grows slowly, tended over time, until one day you notice it's steady beneath your feet. The figure stands in her own garden, surrounded by what she planted. Not waiting, not asking, just being. It isn't loneliness. It is solitude chosen on purpose. And there's power in that.

The Card, As I Lived It:
I didn't land here all at once. It came slowly, after years of stretching every resource, of scraping by, of surviving more than thriving. Then one day I looked around and realized: I had made something. Not perfect, not shiny, but steady, soft, and mine.

It showed up in the mornings on my porch, coffee warm in my hands, watching flowers I planted move in the wind. It showed up in the kitchen, in the way cooking or cleaning stopped feeling like chores, and started carrying a sense of rhythm I could rest inside. In the clothes I wore because I loved them, not because anyone else would. In the silence that once felt sharp, but now stretched wide and spacious.

The Nine of Pentacles wasn't about luxury, not really. It was about noticing I had built a life with my own two hands. It was when I stopped shrinking around comfort, stopped questioning whether I had earned my rest, and started letting joy slip in without apology. Prosperity, I learned, isn't only a number on a page. It can be a feeling, simple and quiet, the kind that whispers, *You're safe here*. And for once, I believed it.

Ten of Pentacles
"When You Build a Legacy, Grounded in Love, Abundance, and Security"

The Card, As They Say:
The Ten of Pentacles is generational wealth, family ties, and the closing of a long cycle. It's the family gathered in front of a grand estate, symbols of stability, shared values, and blessings passed from one generation to the next. It isn't flawless. It's foundation that lasts.

The Card, As I Lived It:
I met this card in the moments when survival shifted into something else. When I realized I wasn't just building for myself anymore. I was shaping traditions. Bringing laughter back into rooms that once held only silence. I saw how healing could become shelter, how love, when tended, could turn into legacy.

It was in my son's voice as he spoke of his childhood, not with fear, but with warmth. The life I worked to build had become soil where his confidence could grow. Our home, our rituals, our resilience… all of it turned into his compass. I noticed it again in community work, when the values I'd carried, steadiness, care, and integrity, came back to me in the lives I had touched.

The Ten of Pentacles reminded me that abundance has a way of growing when it moves between people. Legacy isn't about wealth alone. It's about what carries forward because you began it. And real wealth? It's the love that keeps echoing long after you're gone.

Page of Pentacles
"When You Nurture a New Path, With Curiosity and Practical Vision"

The Card, As They Say:
The Page of Pentacles carries fresh beginnings. Curiosity you can touch. The first seeds of a goal that's more than a dream. This is the student: willing to learn, willing to work, steady enough to keep showing up. It isn't naïve. It's eager, but grounded.

The Card, As I Lived It:
I crossed paths with this Page in those shaky starts, the times I didn't have a map, but I had direction. It was there when I signed up for my first college class, notebooks stacked, heart pounding. I wanted to prove, mostly to myself, that I wasn't only capable, I was committed. Every lesson I took in felt like a step toward a future I was only beginning to believe in.

It was there when I opened my first tarot deck and made a small ritual of pulling cards each morning. Back then it wasn't about mysticism. It was about building a habit, reflection, curiosity, a rhythm that kept me rooted in who I was becoming. And it was there in the early mornings and long nights at the sheriff's office. Learning the rules. Taking on weight I hadn't carried before. Showing up not because I knew enough, but because I was willing to learn what I didn't.

The Page of Pentacles taught me I didn't need a polished plan to begin. Just the nerve to plant a seed, and the patience to keep tending it.

Knight of Pentacles
"When Steadfast Patience Turns Dreams into Tangible Reality"

The Card, As They Say:
The Knight of Pentacles is steady motion. Slow, deliberate. He's discipline over drama. Loyalty over shortcuts. The one who keeps showing up, even when it's thankless. This isn't rushing. It's persistence, quiet, shaping, long-term. Not stagnation. Cultivation. Careful. Earned.

The Card, As I Lived It:
I've known this Knight in the seasons where progress barely showed on the surface, but I could feel it stacking underneath. He showed up in the early mornings at the sheriff's office, before phones rang, before anyone else arrived. I logged in, mentored interns, fixed

broken systems. Trust didn't come from flash. It came from repetition. From being there. No glory. No shortcuts. Just rhythm. And over time? Results.

He showed up again in writing. Not muse-lit epiphanies, but nights of tired sentences, scribbles that didn't always sing. Still, page by page, the words piled up. A book took shape, not from waiting, but from keeping the pen moving. And he was there in the garden too. My hands in dirt. Watering. Weeding. Hoping. Not everything grew. But enough did.

That's when I understood: growth isn't loud. It doesn't flash. It endures. The Knight of Pentacles taught me that devotion doesn't need an audience. It asks for patience. It asks for practice. And those two things, unremarkable as they seem, are what make a life hold steady.

Queen of Pentacles
"When Nurturing Abundance Becomes an Act of Self-Care"

The Card, As They Say:
The Queen of Pentacles is resourcefulness with heart. Practical care. Steady warmth. She blends homemaking with self-worth, tending both the outer and inner spaces. Her message? Prosperity grows through attention and love, not only through numbers on a page. She isn't about indulgence. She's about security, rooted, lived, and real.

The Card, As I Lived It:
I crossed paths with her in seasons when care was demanded of me, for my family, yes, but also, finally, for myself. She appeared in the soft kitchen light after hospital nights, when I stirred soup with tired hands and fierce love. The meals weren't fancy, but they mattered. They said: nourishment is a kind of protection.

She showed up when I paid the bills, stretched every dollar, and still lit a candle, pulled on a sweater, or opened a new notebook. Not splurging, choosing. Reminding myself that tending to my own needs was sustainable, not selfish. I felt her in the way I shaped our home. Blankets within reach. Lamps glowing softly instead of harshly. A desk cleared enough to invite focus. A space that let my body unclench. A space where I could finally exhale.

Nothing had to be earned. Nothing had to be justified. The Queen of Pentacles didn't frame wealth as excess. She reframed it as enough. She showed me that steady care, for my space, for my people, and for myself, was the kind of richness that lasts.

King of Pentacles
"When Leadership Means Wealth with Integrity"

The Card, As They Say:
The King of Pentacles is strategic stewardship, grounded prosperity, and authority rooted in care. He works with what he has wisely, stretching it where it can grow, and anchoring it where it needs to hold. His energy isn't about clinging; it's about letting things circulate and still remain steady. He's about building abundance that can last and serve.

The Card, As I Lived It:
I met this King not in boardrooms or portfolios, but in the quiet, deliberate shaping of a life that could hold steady in storms, and offer shelter to others, too. He sat with me at the kitchen table, where envelopes and notebooks were stacked high. I wasn't scraping by for the month; I was sketching a future where my son would stand on firmer ground than I ever had. Every dollar had direction. Every plan, a reason. Security wasn't a prize. It was the gift I wanted my family to inherit.

I felt his presence at work when I gathered resources for families in crisis, turning my role into a bridge for community healing. Not because it was required, but because leaving nothing behind felt empty. His influence reached into my long-term choices too: investing in my writing, in rest, in the kind of learning that pays dividends no account can measure.

It wasn't about recognition. It was about building something true. Something steady enough to hold others, even when I'm no longer in the room. The King of Pentacles reminded me that wealth wasn't about what I could collect. It showed up in the things I managed to keep going, in the way care slowly turned into structure, in the small choices that added up over time. And when I looked back, I could finally see: I had built something that could last. And I allowed myself to believe it mattered, not just for me, but for others too.

My Interpretation of Oracle of the 7 Energies

"When the mind quiets, the soul speaks."

All through the writing of this book, I leaned on more than memory. I leaned on mirrors. Tarot cards. Dreams. The quiet intelligence of the body. And oracle decks that reminded me to stop and notice what was rising from within.

Among those companions, *The Oracle of the 7 Energies* by Colette Baron-Reid became a steady presence. Not because it promised to tell me what was coming, but because it kept me rooted in what already was.

Every card I pulled didn't hand me an answer. It offered a doorway. A pause. A shift in light that made me ask a different kind of question. These weren't predictions; they were invitations. Invitations into presence. Into emotion. Into story.

The reflections that follow aren't copied from a guidebook. I wrote them from the inside, from lived experience, from late nights, from small, stubborn awakenings. Some cards showed up quiet, like a hush I almost missed. Others landed hard, impossible to ignore. Together they helped me notice the subtle patterns running under everything else, the threads I hadn't seen until I slowed down enough to listen.

You don't need to know this deck to step into what's here. These words aren't here to instruct. They're here to resonate. To find you where you are, in stillness, in seeking, or in some sacred in-between.

You might hear your own question echoed back.
You might feel seen by a single line.
You might recognize a weight you didn't realize you'd been carrying.

Whatever rises, trust it.

Because these cards, like all true teachers, don't tell you who you are.
They remind you.

1 Earth Magic

Remember what's real. Not the kind you have to figure out, the kind you can feel. Bare feet pressing into dirt. Wind moving your hair. Roots running quiet and deep where no one bothers to look. Your body knows these things, even when your mind forgets. That knowing? That's the magic. Ordinary, ancient, waiting right here with you.

2 Roots of Abundance

Strength isn't always loud. Not everything strong makes a sound. Sometimes it's the steady stuff under the surface, an old prayer, a choice you forgot you made, the systems that keep you upright when you're tired. This card reminds you: something solid is holding you. You don't have to hold on so hard. You don't have to grip so tightly anymore. The roots are already there, and they're enough.

3 Time Machine

Ever feel déjà vu tug at you? Like life is looping back around. This card asks you to notice when old patterns try to pull you under. Maybe you've stood in this doorway before. But this time, you're not the same. You get to pause. You get to choose differently. You get to walk forward with eyes wide open.

4 Great and Full

Gratitude doesn't always come with fireworks. Sometimes it's the quiet "thank you" breathed into your morning coffee. The way your shoulders drop when the air feels lighter. The text that arrives when you needed it. Fullness doesn't always shine, sometimes it rests. And resting in it is more than enough.

5 Body and Soul

You are not separate from your body; you're in a relationship with it. This card is an invitation to tend to both the vessel and the spirit, with tenderness. Wholeness grows when they listen to each other, when you care for each like you would a beloved. Softly. Consistently. With trust.

6 It Is What It Is

There's a strange relief in not fighting anymore. This card doesn't ask you to give up. It asks you to stop wrestling with what already happened. That door closed. That person was who they were. There's grief in that, yes, but also freedom. Because now, you get to choose how to meet it. Sometimes wisdom begins in the pause, in the breath that says, "Okay. Now what?"

7 A Deep Breath

Before the fix, before the plan, before the spiral, stop. Inhale. This card brings you back to what hasn't left: your breath, your body, the now. It won't solve everything, but it steadies you long enough to make it through this moment. Sometimes the holiest thing you can do is place a hand on your chest and whisper, *I'm still here*. One breath. Then another.

8 Into Me I See

This one's tender. It's not about connection out there, it starts in here. Sitting with yourself, no flinching, no performing. Letting the masks slip. Saying, *Alright. This is me. All of it.* It's not always comfortable, but it's real. And the intimacy we crave with others? It begins with the courage to meet your own reflection and stay.

9 The Rose's Kiss

This card says, "Let beauty in." Not just because it looks nice, but because it feeds you. Pleasure isn't shameful. Softness isn't weakness. The rose doesn't apologize for blooming, and neither should you. Let sweetness be part of your survival. Let joy be simple.

10 Close Encounters

Here's the invitation: let someone see you. Not perfectly, not all at once. Just enough to be real. Vulnerability isn't weakness; it's a doorway. There's strength in softening the walls, even if it feels new. Sometimes freedom comes when you stop hiding and let another heart close enough to touch yours.

11 In Perfect Harmony

Harmony isn't about everyone agreeing. It's about when things click, inside you, or between you and someone else. When it feels like music, unforced, flowing. You know it when it happens. This card reminds you not to chase it, just notice when it arrives, and let yourself rest in the sound.

12 Bearing Fruit

This is what comes after the hidden labor. The work no one clapped for. The seeds planted in faith. The patience it took to keep going in the dark. This card says something is ready now. Not because you forced it, but because you stayed. Look at what's grown. Let yourself receive it.

13 Feeling the World

Empathy is a gift, but it can weigh heavy. This card asks you to notice what's yours and what you've picked up from others. Sensitivity isn't weakness; it's strength when it's rooted in awareness. Protect your energy without closing your heart.

14 A Beautiful Uncaging

Freedom doesn't always arrive with a bang. Sometimes it's quiet. The day you drop a story that never fit. The moment you realize the shame you carried wasn't even yours. The small breath when you say, *Enough*. This isn't rebellion. It's you, finally letting yourself out of the cage.

15 A Powerful Move

This isn't about big drama. It's about that inner nudge that says, *It's time*. Not reaction. Not scramble. Just a step, maybe small, but steady. A move that's yours. That's where the power is.

16 The Royal You

This energy doesn't brag. It remembers. It's you, walking in your own worth, not above, not beneath. No shrinking, no proving. Just shoulders back, heart steady, moving through the world without apology.

17 The Storyteller

Pause a second. Who wrote the script you're living? Is it still true? This card reminds you, you hold the pen now. You can cross out the fear lines, scribble in softness, write yourself a different ending. You're not stuck in someone else's chapter. You get to shape the next page.

18 The Power of Purpose

Purpose isn't always loud. It doesn't have to be a five-year plan or a polished speech. Sometimes it's that quiet tug in your chest that says, *Remember who you were before all the proving and performing*. This card is that pull. Not for applause. Not to check a box. Just because it matters to you, and that's reason enough.

19 Waking the Lion

This isn't about never being afraid. It's about moving anyway, even with shaky hands. Strength doesn't always roar. Sometimes it stands quiet, heart wide open, saying, I'm still here. I'm not hiding anymore.

20 A Merry Motive

Why are you really doing it? That's the question. Not to scold you, just to bring you closer to joy. Because when your reasons come from that honest place, the place that feels good, even in the mess, your steps start to steady. Let joy be enough.

21 Exposed & Revealed

It happens fast; the mask falls. And suddenly you're exposed. You wonder, what will they think if they see all of it? The ache, the hope, the raw edges. But then you notice… you're still standing. And maybe breathing easier. Being seen isn't always pretty, but it's honest. And honesty has a way of setting you free.

22 Tender Embrace

Not the grand gestures. The small ones. Someone reaching for your hand and not letting go when the tears come. Curling into softness after years of bracing. Care that's steady, no strings. This card doesn't ask you to be strong. It asks if maybe you don't have to hold it all alone anymore.

23 Healing the Heart

Some wounds don't scream. They whisper, in the flinch, in the hesitation, in the way joy feels almost dangerous. This card isn't rushing you. It sits beside you, steady, saying, *Let's tend to this*. Healing doesn't erase the past. It weaves it into a story that doesn't own you anymore.

24 Let It Go

Not a shout. Not a command. A loosening. The hand you didn't know was clenched begins to soften. Letting go isn't losing, it's making space. For peace. For what's meant to reach you, but couldn't while you were gripping so tight.

25 Birds of a Feather

You weren't built to do this alone. This card gathers your people closer, the ones who see you without editing, without masks. The ones who nod because they've lived it too. True connection doesn't ask you to shrink. Just show up. The right ones will recognize you.

26 Great Big Love

Not the kind that needs proof or performance. This love stays, even in the mess. Soul-deep. Soft around the edges. Steady at the core. Maybe it comes through another person. Maybe it's spirit. Maybe it's the way you finally learn to hold yourself. However it shows up, it whispers: *You don't have to earn this.*

27 A Grand Symphony

It's easy to forget you belong when you feel like a single note on its own. But every note is part of the song. Your story, your voice, the way you keep showing up, it adds to the whole. This card says: *Don't stop. You're already inside the music, even if you can't hear the whole thing yet.*

28 Broken Open

Not every crack is a failure. Sometimes pain splits you wide, and it doesn't feel noble. It hurts. But the crack also lets something else in, light, air, room to breathe. This card won't pretend loss is pretty. It says: *Even in the breaking, there can be space for what's next.*

29 Awakening Genius

This isn't about brilliance on demand. It's about letting the spark rise in its own strange way, messy, playful, off-beat. Genius isn't somewhere out there; it's already in you, waiting for permission. Let it surprise you. Let it spill past the lines. Let it remind you of who you were before you started doubting.

30 Shining Through

You don't have to shrink to keep others comfortable. This card is a nudge to let yourself be seen, laugh loud, stand tall, and glow without apology. You weren't made to blend in. You were made to shine. And it's okay if not everyone is ready for the brightness.

31 Call of the Muse

It starts quiet, a line, a color, a sound that tugs at you. Not for applause. Not for outcome. Because it wakes something inside. This card is that tug. It might not make sense, but you follow anyway. Because part of you knows: this is the thread.

32 Quieting the Mind

The world is loud. Thoughts, phones, demands. This card is a hush. Not escape, return. A place where silence isn't empty but alive. Here, feelings rise without pressure. Here, you can just be. And in that being, something gentle unfolds.

33 Ears Wide Open

Listening isn't waiting to talk. This card asks you to hear all of it, the words, the pauses, the tone, the silence between. What truth is trying to reach you? Don't rush to fix. Listen as if the answer is already hiding in the question.

34 Opening to Discovery

A crack in the wall. A maybe. A nudge. You don't need all the answers, just enough space to wonder again. Ask. Stay curious. Something new wants in, if you let it.

35 A Tall Tale

The stories we tell ourselves can feel safer than the truth. This card isn't here to shame you for that. It asks: *Is the story still helping, or is it keeping you stuck?* Let the mask slip. You might be surprised by what waits underneath.

36 Seeing Beyond

This isn't about proof or logic. It's that deep knowing that won't leave you alone. A dream that returns. An idea that circles back. What if you trusted it? What if you let yourself believe what you feel, even if you can't explain it?

37 The Oracle's Gift

Sometimes the gift isn't an answer at all; it's the question that won't leave you alone. This card is like holding up a mirror and noticing not just your reflection, but the way you're looking. Insight comes in pieces, often slow, often quiet. The gift is learning to trust that, the not-knowing, the waiting, and the way meaning slowly grows.

38 Endless Possibilities

You're not stuck with what's been. This card opens the door to what could be, if you stop insisting on certainty. Let curiosity lead for once. Wonder has more room to move than control ever did.

39 Wish Upon a Star

Hope is harder than people admit. This card says it's still alive in you, even if you've learned to hide it. You don't have to shout your wish out loud. Let yourself feel it's still there. That's enough to start.

40 The Land Between

This is the awkward middle, not where you were, not yet where you're going. Wobbly. Uncomfortable. Full of potential. This card reminds you: you're not lost. You're becoming. Don't rush the next thing. Breathe. Let the ground form under your feet as you move.

41 A Higher View

When you're too close, everything tangles. This card says: *Climb higher. Zoom out.* From here, the mess might look different. You might see a pattern, a rhythm, a wider truth. It's not about detaching; it's about remembering the bigger picture.

42 Smoke & Mirrors

Not everything that shines is real. This card shows up when illusion has gotten too comfortable. It isn't an accusation. It's an invitation: look closer. What story are you clinging to for safety? Where have you been outsourcing your knowing? Clear the glass. Return to what's solid.

43 Spirit of Gratitude

Gratitude isn't a checklist. It's a shift in the heart. This card invites you to say thank you, not because it was easy, but because it shaped you. Joy, grief, memory, longing, all of it belongs. Gratitude doesn't make pain disappear, but it makes it feel less lonely.

44 Divine Matrix

Ever notice how some things line up so perfectly it feels impossible to plan? This card is that reminder: threads are weaving, even when you can't see the pattern. You don't have to force it. You don't have to figure it all out. Stay close to what feels true and let the rest reveal itself.

45 Beyond the Ordinary

You've never really fit the mold, and that was never the point. Your intuition, your creativity, your rituals that don't make sense to anyone else… they matter. This card says: *You're not here to blend in. You're here to bring something through that can't be explained by logic alone.*

46 The Uncharted Sea

This is the open water. No map. No landmarks. Just the compass inside you. It's scary, yes, but also full of possibility. Think of those who came before, trusting stars and tides more than certainty. You're not lost. You're navigating like they did, by something ancient in you that still remembers the way.

47 Sacred Reverence

There's holiness in the ordinary, but only if you slow down to notice. The pause before you speak. The warmth in someone's eyes. The breath you didn't know you were holding. Spirit lives in all of it. Even silence. Even grief. Even you.

48 A Burst of Magic

It sneaks up on you, washing dishes, walking the dog, staring at nothing. A spark. Goosebumps. The idea that feels like it came from nowhere. But it didn't. It rose from the part of you still plugged into mystery. This card reminds you: not every gift has to be earned. Some just arrive. Let them.

49 Willing Release

Letting go rarely happens all at once. It's slow. Fingers loosening. A breath you didn't realize you were holding has finally been exhaled. This card says: *You're ready.* Release isn't defeat. It's alignment. The moment you stop gripping what no longer fits, space opens for something softer to land.

My Interpretation of Animal Spirit Reflections

"Every instinct is a teacher. Every creature carries a truth."

Throughout this journey, I didn't walk alone. Beneath the tarot, beside the dreams, beyond the journaled pages, the animals began to speak. Not in words, but in energy, in metaphor, in knowing.

The *Wild Unknown Animal Spirit* deck became more than a tool; it became a quiet companion. A way of engaging the deeper rhythms of each year, not only through analysis but through embodiment. These creatures didn't arrive to forecast the future or label the past. They appeared to reveal what was stirring within me: resilience, fear, intuition, hunger, softness, rage. They came as messengers from the unseen, guardians of shadow and light, instinct and memory, spirit and form.

Each one showed up different. Some with an edge, some with comfort. Every single one had something sacred to offer. They reminded me that healing is not always articulate. It is primal. Felt in the breath, in the bones. In the body's pause before a decision. Clarity isn't always a thought. Sometimes, it's a flick of the tail. A coiled presence. A cry. A stillness.

Each reflection is written in my own words and voice. They are my own, born from meditation, from lived experience, from soul-language that arrived on breath and in silence. Each reflection became a dialogue between myself and the energy the animal held. Some came gently. Some cracked me open. All asked me to listen.

You don't need to know this deck to understand the medicine it offers. These spirits are archetypes. Echoes. Mirrors. Meet them as you are, curious, closed, uncertain, open. Let the ones who call to you linger. Let the others wait in the shadows until you're ready.

Some will comfort.
Some will confront.
All will ask you to remember something ancient in yourself.
Something that was never broken, only buried.

Let them find the part of you that knows, and has always known.

Bat

The Bat energy calls you to move through endings with grace. This energy lives in the space between dusk and dawn, the quiet, the unknown, the moment before transformation. Let go of what has passed. A new day waits, and your wings are stronger than you remember.

Bear

The energy of the Bear spirit rises from hibernation, blinking into the light of a new chapter. Bear energy marks the start of a transformation, not flashy or fast, but steady and soul-deep. The beginning may feel heavy, uncertain, even lonely. But the thaw has already begun. Spring is calling. You don't have to know the way. You only have to begin.

Beaver

Beaver energy is of sacred devotion. Not flashy. Not loud. But steady, loyal, and committed to the long haul. Beaver reminds you that love is built through presence, protection, and patient effort. What you nurture now will shape your foundation.

Bee

The Bee energy works with joyful devotion. This energy is communal, focused, and filled with purpose, but when unbalanced, it can tip into burnout. You give and give, forgetting to taste the sweetness you've helped create. This card asks: *Can you pause long enough to receive what you've built? Let nourishment meet your effort.* Even the busiest heart deserves to rest in its own honey.

Black Egg

The Black Egg energy holds the sacred center of your voice, the place where truth hums before it ever becomes sound. This energy invites you to speak from deep within, without apology or performance. Not to be loud, but to be real. When you return to this knowing, your words resonate. When you stray, they scatter. This is the birthplace of your voice. Come back to it. Speak what only you can say.

Buffalo

The Buffalo energy walks in reverence. This energy carries strength and humility in equal measure, grounded in earth but listening to sky. When you meet life with gratitude, even in hardship, you unlock a kind of wisdom that can't be forced. This is sacred endurance, the kind that honors your journey as sacred. Bow your head, raise your eyes. The storm is not against you. It is part of you.

Butterfly

The Butterfly energy moves through metamorphosis, delicate, disoriented, becoming. This energy reminds you that transformation isn't a straight line. It's messy, magical, and often uncomfortable. Be patient with yourself as you shift. Let softness be your shelter. You don't need to rush the emergence. The wings will come when it's time.

Camel

The Camel energy walks through fire without burning. This energy is deeply self-sustaining; it knows how to draw from inner reserves when the world runs dry. Even under pressure, it stays calm, composed, steady. Camel reminds you that you carry more inside than the world can take from you. Even when the pressure rises, you have a well that doesn't run dry. Strength doesn't always show itself as fire. At times, it's the steady calm that lets you keep moving. Trust what's already rooted within you.

Cheetah

Cheetah energy moves with sacred speed, fueled not by chaos but by purpose. This energy is focused, radiant, and alive with direction. When this card appears, it's time to move, but only from your core. Not from panic. Not from pressure.

Cobra

Cobra waits, not in threat but in patience. There's a stillness to it, the kind that makes you aware of your own breath. It's less about striking and more about listening, holding space until the moment is truly ready. The lesson isn't in the strike but in the waiting. Be teachable. Be open. The next guide may already be nearby. Sometimes, the most sacred lesson begins with a pause.

Cosmic Egg

Cosmic Egg energy holds the final truth: you are whole. This energy surrounds you with completion, unity, and sacred containment. It marks the end of one journey and the quiet beginning of another, not because something is missing, but because you're finally ready to hold all that you are. You're not searching anymore. You're arriving.

Crocodile

Crocodile energy waits beneath the surface, still and watching. This energy reminds you that rest is not weakness, it's strategic. Pull back. Conserve. Let the external noise pass. Your time will come. Its stillness isn't idleness; it's storing strength. Power gathers quietly beneath the surface, waiting for the exact moment to move.

Crow

The Crow energy sees between worlds, catching the patterns others pass over. Signs. Symbols. Strange little repetitions that tug at your attention. Notice what runs under the surface, the part most people glance past. Magic runs through the ordinary; trust the nudge of your intuition. This card signals magic woven through the mundane. Trust your intuition. Something hidden is trying to get your attention.

Deer

Deer moves with a hush, gentle but steady. Its strength shows up in softness, the kind of presence that doesn't need to be loud to be real. However, being gentle doesn't mean being naïve. Deer sees clearly. It simply chooses to meet the world with compassion anyway. This card invites you to return to tenderness, even when the world tempts you to close off.

Dolphin

Dolphin's joy heals without effort. It moves with a kind of lightness that lifts everyone around it, often without knowing it's doing so. It reminds you that spirit speaks in laughter too, and that play can be sacred. You don't have to try so hard to be powerful. Just be present. That's more than enough.

Dragon

Dragon energy guards your innermost self. This energy watches from the center of your being, the quiet witness who sees all without judgment. When this card appears, you're being invited inward, beneath roles, wounds, and defenses, to the part of you that has never been lost. Sit with yourself. Ask nothing. Just observe. The soul speaks here, without words, and it's time you listened.

Dragonfly

You catch it for a second, a shimmer, a truth that feels close and then slips away. Dragonfly energy is like that. Quick. Hard to pin down. It asks you to stop gripping so tight, to soften your gaze and look again. What you thought was fixed might not be. What changes shape could be showing you what's real.

Eagle

Eagle doesn't get lost in the noise below. It climbs higher, steady, circling until the view clears. From up there, you see more, the patterns, the openings, the thing that matters most. This isn't about rushing in; it's about focus. Eagle asks: *What are you circling right now, and are you ready to give it your full attention?*

Earthworm

The Earthworm energy speaks to the beginner, the one just starting to stretch into visibility. This energy is humble, tender, and often unsure. When this card shows up, you're being asked to honor your inexperience, not as failure, but as fertile ground. Don't rush to mastery. Let yourself be new. There's beauty in what's still unfolding.

Elk

Elk carries a steady kind of strength. Protective. Providing. Enduring. But even the strongest back can tire. You may be holding space for many right now, and that's sacred work. Don't forget yourself in the process. Even leaders need rest. Guardians need care. Don't forget you are part of the circle you protect.

Elephant

The Elephant moves slow but certain, clearing the way with ancient strength. It remembers what others forget. The path may look blocked, but Elephant knows how to keep going, step by step, with quiet wisdom. When this energy shows up, it's a reminder: you're being guided by something bigger than logic. What's in the way isn't stronger than what's already inside you.

Fire Ant

The Fire Ant energy sparks when tension builds and boundaries blur. This energy pulls you into conflict, reactive, restless, easily inflamed. It feeds on gossip, blame, and the illusion of control. But underneath the fire is sensitivity. You're allowed to feel overwhelmed, but you're not meant to stay there. Step back. Cool down. Not every battle is yours to fight.

Firefly

Firefly energy flickers with brilliance, quick, wild, and luminous. This energy arrives like a sudden idea, a rush of clarity, a creative whisper that won't linger long. You don't get to hold it forever, but you can *catch* it, if you're paying attention. Keep a pen nearby. Keep your heart open. Some of the brightest truths come in flashes.

Fish

Fish energy moves with emotion, sensitivity, and subtle strength. This energy is adaptable, intuitive, and deeply feeling, but when unmoored, it drifts. Sometimes you drift without noticing, carried by currents that don't even belong to you. That's when it's time to pause and ask: *Is this feeling mine, or something I picked up along the way?* This card invites you to pause. Anchor. Breathe. Let your direction come from within, not just from the currents you're caught in. Depth doesn't demand drowning. It asks for presence.

Fox

Fox energy moves with quiet brilliance, clever, observant, magnetic. This energy adapts easily and teaches through presence more than words. Fox can be fiercely loyal, the kind that sticks close to what it loves. But left without care, it grows uneasy, slipping back, second-guessing if it's safe to come forward. What helps is not a rule, but a return to the roots, the people, the places that steady you. To the people and places that bring you back to yourself. You don't need to be perfect before you show up. Just be real. That's where the magic lives.

Frog

Frog shows up when it's time to let go, to shed what's been sticking to you. It's a call back to breath, to water, to beginning again. This energy is sensitive and easily weighed down by the world. It reminds you that rest isn't a reward, it's a requirement. Cleanse. Cry. Submerge. Let the water carry what you were never meant to hold. You're not here to carry the weight. You're here to heal.

Gazelle

The Gazelle energy moves with grace, but carries a nervous heart. This energy is alert, aware, always scanning, but that same sensitivity can keep you from resting in the beauty you've created. You don't have to brace all the time. Not every shadow holds danger. Breathe. Receive. Let the present nourish the part of you that's always been preparing to survive.

Golden Egg

The Golden Egg energy holds the quiet truth of your heart. This energy is tender, radiant, and often overlooked in the rush of doing. It asks: *Can you hear what's softly pulsing beneath the noise?* This is the voice that doesn't shout. It hums. It waits. It knows. When this card appears, return to stillness. Place your hand on your chest. Listen inward. The answer you seek is already within you; it just needs space to be heard.

Hawk

Hawk energy watches from above, focused and clear. This energy is a messenger of insight, perspective, and divine timing. When this card appears, you're being asked to rise above distraction and look again. Patterns are forming. Truth is circling. Stay alert, not anxious. Listen for what repeats. There's meaning in the movement, and something important is trying to land.

Horse

Horse energy runs with freedom born of grounded strength. This energy is powerful, but not forceful; its motion comes from deep within. When this card arrives, it's not about escape. It's about sovereignty. The will to move, to rise, to begin again, lives in your bones. You are not trapped. You are gathering. When you're ready, run toward what calls, not from fear, but from power reclaimed.

Hummingbird

Hummingbird is drawn to sweetness, sipping from one small joy and then another. Quick, restless, always on the move, yet it keeps coming back to the flowers that truly feed it. This energy asks you the same: *What gives you life right now, not just for a moment, but in a way that sustains you? What beauty have you rushed past in search of something bigger?* Return to the nectar. Even the tiniest moment can become holy if you let it linger.

Hyena

Hyena energy wears a grin, but it isn't always laughter underneath. This energy deflects with wit, using humor to shield what still aches or longs to be seen. Sometimes it's easier to crack a joke than to face what aches. Humor keeps the room light, but it doesn't always keep you honest. Hyena asks: *What's hiding underneath the laugh?*

Lamb

Lamb speaks with a quiet voice, but there's weight in what it carries. Innocence here isn't emptiness; it's a different kind of wisdom, tender and often missed in a noisy world. Softness isn't the same as weakness. The Lamb carries ancient knowing, the kind that arrives in stillness and speaks in whispers. When this card appears, it's time to listen to your intuition, your inner child, your soul's original voice. The message won't shout. But it will be true

Lion

The Lion energy rules not through noise, but through presence. This energy is disciplined, centered, and entirely unshaken by chaos. It watches more than it speaks. It moves only when it means to. You don't need to prove your strength; it lives in your stillness, your restraint, your devotion to growth. True mastery isn't loud. It's rooted, patient, and precise.

Lizard

Lizard energy senses everything: energy, mood, the subtle shifts in every room. This energy is intuitive, creative, and alert, but when overstimulated, it retreats. This card asks you to check your boundaries. Have you been too exposed? Too attuned to everyone but yourself? Pull back. Rest your nervous system. Your sensitivity is a gift, but only when it's protected.

Moth

The moth wanders toward light, pulled without always knowing why. Sometimes it's hunger. Sometimes it's hope. Sometimes it's just the nearest glow in the dark. Not every shine will warm you. Some singe. Some vanish. This card is a reminder that you don't have to chase each flicker. Stay with what is here. Give the unfinished room to breathe. Change doesn't always rush in; sometimes it waits, quiet, while you learn how to stay put.

Mouse

Mouse spirit notices what others miss, every detail, every thread, every crack in the plan. Mouse energy is precise and prepared, but when overwhelmed, it shrinks into worry and control. The world can start to feel too big, too chaotic. This card invites you to zoom out. Your careful eye is a gift, but only when pointed toward something that matters. Choose purpose over perfection.

Nightingale

The Nightengale is a gentle messenger reminding you that your voice is medicine. Not because it's perfect, but because it's *yours*. Nightingale energy asks: *What truth wants to rise from your chest into sound? What ache could soften if only it were sung?* Speak with honesty. Sing without apology. Somewhere in that song, healing begins.

Octopus

Octopus picks up on everything: the mood in the room, the unspoken needs, the weight no one else names. Its gift is empathy, but that same gift can knot itself tight if there are no boundaries. What starts as closeness can blur until you're exhausted, stretched in too many directions. This card is a reminder: step back. Not every feeling belongs to you. Let your own breath clear space, so your intuition can move freely again.

Otter

Otter energy brings play, connection, and unguarded joy. This energy reminds you what it feels like to be light, not because life is easy, but because love is present. When this card appears, it's an invitation to let delight back in. Laughter heals. Touch matters. You don't have to earn belonging. You just have to allow it. Let yourself be held without apology.

Owl

Owl energy sees what others miss, through darkness, through illusion, through to the heart of what matters. This energy arrives with quiet gifts: insight, clarity, and sometimes, tangible abundance. But this isn't about luck. It's about alignment. You've earned what's arriving. Trust your instincts to receive it with grace, and to use it in service of something greater.

Oyster

Oyster keeps its treasure tucked away, layered in silence, wrapped in protection. Sometimes that guarding is wise; not everything is meant for the world. But sometimes the shell stays closed long after it's safe to open. This card asks you gently: *What beauty have you been keeping hidden?* You don't have to perfect it before you share it. The world doesn't need polish. It needs what's real, raw, and alive in you.

Panther

The Panther energy arrives like a storm, loud, disruptive, uncompromising. But Panther doesn't come to destroy you. It comes to destroy what no longer serves you. When this energy pounces, it may feel like chaos, but beneath the upheaval is clarity. What's unnecessary must go. What's real will remain. Trust the mess. It's making room for your next becoming.

Peacock

Peacock doesn't glow to get attention. It shines because that's its nature. The feathers open because that's what they do. They don't pause to ask if it's okay, and they don't shine brighter just because someone is watching. Your radiance works the same way. It's been shaped by the hard things, by the lessons you never asked for, by the ways you've kept going. You don't have to prove it or package it. Just let yourself be as you are, and notice how much room that gives you to breathe.

Phoenix

Phoenix shows up after something has burned down. The smoke still clings, the loss is real, but there's movement in the rubble too. Fire doesn't only destroy. It also clears. What's left behind might look bare at first, even hollow, as if the story has burned out completely. But that isn't the whole picture. The loss clears room you couldn't make on your own, space where something else can take root. This is the middle place, the unsettled stretch where something new is already starting to form, even if you can't see it yet.

Rabbit

The Rabbit energy reveals what happens when fear begins writing the story. This energy is tender, intuitive, but when overwhelmed, it loops in worry, speaking the danger into being. The mind races, the breath shortens, and safety feels out of reach. But stillness is a medicine too. Quiet the noise. Come back to your body. You are not what you fear. You are the one who can listen beyond it.

Raccoon

Raccoon energy is gifted and guarded, brilliant behind the mask. This energy is artistic, resourceful, and often hidden, holding back its talent out of fear it won't be received. When this card appears, ask yourself: *Where are you dimming what's meant to shine?* You don't have to perfect it before you share it. Trust the raw. Trust the real. Your gifts aren't accidental. They're waiting to be seen.

Scorpion

Scorpion energy holds a heat that doesn't always show on the surface. At times, it feels sharp. Other times, it hides, keeping quiet and waiting. Either way, it simmers until it finds a way out. Sometimes it's old wounds that stir it, reminding you what still aches, what still needs care. Speak it. Burn clean. This isn't about unleashing the venom; it's about transforming it. The heat you carry can heal or consume. Choose to let it free you.

Sea Serpent

Sea Serpent wraps itself around the tender places, the spots where expression, desire, or emotion have been held back too long. This energy invites you to move what's been frozen, to let feeling rise without apology. There's no need to rush. Healing doesn't happen all at once; it comes in waves. Through it all, you are held.

Shark

Sometimes you can sense it before you see it, the ripple, the unease, the way the room feels heavier. That's Shark energy. It doesn't mean attack. It means something unspoken is swimming close. Its presence can be unsettling, circling close, carrying the weight of unspoken needs. You may try to hide it, but its presence is felt in every room. Honesty is the only way to calm the waters. Say what you mean. Name what you want. What you've been afraid will destroy you might be what finally sets you free.

Snake

Snake energy sheds to grow, again and again. This energy is ancient, healing, and ever-evolving, a reminder that transformation lives in the body first. When this card appears, it's time to release what no longer fits: identities, patterns, protection that once served but now constrains. You are not starting over. You are growing into your next skin. Trust the rhythm. Trust the renewal.

Spider

The Spider is the weaver, the quiet architect of meaning. Spider energy reminds you that your life's work is sacred, and every thread matters. It reminds you that what you're weaving matters, even if it looks small. Creation has its own rhythm, slower than you'd like sometimes, but sacred all the same. Keep weaving. The beauty is already in motion.

Starfish

The Starfish energy dazzles, radiant, magnetic, admired. But Starfish energy asks you to look beneath the surface: are you shining from your essence, or performing for approval? Beauty is not the problem; forgetting your depth is. Return to what's real. Reclaim the dreams you shelved to stay beloved. You are more than the reflection others see. You are the tide itself.

Stingray

The Stingray energy rises when you're caught between comfort and calling. This energy invites you to feel the tension, not as failure, but as a sign that you're evolving. Sometimes growth feels like a stretch you don't want to make. It stirs the waters, shakes your balance, and asks you to stand anyway. Not with armor, not with a shell, but with the spine you're growing piece by piece. That quiet strength is already inside you; let it move you forward.

Swan

Swan moves slowly, gliding across the reflection until something deeper shines through. There's elegance in it, yes, but also a kind of quiet knowing, creative, intuitive, more than surface beauty. Swan asks you to see yourself that way, too, not as performance, but as presence. What you create now carries the echo of who you truly are. Let it flow. Let it be enough.

Tarantula

Tarantula waits, still but watchful. A choice is near, and you can feel it pressing in. It doesn't hand you a map, only a pause, asking you to listen before you move. This card doesn't offer a map. It offers a moment. Listen inward. The right path won't scream. It will hum. You'll feel it in your chest when it's time to move.

Tiger

Tiger energy hunts in silence, led by instinct, not impulse. This energy is lunar, powerful, mysterious, and attuned to the dark. It doesn't chase. It watches. It waits. When this card appears, you're being asked to trust your inner wildness, not as chaos, but as wisdom. Let your desires come into focus without explanation. Move when it's time. Not louder. Just deeper.

Turtle

At first glance, Turtle looks plain, just a slow step, just a heavy shell. But there's more carried there than meets the eye. Age. Memory. A kind of patience most of us forget. When Turtle turns up, it isn't urging speed or proof. It's pointing you toward a slower rhythm, the kind that doesn't break when the road drags on. A step may feel small, even forgettable, but it adds up in ways you'll only see later. Each pause gathers meaning. You don't need to run to arrive. You're already in the story.

Whale

With Whale, everything slows. The surface noise fades, and you're pulled into deeper water. Down here, healing isn't fast. It takes time, storms, and silence. Whale carries both survival and tenderness, showing that strength can be quiet too. You don't need to push against every wave. Sometimes letting the current hold you is the way back to yourself. You don't have to fight every wave. Sometimes the current knows where you need to go.

Wolf

Wolf energy guards what matters most: family, truth, tradition. This energy is protective, wise, and purpose-driven. It leads with integrity, but can become rigid when it forgets that each path is sacred in its own way. You are not here to control the pack; you are here to model freedom within belonging. Guide with love, not expectation. The strongest leaders know when to release the reins.

Unicorn

Unicorn energy stirs when you begin to remember that there is more. More than logic, more than form, something deeper, wiser, and beautifully inexplicable. Unicorn energy invites you to trust what your spirit already knows, even if your mind still doubts. You are not chasing magic. You are the magic. Let the questions guide you. Wonder is a form of devotion.

Vulture

The Vulture energy purifies what others discard. Vulture energy is sacred cleanup, not glamorous, but essential. It teaches that nothing is wasted when tended with care. When this card appears, you're being asked to metabolize what has been left behind: grief, regret, remnants of old versions of you. This isn't about dwelling. It's about transmutation. You're not carrying rot. You're composting it into wisdom.

Zebra

Zebra energy walks the threshold, wild and wise, strange and sacred. Zebra energy thrives in contrast, refusing to flatten into one identity. When this card appears, it asks: *Where have you been hiding your eccentricity, your color, your depth?* You were never meant to blend in. You were meant to illuminate the spaces between. Let your contradictions speak. That's where your magic lives.

Acknowledgments

I want to acknowledge the tarot, oracle, and animal spirit cards that walked beside me in the making of this book. They aren't named directly in the chapters, but their presence shaped the stories.

If you're curious, you can follow the breadcrumbs through the descriptions and titles. The full list appears below.

The following decks were used as companions for reflection and spiritual insights:

- The Rider-Waite Tarot

- The Relative Tarot by Carrie Paris

- Oracle of the 7 Energies by Colette Baron-Reid

- The Wild Unknown Animal Spirit by Kim Krans

All interpretations offered here are my own,
shared in the spirit of self-reflection and personal growth.

About the Author

Rowena Sowders is the author of The Seeker's Lessons, a hybrid memoir weaving healing, spiritual reflection, and intuitive reclamation. A former mental health therapist with a Master's in Counseling, she brings a trauma-informed lens to her storytelling, braiding together embodied insight, dream symbolism, and the quiet power of tarot.

With a background in psychology, energy work, and public service, Rowena weaves wisdom from the clinical to the mystical. Whether serving her community, guiding others through crisis, or mothering with fierce devotion, she has spent her life turning pain into purpose.

Her writing is rooted in personal experience, raw, lyrical, and fiercely honest. She believes that every story is an altar, every wound a doorway, and every seeker a teacher in disguise.

She lives in the American Southeast with her husband and son, surrounded by books, yarn, an ever-growing collection of tarot decks, mugs, and the comfort of everyday magic.

Wherever you are in your story,
may you keep choosing softness over silence,
and curiosity over fear.

You were never lost.
You were always becoming.
Thank you for letting me walk beside you awhile.

QUIET CUP
PRESS